Rituals of Conflict

RITUALS OF CONFLICT
Religion, Politics, and Public Policy in Israel

Ira Sharkansky

LYNNE
RIENNER
PUBLISHERS

BOULDER
LONDON

Published in the United States of America in 1996 by
Lynne Rienner Publishers, Inc.
1800 30th Street, Boulder, Colorado 80301

and in the United Kingdom by
Lynne Rienner Publishers, Inc.
3 Henrietta Street, Covent Garden, London WC2E 8LU

© 1996 by Lynne Rienner Publishers, Inc. All rights reserved

Library of Congress Cataloging-in-Publication Data
Sharkansky, Ira.
   Rituals of conflict : religion, politics, and public policy in
Israel / by Ira Sharkansky.
       p.   cm.
   Includes bibliographical references and index.
   ISBN 1-55587-678-1 (hardcover : alk. paper)
   1. Judaism and state—Israel. 2. Judaism—Israel. 3. Judaism and
politics—Israel. 4. Religion and politics—Israel. 5. Orthodox
Judaism—Relations—Nontraditional Jews. I. Title.
BM390.S5113 1996
322'.1'095694—dc20   96-36342
                                                                    CIP

British Cataloguing in Publication Data
A Cataloguing in Publication record for this book
is available from the British Library.

Printed and bound in the United States of America

∞ The paper used in this publication meets the requirements
   of the American National Standard for Permanence of
   Paper for Printed Library Materials Z39.48-1984.

   5 4 3 2 1

Contents

Preface · vii

1 The Power and Limits of Religion · 1
    Proclamations of God's Death Have Been Premature, *2*
    Religion in the Jewish State, *5*
    The Symbols and Substance of Public Policy, *11*
    Are Some Problems Truly Insoluble? *13*

2 The End of Religion? · 21
    Plurality of Doctrines Within the Hebrew Bible, *24*
    Religious Creativity Beyond the Hebrew Bible, *28*
    The Power of Faith, *31*

3 Judaism(s) · 37
    Political Representatives of Israeli Orthodoxies, *38*
    Orthodoxies and Other Judaisms, *41*
    Legitimate Criticism in the Hebrew Bible, *45*
    Stress, Ambivalence, and Coping in the Hebrew Bible, *52*
    Beyond the Bible, *61*

4 Israeli Politics · 75
    Israeli Society and Government, *76*
    Explaining Israel's Democracy, *81*
    Ethnocentric Versus Universalistic Perspectives in the Bible and Modern Israel, *83*
    Violence Among Jews, *85*
    Religious and Secular Israelis and Their Political Institutions, *86*
    On the Style of Israeli Politics: Coping with Multiple Adversities, *95*

5 The Intensity of Religious Politics · 101
    Religious Issues of High Emotional and Political Content, *102*

6 Religion and Public Policy   133
   Rituals of Dispute About Religion and Public Policy, *134*
   Who Wins? Tied Score, More or Less, *142*
   How Different Is Israel? *151*
   A Summary of the Argument and a
      Look to the Future, *152*
   The Implications of International Peace
      for Domestic Peace, *154*

Bibliography   159
Index   169
About the Book   172

Preface

As I write this preface, even after the election of a new prime minister, Israel has not completely recovered from its shock over the murder of Yitzhak Rabin by a religious Jew; and the nation is still reeling from three suicide bombings by Muslims that followed within eight days of one another, killing more than sixty and injuring hundreds. Inquiries into the assassination include investigation of rabbis who called Rabin a traitor for transferring parts of the Land of Israel to Palestinians, likened him to the Nazis, and proclaimed him a fit target for killing. Muslim terror appears to be the work of organizations that oppose the efforts of the Palestine Liberation Organization to make peace with Israel and prefer a state for Arabs ruled according to Islamic law.

Religion is important in the Holy Land, and Israeli conflicts over religion provoke questions that also have relevance for other countries. This book focuses on disputes within the Jewish sector but cannot overlook tensions among Jews, Muslims, and Christians, as well as quarrels between Muslims and Christians. Yet while blood continues to be shed for religion in the place of David's kingdom, the Crusades, and the twentieth-century Israeli-Arab conflict, the picture is not one of simple mayhem. There is a combination of religious intensity and moderation in practice that results from competition among religious interests and between the religious and the secular. Religious issues are nearly always on the public agenda, with shrill demands from both religious and antireligious activists. Typically, neither side wins, and both remain frustrated.

Immediately after the assassination of the prime minister, leaders of Jewish religious and secular communities sought accommodation with one another, but their efforts did not stop several thousand ultra-Orthodox men from gathering in Jerusalem to protest the work of archaeologists studying coffins and bones unearthed at a construction site. (The remains were associated with the Hasmoneans, who ruled Judea for about 100 years from 160 B.C.E.) The leaders of the demonstration invoked curses on the archaeologists that they be stricken with disease and deformities.

Until the assassination, many Israelis—including, apparently, those in the security services—saw religious curses as expressions of spiritual intensity and not as operational plans. A friend with a religious education claims that the ultra-Orthodox are harmless. "They are praying that God will bring a calamity upon the archaeologists. They know 'Thou shalt not murder.'" Yet he cannot promise that individuals among the ultra-Orthodox will not absorb only part of their rabbis' message and do the Lord's work by killing an archaeologist.

Political scientists cannot predict the future. Our craft is to draw lessons from the past that have relevance for the evolving present.

Details of the killing will keep conspiracy thinkers busy for decades. The young man who killed Rabin is a religious Jew and was a law student at Bar-Ilan University, which is governed by religious Jews. The act seemed to be the work of educated individuals motivated by doctrine rather than of a marginal, mentally unbalanced character. It is not clear how many of the young and well-educated religious Jews interrogated by the police in the days after the assassination knew about the plans to kill the prime minister and participated in them. The media reported that one religious nationalist who was active in antigovernment demonstrations was a paid informant of the security services and may have contributed to anti-Rabin sentiment as an agent provocateur. Some left-of-center politicians used a broad brush to paint religious Jews, nationalists, and many right-of-center secular politicians as indirectly responsible for the crime. Rabbis and right-of-center party leaders said that leftist secular Jews who do not understand rabbinic writings were carrying out a witch-hunt that threatened religious freedom and political opposition.

Should the curses of the ultra-Orthodox against the archaeologists be viewed as serious threats or dismissed as just another demonstration in the running conflict between the pious and the archaeologists? Does the confluence of the assassination and the demonstration of the ultra-Orthodox mark Israel as a remnant of the dark ages that should be disqualified as a democratic regime? Or is it similar to the United States, where religious extremists threaten and occasionally kill abortionists, but where state institutions prosecute illegality and maintain a reasonable degree of civil order?

A substantial majority of the Israeli population is indifferent to religion or opposed to the religious agenda. But Israel has prominent religious sectors; those sectors do not agree on issues of doctrine, political strategy, or tactics. Ritualized conflict appears time and again. Religious and antireligious activists both charge that their opponents have violated the declared policy of status quo—no change in public activities concerned with religion. The conflict may rise from a demand to close a road on the Sabbath and religious holidays, opposition to the sale of nonkosher food, the display of immodest posters in public places, or opposition to the work of archaeologists. The ritual includes demonstrations and counter-demonstrations, with each side accusing the other of anti-Semitism; great noise and terrible curses; a low level of violence with fists, sticks, stones, and garbage; and efforts by religious and secular leaders to calm their followers by referring to ancient civil wars that weakened Jews in the face of foreign enemies. Subsequent stages involve leaders' efforts to reach an accord and a cooling of tempers. The resolution is not likely to satisfy either religious or secular activists, and the same basic issue will surface again in different circumstances.

The stalemate that has marked religious-secular disputes in Israel resembles that in other democracies. Zealous Jews are strong enough to put their issues on the public agenda, create occasional disturbances, and win concessions on individual issues, yet they do not dominate Israel any more than zealous Christians dominate the United States or other democracies.

Like other lessons of political analysis, this one is subject to re-examination and revision. We will know the lesson has been learned only when Israeli governmental institutions prove themselves capable of isolating extremists, and a significant proportion of religious leaders do what they have promised in the aftermath of the prime minister's assassination: emphasize the value of human life in religious education and exclude deadly violence from religious disputes.

At least in the short run, the work of Muslim extremists has helped the Jews deal with their religious problems: Both religious and antireligious Israelis have issued calls for Jewish unity against the common enemy. The government has responded to Arab terrorism by indicating that Israeli security forces will continue to operate in areas transferred to the Palestinians.

Terrorism seems to have been one of the elements in the success of the Likud candidate for prime minister in the elections of May 1996. The election was the first to use a system that provided Israel's voters with two choices: one a direct selection of the prime minister, and one a choice among the political parties contending for control of the Knesset. The change in the electoral system complicates any analysis of why Israelis voted as they did. Issues in the campaign may provide some of the explanation, but also important may have been the voters' response to the electoral reform in a way that added to the strength of small parties, including the religious parties.

Religion per se was not a prominent issue in the campaign, but it may have figured in how some voters viewed the issues of peace and security. Likud was a party with a traditional nationalist appeal, with a historic concern to maintain Jewish control over the Land of Israel. Benjamin Netanyahu won by the thin margin of 50.4 percent of the valid votes (against 49.5 percent for the Labor Party candidate, Shimon Peres). Almost 5 percent of the voters cast blank ballots, indicating dissatisfaction with both candidates. Early analyses indicated that support for Netanyahu was especially strong among "religious" and "traditional" Jews (terms we will clarify in succeeding chapters) and indicated that he outpolled Peres among Jews generally by about 11 percent.

This book went into production just as the prime minister elect was preparing his government and its program for the Knesset's endorsement. Netanyahu's rhetoric promised a continuation of the peace process, but with a more cautious approach than that of the preceeding government. The election results increased the number of Knesset seats held by religious parties from sixteen to twenty-three. The statements of their leaders indicated both a concern to achieve key items on a religious agenda, and a desire to calm secular Jews who feared a threat to their lifestyles. Secular members of Likud, as well as members of other parties likely to be in the government coalition, were poised to resist any far-reaching moves by religious politicians.

It was not a time to risk prophecy, except to predict that religious issues would continue to excite the state created by Jews in the Promised Land.

—I. S.

1

THE POWER AND LIMITS OF RELIGION

Sometimes, religious Jews have used violence in an attempt to thwart a peace process that was transferring parts of the Land of Israel taken in the Six Day War of 1967 to a Palestinian Authority. And Muslim suicide bombers have acted against Jews, apparently because the Palestinian Authority was willing to accept only part of "Palestine," or because the Palestinian Authority would not be governed as a religious Islamic state. More than sixty people were killed in Jerusalem and Tel Aviv during an eight day period in March 1996. In both Jewish and Muslim sectors, there were religious leaders who condemned violence (or waffled as they expressed understanding for the suffering of killers that led them to violence).

The assassination of Prime Minister Yitzhak Rabin in November 1995 by a religious Jew led some Israelis to fear that violence would overwhelm the already tense relationship between religious and secular Jews. However, what had the potential to begin another religious war in the Promised Land may prove to have been only a blip in a setting where there is much conflict about religion, but where religious interests seem unable to determine major issues of public policy. Religious Jews are themselves divided on the issue of giving up parts of the biblical Land of Israel for the sake of peace; they also encounter strong opposition from secular Jews, some of whom are markedly antireligious.

Conflict about concessions to Palestinians set competing clusters of religious and secular Jews on each side of the debate as to whether Israel should offer more or withhold further agreements pending a cessation of Palestinian violence. It appears that most religious Jews oppose any transfer of the Land of Israel to non-Jews, but some do support such a trade. Many ultra-Orthodox Jews are indifferent to the peace process. They can live under any secular regime that allows them to practice their faith, in homogeneous neighborhoods. Muslim extremists may have settled, at least for a while, the conflict among Jews about the Land of Israel: If Israelis generally come to regard themselves as locked in another struggle with Arabs, the further transfer of land to Palestinians may come to a halt—and with it the peace process.

Most Israeli disputes about religion do not involve land or international politics. They concern public policy about Sabbath observance, kosher food, opportunities for secular marriage, divorce, burial, abortions and other medical practices, archaeological research at ancient graves, the definition of who is a Jew, and the rights of non-Orthodox congregations and their rabbis. If we focus on the plight of individuals, we can see many Jews who suffer because the state does not enforce religious law strictly enough. Others suffer because the state is too Jewish in character. If the focus is on the society as a whole, we find a standoff between religious and nonreligious activists.

This book concentrates on issues of religion and public policy disputed among Israeli Jews and includes other religious issues in Israel involving Muslims and Christians; and it links the discussion of Israel to what occurs in other societies. Even though Israel's place in the Holy Land and its status as a Jewish state appears to ensure religious activists prominent roles in policymaking, my thesis is that the politics of religion in Israel resembles the situation in many other democracies: Religious activists in Israel are powerful enough to put their demands on the agenda but not strong enough to dictate their outcomes. Disputes repeat themselves often enough to be ritualized. Issues reach a level of considerable intensity, then disappear without a clear resolution. The same basic problem returns again with variations in detail. Both religious and antireligious activists seek to arouse their supporters with claims that their antagonists are gaining control, but neither is able to dominate the other.

PROCLAMATIONS OF GOD'S DEATH HAVE BEEN PREMATURE

A similar picture appears in other Western societies. While some see religion as outmoded, others recite the laws of God that must prevail. Religious issues are prominent topics of public dispute, and both religious and antireligious activists remain frustrated by the outcomes.

For 200 years academics and commentators have proclaimed God's death. The rise of anticlericalism in eighteenth-century France, the twentieth-century Soviet Union, and elsewhere set increasingly powerful states against religion. What authoritarian governments could not do was to be done by the popular education of democracies. However, in some democracies, biblical literalism had a strong hold, as was confirmed by the verdict in the 1925 John T. Scopes trial in the United States.

Religion is a thriving focus of popular observance and academic inquiry. Much religious research is set in the United States, and it describes and explains the continued vitality of faith. The topic is especially fascinating in a society where official neutrality with respect to religion and economic traits that seem to push the society toward secularism exist alongside a high level of religious belief and practice.[1]

Surveys find that over 90 percent of U.S. citizens profess a belief in God, almost 80 percent say that religion is important to them, more than 40 percent are likely to have attended a religious service within the past week, and about the same number say that they pray daily. Between one-third and two-thirds report that they have witnessed a miracle, felt the direct presence of God, or had one of their prayers answered.[2] Harold Bloom used the terms "religion-soaked" and "religion-mad" for U.S. society.[3] Violence in the name of religious belief occurs not only in the Middle East and Northern Ireland but also in the United States with the killing of physicians and others working in abortion clinics.

The United States has a reputation as an advanced industrial society extreme in its religiosity, and in that regard it is not unique. Table 1.1 is based on data from surveys conducted in the 1980s; the majority of countries studied were Western, economically advanced, democratic societies. In nine countries, more than 30 percent of the respondents claimed to attend church weekly; in seven, at least 65 percent felt religious; and in six, at least 90 percent said they believed in God. Even in the Scandinavian countries, where the level of church attendance was low, over 50 percent of the respondents claimed to believe in God.[4] Emile Durkheim may have been right when he wrote in 1915 that no society is without religion.[5]

Enlightenment is a term used to summarize events marked by the ascendance of science and education and the expected retreat of religion. When discussing the Enlightenment, it is common to focus on the eighteenth century, but important episodes occurred as early as the sixteenth century, and they continue to occur in the late twentieth century. Luther, Copernicus, and Galileo did their work in the sixteenth century; Newton in the seventeenth century; Darwin, Freud, and genetic engineers in the nineteenth and twentieth centuries. Parallel to scientific development has been the achievement of greater individual freedom in the political sphere, such as that gained by the American and French revolutions, and the realization that concepts

Table 1.1 Measures of Religiosity: International Comparisons from 1981–1983

	Percentage attending church weekly	Percentage who feel religious	Percentage expressing belief in God
Australia	17	58	80
Belgium	30	69	76
Britain	14	53	73
Canada	31	74	91
Denmark	3	56	53
Finland	3	51	—
France	11	48	59
Germany	19	54	68
Hungary	11	42	44
Iceland	2	67	77
Ireland	82	63	95
Italy	32	80	82
Japan	3	24	39
Mexico	54	74	97
Netherlands	25	63	64
Northern Ireland	52	58	91
Norway	5	43	68
South Africa	43	69	95
Spain	40	62	86
Sweden	6	32	52
United States	43	81	96

Source: Adapted from Robert A. Campbell and James E. Curtis, "Religious Involvement Across Societies: Analysis for Alternative Measures in National Surveys," *Journal for the Scientific Study of Religion* 33, no. 3 (1994): 215–229.

like *good* and *justice* do not come fully prescribed from the Almighty or ancient religious doctrines but vary in character from one cultural setting to another.[6] The direction of these movements has not been unidimensional; there have been changes in pace and steps backward. We should remember that historians and social scientists describe reality by means of abstractions that are never perfect and vary greatly in their capacity to incorporate all the important details.

It appears that science has gained the upper hand over religion, but its victory is by no means total. There is widespread respect for verifiable material observation that derives from science on the one hand and faith about basic truths derived from religious doctrines on the other hand. If there is a conflict between religion and science, it appears to be a standoff or a game with a chronically tied score.

Reports of religious resurgence seem to be as far off the mark as descriptions about God's death. Some major Western denominations have been losing members, while others are gaining. New religious movements tend to lose many of their affiliates after a year or two. Eastern European churches have shown increased vitality after the Soviet collapse. Rather than a clear trend toward secularism or religion, an overall stability of religiosity, along with indifference toward religion, anticlericalism, revival, and religious creativity, seems to characterize Western societies.[7]

It is part of the U.S. puzzle that religious interests can keep issues of the greatest emotional content on the political agenda but not to achieve their enactment. Shifting alliances of groups with contrasting doctrines occur alongside head-on clashes among opposing camps.[8] Issues of abortion, school prayer, sex education, the teaching of evolution, pornography, and the rights of homosexuals are given religious overtones. A lack of clarity or finality in court decisions about placing a manger scene or a menorah in a public place add to the sense of unresolved tensions among religious communities and between the religious and antireligious. The rhetoric of activists emphasizes a struggle of polar extremes. However, the reality is negotiations, partial victories, and continued frustration rather than stunning achievements of either religious or secular interests.

RELIGION IN THE JEWISH STATE

Israel is an intriguing site in which to examine the role of religion in politics. In several ways it is a polar opposite of the typical Western democracy. Founded in 1948 and declared a Jewish state, Israel stood against the trend of breaking the church-state nexus that had prevailed for more than a century in Europe and North America. The forms and practices of government render Israel a democracy, but several of its population groups are not Western, or only recently so. Jews who migrated in the 1940s and 1950s from North Africa, the Balkans, and Asia, together with their descendants, now comprise more than one-half of the Jewish population. These groups are called "Oriental (i.e., Eastern) Jews" or "Sephardim" (after the Sephardi, or Spanish ritual followed in their synagogues). Sociologists who study Israeli communities find that these Jews are experiencing a similar acculturation of post-Enlightenment influences in Israel that many European Jews experienced a generation or more before migrating to Israel.[9] Seventeen percent of the population is Arab, and some 10 percent of the Jewish population is ultra-Orthodox (or *haredim*, meaning awe-inspired or God-fearing). Ultra-Orthodox youth learn little or no science, mathematics, secular history, or humanities.

Israel's history ensures a prominent role for religion. It is located more or less in the same place that produced the Hebrew Bible and set the Jews on their course. Its independence in 1948 came only three years after the Holocaust, whose religious significance is an issue of dispute and pain. The period 1945 to 1967 saw a change in Jewish fortunes from victims to victors, a mass migration of Jews that recalled the return from Babylonian exile described in the biblical books of Ezra and Nehemiah, and the uniting of Jerusalem under Jewish rule for the first time in two millennia. Believers saw these events in the context of Judaic themes of redemption. Nonreligious and antireligious Zionists also saw parallels with the Hebrew Bible. Even those Israelis who were uncomfortable with the extent of the success viewed it in the context of Jewish history: They worried about the intensity of Arab enmity toward Jewish conquerors and the capacity of Jews to govern non-Jews.[10] Israel's Declaration of Independence defined the state as Jewish and promised equality to Israelis regardless of ethnicity, religion, or sex.

Religion and Judaism

Religion and *Judaism* are terms too complex for simple definition, especially when each is viewed in the context of the other. The dictionary defines *religion* as a recognition or belief of some higher unseen power that is entitled to reverence, worship, and obedience. Scholars quarrel as to whether the power must be supernatural: Must some form of God be involved, or may the unseen power be a moral value, as viewed by humanists, or a dynamic of history, as viewed by Marxists?[11] There are also quarrels about differences between *religion, sect,* and *cult.*[12] Another set of controversies focuses on whether the doctrines of religion actually guide their communities' beliefs and behaviors. By one view, culture is likely to be dominant: Religious leaders pick and choose among the variety of doctrines and emphasize those that suit their surroundings.

More clearly than any other major religion, Judaism combines ethnicity with doctrines in ways that challenge simple description. Jewish humanists, agnostics, and atheists are no less at home in Israel than the ultra-Orthodox and mildly religious. A great diversity of doctrine and practice reflects the long history of Judaism and its spread through many cultures. Jacob Neusner claims to identify eight varieties of Judaisms, but he seems to identify at least ten: that which preceded the Judaism of the dual Torah, which Neusner dates from the fourth century C.E.; the Judaism of the dual Torah; Reform, Orthodox, and Conservative Judaisms; Zionism; Jewish socialism; American Judaism; Israeli Judaism; and a Judaism of "reversion" that advocates a fresh encounter with the Judaism of the dual Torah.[13] The dual Torah refers to the written Torah—that is, the first five books of the Bible—and the oral Torah. The oral Torah is the accumulation of rabbinical commentaries on the written Torah and religious law derived from it. In writing about the Jewish experience in the United States, Neusner confuses his own concepts by asking if it is Jewishness without Judaism. He calls some efforts of American Jews "grotesque" but concludes nonetheless that they represent the efforts of Jews to survive that so far have been successful.[14]

The Hebrew Bible marked the birth of Judaism and is its root document.[15] Many see it as the source of revealed truth, but its truths are plural in the extreme and more likely to be topics of dispute than of agreement. Ancient and modern rabbis assert that a complete Torah (oral and written) was provided to Moses in Sinai and that they only add commentaries on their understanding of Torah. These claims should be viewed as statements of faith and doctrine. Scholars make a persuasive case that the written Torah as well as other portions of the Bible changed over the course of ancient history and that the oral Torah continues to change. A modern rabbi writes that the approaches used to interpret the Bible are too many to summarize and that the concept of the oral Torah serves "the function of keeping the canonical written Bible a fluid text through endless commentary and interpretation."[16] A related view is that the Hebrew Bible reflects numerous streams in the evolution of ancient Judaism and that rabbinical Judaism has continued the evolution in a plurality of streams.[17]

The Bible introduces numerous disputes and leaves them unresolved; it is as if the editors agreed to disagree. The text we read emerged from a process of tales that were transmitted orally, written, and rewritten over a millennium or more. The Bible both glorifies and condemns the monarchies of the Israelites. Some books and verses emphasize ethnocentrism (the benefits to be received by God's chosen people), while others are universalistic. Universalistic passages express God's concern for Israel's neighbors, and the roles that converts and their descendants have played in Israel. Scholars have been writing about the Bible since ancient times, seeking to convince one another of their interpretations.

The character of the Bible is a fitting beginning to the Jews' history. From their first appearance in the Promised Land, the people who were first called Hebrews, then Israelites, and then Jews have had to accommodate themselves to foreign neighbors and outsiders more powerful than themselves. Jewish survival has been maximized by intellectual flexibility, creativity, and a capacity to deal with ambiguities and uncertainties. Several scholars believe the Hebrew Bible and Judaism provide provocative questions without final answers. Gabriel Josipovici writes: "Christianity expresses profound desires and suggests that these can eventually be fulfilled. The Hebrew Bible refuses that consolation."[18] Aaron Wildavsky makes a similar point when writing about Moses' leadership:

> [There was not] a series of successful solutions but rather a set of perennial problems that may be mitigated from time to time but can never be resolved. [In his search for the ideal style of leadership] Moses moves through several political regimes, seeking but never finding the ideal balance among them. In the same way, Jews are commanded to seek God, though they will never find him; the journey is as important as the destination.[19]

Since the biblical period, there have been changes in the Jews' rituals, doctrines, communal governance, issue agendas (i.e., the problems that Jews argue about), and styles of politics. Studies of Jewish communal government in different periods and countries show varieties of self-rule, dependence on, and autonomy from Gentile authorities. Jewish communities in ancient times, in both the Promised Land and the Diaspora, began the process of finding in the Bible the themes that served their needs. Lionel Kochan adapts a Talmudic passage, based on a phrase in Deuteronomy, to his own study of Jewish communities in Berlin and London: "The Torah is not in heaven, but it is in Berlin and London, as much and as little as anywhere else."[20]

With hardly less vitality and creativity than their biblical ancestors, modern Jews have adapted to a variety of cultures and have developed numerous perspectives about themselves and their surroundings. According to the U.S. rabbi Abba Hillel Silver:

> In the Bible and Talmud the doctrines of Judaism are nowhere presented in the unified form of a treatise. They are broadly diffused in prophetic utterances, legal codes, history, poetry, precept, parable, and drama. . . . Men enamored of compact systems will have difficulty in grasping the essence of Judaism. . . . Judaism is no more the product of any one country than it is the product of any one age. . . . It is the emergent spiritual way of life of a historical people. . . . It possesses the unity not of a system but of a symphony.[21]

The categories of Conservative and Reform Judaism describe most of the Jews in North America. Surveys of Israeli Jews tend not to use these terms. Much of the Israeli population may be unfamiliar with them or perceive in them a meaning substantially different from what they signify to North Americans.[22] There are Conservative and Reform congregations in several Israeli cities, but they do not account for much of the Israeli population. Their members tend to speak to one another in English or American-accented Hebrew. One survey of Israeli Jews found 10 percent of the population within each of the ultra-Orthodox and Orthodox categories, 29 percent traditional, and 51 percent secular.[23] Israelis who consider themselves traditional are typically from North African or Asian backgrounds. Many of them observe dietary laws and Sabbath and wear *kipot* (yarmulkes) but are not as rigorous about observances as those who consider themselves Orthodox.

Ultra-Orthodox communities of Jerusalem, Bnei Brak, New York, London, Melbourne, and Antwerp express their otherness by distinctive clothing and their adherence to their own rabbis' rulings with respect to law and custom.[24] Individual rabbis continue the age-old tradition that each scholar learns the Torah and other sources. They view disagreement as natural, something that will contribute to the greater understanding of each scholar. By argument with others who are learned, a rabbi increases the likelihood that he ultimately sees God's view and not his own.

Jewish ethnicity allows diversity of doctrine and has proved useful for community survival. While individual rabbis may be outspoken in their intolerance of certain ideas, the community has been willing to accept as Jews individuals of widely variant beliefs and practices, as well as nonbelievers and those who do not practice any conventional rituals. A Christian historian of Christianity expressed his admiration of Jews for their intercommunal tolerance without the warring factionalism of Christian sects: "Countless varieties of Christianity have fought about matters of doctrine and interpretation, with each claiming to be a universal faith, more advanced doctrinally than tribal Judaism."[25]

Jews dominate modern Israel. They amount to some 83 percent of the population, and a larger percentage of the national parliament (Knesset). Non-Jews have reached positions as judges in lower courts and appellate courts, consuls in major postings of the Foreign Service, deputy ministers in government departments, and the rank of brigadier general with command over large units in the army.[26] To date there has not been a non-Jewish minister in any Israeli cabinet, a non-Jewish member of the Supreme Court, or a non-Jew with the rank of director general in a ministerial bureaucracy. (The Foreign Ministry sought to appoint the first non-Jew to the rank of ambassador in 1994. It offered the post in Finland to a candidate who subsequently admitted to the press that he occasionally slapped his wife. After a few days of media sensation, the candidate withdrew his name, saying that he could not defend certain policies of the Israeli government.)

The non-Jews of Israel include Muslims (11 percent of the population), Christians (3 percent), and Druze (an Arab-speaking community that traces its religion to a split from Islam in the eleventh century, with less than 2 percent of the population). In each of these groups there are internal divisions of doctrine, ethnicity, or loyalties to extended families. Just among the Christians in Jerusalem, there are churches of the Armenian Orthodox, Armenian Catholic, Greek Orthodox, Greek Catholic, Roman Catholic, Ethiopian, Copt Orthodox, Copt Catholic, Syrian Orthodox, Syrian Catholic, Maronite, Anglican, Lutheran, Baptist, other Protestants, and Mormons.[27]

The plurality of Judaisms produces a great deal of dispute in Israel about religion, ethnicity, and politics. Israel's character as a Jewish state appears more in the preoccupation of political activists with Jewish issues than with any consensus about religion or what is good for the Jews. The agenda of public dispute includes:

- The significance of the biblical Land of Israel and how much of that imprecise landscape should be insisted on or bargained away for the sake of peace: An important issue in this category is Jerusalem, with its Jewish, Christian, and Muslim holy places. The city's history has rendered religious and secular Jews suspicious of Gentile intentions.
- Which aspects of religious law should be enforced by state authorities, and which bodies should have the final say in determining the nature of religious law and its application to individual cases? This group of issues includes the application of religious law to what is permitted on the Sabbath and religious holidays; the sale of nonkosher food; rules of modesty and decency; abortions, organ transplants, and other medical practices; the treatment of ancient Jewish graves uncovered in construction projects; who should be considered a Jew; and who should be given the designation and authority of rabbi to perform marriages, divorces, and conversions to Judaism.
- What are the rights and privileges of non-Jews? Should they have access to public positions and other benefits of public policy?
- What are the rights and privileges of various categories of

Jews? Religious and secular Jews, ultra-Orthodox, and non-Orthodox, as well as Jews from North Africa, Ethiopia, and Asia, feel that they have been treated unfairly by other Jews.

All of these controversies simmer without clear resolution. Individual cases are placed on the public agenda, cause a commotion for days or weeks, and are more or less resolved. Before too long, another issue emerges to reflect the same underlying disagreement.

These ongoing and unresolved disputes are the focus of this book. Virtually every policy issue that reaches the agenda of Israel's cabinet has a Jewish component attached to it, even though not all involve religious issues per se. The different sides in an argument about welfare policy, fiscal policy, or defense may refer to the well-being of the Jewish state or wrap their demands in what they call Jewish norms or tradition. No government budget can pass without religious parties demanding more money for religious education and secular activists arguing that religious parties are using an unfair electoral advantage to blackmail the secular majority. Any program that involves construction is likely to generate a concern among religious politicians that their voters get a fair share of housing and to arouse religious activists with the threat of excavation to ancient Jewish graves. When there is a dispute between religious and secular interests, each side is likely to begin the process by accusing the other of anti-Semitism and of trying to alter the policy of status quo, or no change on matters of religion. It is not easy to determine which topics are truly religious disputes and which are merely colored by religious rhetoric. Nor is it easy to determine who wins and loses each confrontation about religion.

Religion appears to be at least as prominent in Israel as it is in other democracies, and perhaps more so. Yet even in Israel, secular interests keep religious interests from determining outcomes of issues of great intensity. Religion is strong enough to ensure its respect and occasional victories, but it falls short of dominating important policymaking issues. The public agenda in the Holy City of Jerusalem is more affected by religious issues than that of Israel as a whole, but in Jerusalem, too, there is an unresolved stalemate between religious and secular interests.

THE SYMBOLS AND SUBSTANCE OF PUBLIC POLICY

Just what is meant by *public policy, symbols,* and *substance* is a matter of some dispute, especially in the context of religion. *Public policy* refers to what government does or proposes to do, with an emphasis on what is widely viewed as the "important" actions of government. An issue may be important on account of the resources involved, the number of people affected, or the sensitivity of the issues.[28] *Symbols* involve things or statements that represent abstract ideas, often with high emotional value, although not necessarily high financial value: the design of a flag, the words of a song or speech, or the content of a ceremony. *Substance* refers to the money or the tangible goods and services that are distributed as a result of public policy.[29]

There is no doubt that religion affects issues with high symbolic content. Stormy debates in the Knesset focus on whether a government official has covered his head when appropriate, has been seen eating in a nonkosher restaurant, or has been found violating the prohibitions against working on the Sabbath. What is less certain is the capacity of religious interests to determine the outcome of issues with significant material implications. These include detailing the services that citizens receive from the government, imposing controversial behaviors on the entire population with the force of law, and determining the division of substantial public resources among religious and secular interests. The failure of religious interests to dominate these outcomes is a common thread that links the chapters of this book, and it is what makes Israel similar to other Western societies.

There are problems with the categories of symbolic and substantive issues. A policy that distributes money, services, or regulations is not necessarily more important than a policy concerning the design of a nation's flag, the words of a prayer in an official ceremony, or the statement of a national leader about what is good, true, or just; such symbolic matters may be of the utmost importance to some citizens. Some issues combine symbolic and tangible elements. The unity of Jerusalem under Israeli rule not only is a slogan pronounced by several political parties but involves tangible issues of municipal boundaries and public services. The location of the U.S. Embassy in Jerusalem may seem a symbolic site for an office building but the issue carries weight in international politics.

This book is about religion, politics, and public policy in Israel, but its findings are relevant to other Western democracies. In both Gentile countries and Israel, religious activists speak with great emotion about the catastrophes that occur in godless societies, and antireligious activists see powerful and intolerant coalitions of believers. Yet the reality is far from these extremes. While religious disputes thrive, victories of either religious or antireligious activists are rare.

Judaism as a religion affected by national culture may appear unusual, but it is not unique. Varieties of Christianity are local in character despite their assertions of being universalistic. Scholars describe numerous amalgams of pagan and Christian traditions, as well as how cultural norms and the personal tastes of Christian clerics affect their interpretations of Holy Scripture and the contents of religious teaching.[30] Variants of Islam also exist. The plurality in each of these religions lessens the strength of religious blocs in the politics of Israel and other democracies.

The empirical approach used in this book resembles that used in numerous works of scholarship from the United States and other Western societies. Social scientists using different concepts and research methodologies have produced similar findings about the vitality of religion and its failure to dominate democratic countries. In Israel, as elsewhere, however, the results of dispassionate analysis of religion and politics encounter much opposition. Some researchers are obsessed with an exaggerated view about the power of the believers or nonbelievers, and the findings of this book are unlikely to calm them. Although the reality seems far from a true Kulturkampf, reality has a limited role in spiritual disputes.

ARE SOME PROBLEMS TRULY INSOLUBLE?

The discussion about insoluble problems is clouded by some confusion of concepts.[31] Individual issues may appear to be solved, but they return time and again with variations in character or other detail. A problem can appear to be insoluble for years, then change its status along with political constellations and norms. Analysts must be wary about the concept of an insoluble political problem in an age when the Cold War has ended after more than forty years, the African National Congress is governing South Africa, and the Israeli government and the Palestine Liberation Organization have conducted negotiations.

The Israeli-Arab conflict has been difficult even at the best of times. Israel has its doves and hawks, including some with the religious conviction to hold every inch of the Land of Israel that Israel occupied in the Six Day War. The governments of Arab states and Palestinian organizations have their separate interests with respect to Israel over issues of water, refugees, and boundaries. Problems between the Arab entities that do not concern Israel have on occasion led one such entity to frustrate another in its efforts at accommodation with Israel. Now that Israel and the PLO are negotiating, there are severe tensions and occasional bloodshed between Palestinian and Jewish accommodationists and rejectionists. The rejectionists have directed campaigns of terror that threaten the capacity of other Palestinians and Israeli officials to negotiate further.

The terms *predicament* and *dilemma* are used to describe difficult problems. A predicament is a situation in which all the apparent options are undesirable; a dilemma, a situation in which they are equally undesirable. Both terms appear to be fragile and alterable by a change in rhetoric. Participants in a dispute can reduce a dilemma to a predicament or solve it altogether if they expand the time frame in which they want satisfaction or moderate the adjectives used to describe their demands. While it is impossible to achieve an immediate end to drug abuse, it may be possible to reduce drug abuse considerably over a period of time devoted to popular education.

There is much ambiguity about problems that have proved difficult. Policymakers and researchers quarrel about their definitions of a problem, the benefits and costs of policy options, and how to describe policy-relevant events. Analysts argue whether the war in Lebanon that began in 1982 was primarily a misguided Israeli adventure that wasted human and material resources and caused a loss of international good will or whether it weakened the Palestinians to the point where more of them were willing to negotiate the terms of coexistence with Israel. Also a matter of dispute is whether Israel or the Palestinians won or lost the intifada that began in 1987 or whether it convinced leaders on both sides that they could not impose their will on the other by force alone.

Several criteria may be useful to judge the insolubility of problems. They include the refusal of adversaries to accept compromise; the price adversaries are willing to pay in missed opportunities, lost treasure, or lives; and the persistence with which unresolved issues remain topics of discussion among policymakers or in the mass media.

The claim for the insolubility of religious policy disputes among the Jews of Israel rests on their longevity. Different groups of Israeli Jews have argued some of the same issues—albeit with changes in details and personalities—since the state gained its independence. Some disputes still on the political agenda were apparent in the prestate period of the British Mandate in Palestine and in the nineteenth and early twentieth centuries among the Jews of Europe. Some conflicts have roots in the clash between Jewish zealots and cosmopolitans during periods of Greek and Roman rule in Judea from the second century B.C.E. through the first century C.E.[32]

The costs involved in the failure to solve intra-Jewish religious conflicts contribute to their insolubility. Paradoxically, the costs to antagonists of compromise are high, while the costs of continued conflict are low. At issue are not so much material resources but having to change principles. Spiritual truth may be the most weighty possession of individuals committed to religion or antireligion. For the religious Jew, compromising the sanctity of the Sabbath touches the core of religious law in the Ten Commandments. For the antireligious Jew, the threat of Jews to deny work, travel, or entertainment on the Sabbath is also important. If the religious are allowed to govern that part of one's life, they may demand further encroachments of religious law governing who may marry whom (religious law forbids marriage between a man with the name of Cohen and a divorced woman), what clothing may be worn (religious law forbids the interweaving of wool and linen), and what food is eaten.

While the spiritual cost of compromise is high for both the religious and antireligious Jew, the cost of continued conflict has been low. Religious and antireligious sectors have worked out rituals of protest and disturbance with minimum consequences for human suffering or loss of property. In the background is the possibility of substantially increased costs if one side escalates the struggle beyond the conventional ritual, but religious and secular leaders call for tolerance and patience in times of conflict. They recall past conflicts that have exposed the community to attack from without. The last serious Jewish civil war occurred when the Romans occupied Jerusalem in the first century C.E., but Jewish memories are long. What Josephus called the Jewish war is still a topic of political discussion in Israel.

The Holocaust, along with all the lesser episodes of persecution, also moderate Jewish conflicts about religion. The Gentile threat remains relevant despite talk of peace between Israel and the Arabs. Jewish history has seen good and bad times, tolerant and even pro-Jewish Gentiles (Judeophiles), and Judeophobes consumed with hatred. Continued acts of Arab terror and graveyards desecrated by German or U.S. anti-Semites lead Jews to unite no matter what their internal animosities. An epigram heard from some Jewish atheists is that they will remain Jewish and tolerate the ultra-Orthodox as long as one anti-Semite remains alive.

The concept of coping is associated with the stresses of difficult policy problems, including those affecting religion and the state in Israel. Coping indicates something less than solving problems.[33] It concerns contrasting demands when no simple solutions are apparent.[34] It involves adapting, managing, dealing with, and satisfying.[35] It implies decisions that are good enough, even if they are not what any of the participants really want.

Israel is a country of intense stresses, resulting not only from the competition between religious and secular Jews but even more so from the external threat associated with the Israeli-Arab conflict. As a percentage of national resources, the country's outlay on security has generally been more than five times greater than that in other Western democracies. These expenditures produce additional stresses of resource shortages. Heavy immigration was a major source of stress from 1948 through the mid-1950s, when the population more than doubled. The phenomenon returned with the collapse of the Soviet Union and the opening of Ethiopia; a spurt of immigration added more than 10 percent to the national population in 1988–1995.

Israel's political system is another source of stress. An electoral process of proportional representation reflects and reinforces a multiplicity of voices. More than twenty parties have competed in recent national elections, and about ten have garnered the minimum votes required to receive at least one seat in the 120-member Knesset. No party has ever won a majority. The result is that each cabinet has been a coalition among parties whose members quarrel and compromise while they govern.

Policymakers have coped with the demands of religious and antireligious activists by using several tactics, none of which has thoroughly treated the underlying problems. They offer concessions on details, engage in prolonged discussions, and delay projects rather than canceling them outright. Sometimes a delay provides time for splits within the religious or secular camp or wears down those who have put the issue on the agenda. Religious disputes produce an occasional flare-up with shrill rhetoric, mass demonstrations, the use of nondeadly weapons, and some bruises. More typically, there is chronic tension, with complaints from religious and antireligious activists. Both camps express dissatisfaction with the status quo and what they see as their opponents' successes.

The costs of dispute in treasure and blood provide an incentive to solve other issues and remove them from the agenda. The accommodations reached between Israel, Egypt, Jordan, and the Palestinians—imperfect as they may appear—reflect the capacity of policymakers to alter their conceptions or the terms of discourse and to solve at least partially what had seemed insoluble. Religious conflicts among the Jews of Israel suggest that some issues are chronic to the point of being permanent. The length of the disputes and the Jews' experience of common ethnic suffering moderate these conflicts and minimize the prospect that they will be solved once and for all. The costs of a solution to these religious disputes are high, insofar as they would involve doctrinal changes among those who are intensely religious or antireligious. In contrast, the costs of continued conflict are low, involving tolerable levels of frustration, property damage, and lost economic opportunities. The concept of ritual is appropriate to flare-ups, not only because such occasions concern religion but because a similar process repeats itself time and again, with many of the same assertions and actions.

Subsequent chapters cover several topics meant to clarify the issues introduced here. Chapter 2 focuses on issues of religion and politics in Western democracies and contributes to the theme of similarity between Israel and other countries. Chapter 3 describes the plurality in contemporary Judaisms. Chapter 4 reviews the character of Israel politics and policymaking. Chapters 5 and 6 contain a survey of issues that have set religious and secular interests against each other in Israel and a description of outcomes that have not satisfied either the religious or the antireligious.

NOTES

1. David C. Leege and Lyman A. Kellstedt, eds., *Rediscovering the Religious Factor in American Politics* (Armonk, NY: M. E. Sharpe, 1993); Kenneth D. Wald, *Religion and Politics in the United States* (Washington, DC: CQ Press, 1992); Stephen D. Johnson and Joseph B. Tamney, eds., *The Political Role of Religion in the United States* (Boulder, CO: Westview Press, 1986); Robert Wuthnow, *The Restructuring of American Religion* (Princeton: Princeton University Press, 1988); R. Laurence Moore, *Selling God: American Religion in the Marketplace of Culture* (New York: Oxford University Press, 1994); and Michael J. Lacey, ed., *Religion and Twentieth-Century American Intellectual Life* (New York: Cambridge University Press, 1989).

2. *Time*, February 6, 1995, p. 48; and Wald, *Religion and Politics*, p. 12.

3. Harold Bloom, *The American Religion: The Emergence of the Post-Christian Nation* (New York: Simon & Schuster, 1992).

4. Robert A. Campbell and James E. Curtis, "Religious Involvement Across Societies: Analysis for Alternative Measures in National Surveys," *Journal for the Scientific Study of Religion* 33, no. 3 (1994): 215–229.

5. Emile Durkheim, *The Elemental Forms of Religious Life* (London: Allen and Unwin, 1915).

6. See, for example, Richard Tarnas, *The Passion of the Western Mind: Understanding the Ideas That Have Shaped Our World View* (New York: Ballantine Books, 1991); Michel Foucault, *Discipline and Punish: The Birth of the Prison*, trans. by Alan Sheridan (New York: Vintage Books, 1979); and Henry J. Aaron, Thomas E. Mann, Timothy Taylor, eds., *Values and Public Policy* (Washington, DC: Brookings Institution, 1994).

7. For example, Daniel Bell, "The Return of the Sacred? The Argument on the Future of Religion," *British Journal of Sociology* 28, no. 4 (December 1977): 419–449: Rodney Stark and William Sims Bainbridge, *The Future of Religion: Secularization, Revival, and Cult Formation* (Berkeley: University of California Press, 1985); Jon Butler, *Awash in a Sea of Faith: Christianizing the*

American People (Cambridge: Harvard University Press, 1990); Barry A. Kosmin and Seymour P. Lachman, *One Nation Under God: Religion in Contemporary American Society* (New York: Crown Publishers, 1993); Karen Armstrong, *A History of God: The 4,000-Year Quest of Judaism, Christianity and Islam* (New York: Ballantine Books, 1993); José Casanova, *Public Religions in the Modern World* (Chicago: University of Chicago Press, 1994).

8. Allen D. Hertzke, *Representing God in Washington: The Role of Religious Lobbies in the American Polity* (Knoxville: University of Tennessee Press, 1988).

9. Avraham Leslau and Mordechai Bar-Lev, "Religiosity Among Oriental Youth in Israel," *Sociological Papers* (Bar-Ilan University: Sociological Institute for Community Studies) 3, no. 5 (December 1994).

10. Meron Benvenisti, *The West Bank Data Project: A Survey of Israel's Policies* (Washington, DC: American Enterprise Institute for Policy Research, 1984), p. 34; also Benvenisti, *The Sling and the Club: Territories, Jews and Arabs* (in Hebrew) (Jerusalem: Keter Publishing House, Ltd., 1988), and *The Shepherds' War: Collected Essays (1981–1989)* (Jerusalem: The Jerusalem Post, 1989); and Yeshayahu Leibowitz, *On Just About Everything: Talks with Michael Shashar* (in Hebrew) (Jerusalem: Keter Publishing House, Ltd., 1988).

11. Stark and Bainbridge, *The Future of Religion,* chap. 1.

12. Geoffrey K. Nelson, *Cults, New Religions and Religious Creativity* (London: Routledge & Kegan Paul, 1987); Robert Wuthnow, "Religious Movements and Counter-Movements in North America," in James A. Beckford, ed., *New Religious Movements and Rapid Social Change* (London: Sage Publications, 1986), pp. 1–28; Thomas Robbins, *Cults, Converts and Charisma: The Sociology of New Religious Movements* (London: Sage Publications, 1988); and James A. Beckford, *Cult Controversies: The Societal Response to the New Religious Movements* (London: Tavistock Publications, 1985).

13. Jacob Neusner, *Death and Birth of Judaism: The Impact of Christianity, Secularism, and the Holocaust on Jewish Faith* (New York: Basic Books, 1987); and Calvin Goldscheider and Jacob Neusner, eds., *Social Foundations of Judaism* (Englewood Cliffs, NJ: Prentice Hall, 1990). This book uses B.C.E. (before the common era) and C.E. (of the common era), which are equivalent to the Christian B.C. and A.D.

14. Jacob Neusner, "Judaism in America: The Social Crisis of Freedom," in Goldscheider and Neusner, *Social Foundations of Judaism,* pp. 130–133.

15. This section borrows from the author's *Israel and Its Bible: A Political Analysis* (New York: Garland Publishing Company, 1996).

16. Burton L. Visotzky, *Reading the Book: Making the Bible a Timeless Text* (New York: Anchor Books, 1991), pp. 226–227.

17. Giovanni Garbini, *History and Ideology in Ancient Israel* (New York: Crossroad Publishing Company, 1988).

18. Gabriel Josipovici, *The Book of God: A Response to the Bible* (New Haven: Yale University Press, 1988), p. 89.

19. Aaron Wildavsky, *The Nursing Father: Moses as a Political Leader* (University: University of Alabama Press, 1984), p. 6.

20. Lionel Kochan, *Jews, Idols and Messiahs: The Challenge from History* (Oxford: Basil Blackwell, 1990), p. 39. On the selective commentary practices by early Greek diasporas, see John J. Collins, *Between Athens and Jerusalem: Jewish Identity in the Hellenistic Diaspora* (New York: Crossroad Publishing Company, 1986). For a collection of literary essays based on the same passage

used by Kochan, see Jason P. Rosenblatt and Joseph C. Sitterson, Jr., *"Not in Heaven": Coherence and Complexity in Biblical Narrative* (Bloomington: Indiana University Press, 1991).

21. Abba Hillel Silver, *Where Judaism Differs: An Inquiry into the Distinctiveness of Judaism* (New York: Collier Books, 1989), pp. 2–6.

22. Eliezer Don-Yehiya, "Does Place Make a Difference? Jewish Orthodoxy in Israel and the Diaspora," in Chaim I. Waxman, ed., *Israel as a Religious Reality* (Northvale, NJ: Jason Aronson Inc., 1994), pp. 43–74.

23. *Jerusalem Post*, January 17, 1992, p. 1B.

24. For an insight into one of the multifaceted branches of ultra-Orthodox Judaism, see Jerome R. Mintz, *Legends of the Hasidim: An Introduction to Hasidic Culture and Oral Tradition in the New World* (Chicago: University of Chicago Press, 1968); and Tamar El-Or, *Educated and Ignorant: On Ultra-Orthodox Women and Their World* (in Hebrew) (Tel Aviv: Am Oved, 1992).

25. Paul Johnson, *A History of Christianity* (New York: Atheneum, 1976), pt. 1.

26. Hillel Frisch, "State Ethnicization and the Crisis of Leadership Succession Amongst Israel's Druze" (manuscript, Department of Political Science, Hebrew University of Jerusalem).

27. Daphne Tsimhoni, "Continuity and Change in Communal Autonomy: The Christian Communal Organizations in Jerusalem, 1948–1980," *Middle East Studies* 22 (July 1986): 398–417.

28. For the author's parsing of this and alternative definitions of public policy, see Ira Sharkansky, ed., *Policy Analysis in Political Science* (Chicago: Markham Publishing Company, 1970), chap. 1; for other approaches, see B. Guey Peters, *American Public Policy: Promise and Performance* (Chatham, NJ: Chatham House, 1993), chap. 1.

29. Murray Edelman, *The Symbolic Uses of Politics* (Urbana: University of Illinois Press, 1964). On the problems in classifying issues involved in policy disputes, see Deborah A. Stone, *Policy Paradox and Political Reason* (Glenview, IL: Scott, Foresman and Company, 1988); Charles E. Lindblom and David K. Cohen, *Usable Knowledge: Social Science and Social Problem Solving* (New Haven: Yale University Press, 1979); and David Dery, *Data and Policy Change* (Boston: Kluwer Academic Publishers, 1990).

30. For example, Edward C. Banfield, *The Moral Basis of a Backward Society* (Glencoe, IL: Free Press, 1958); and Sheila S. Walker, *The Religious Revolution in the Ivory Coast: The Prophet Harris and the Harrist Church* (Chapel Hill: University of North Carolina Press, 1983); James Ault, "Family and Fundamentalism: The Shawmut Valley Baptist Church," in Jim Obelkevich, Lyndal Roper, and Raphael Samuel, eds., *Disciplines of Faith: Studies in Religion, Politics and Patriarchy* (London: Routledge & Kegan Paul, 1987), pp. 13–36. See also Abraham Wolfensohn, *From the Bible to the Labor Movement* (in Hebrew) (Tel Aviv: Am Oved, 1975); and William Safire, *The First Dissident: The Book of Job in Today's Politics* (New York: Random House, 1992).

31. See, for example, Stone, *Policy Paradox and Political Reason;* Lindblom and Cohen, *Usable Knowledge;* and Dery, *Data and Policy Change.*

32. See, for example, Victor Tcherikover, *Hellenistic Civilization and the Jews* (New York: Atheneum, 1959). The First Book of Maccabees (e.g., Chapter 2) describes the onset of the Maccabean revolt as an attack against Hellenized Jews. Josephus' *The Jewish War* portrays the conflict between Romanized and

zealous Jews that preceded and continued during the rebellion against the Romans of 66–73 C.E.

33. George V. Coelho, David A. Hamburg, and John E. Adams, eds., *Coping and Adaptation* (New York: Basic Books, 1974).

34. Ira Sharkansky, "Coping Strategies of Engagement and Avoidance: The Case of Jerusalem," *Policy and Politics* 23, no. 2 (1995): 91–102.

35. Herbert Simon, *Administrative Behavior* (New York: Free Press, 1976).

2

THE END OF RELIGION?

Denying the claim that God is dead are many scholars who believe that we are living in an era of unusual religious creativity. Social scientists who wish to avoid the stigma associated with sects and cults use the label *new religious movements* (NRMs) to describe the Unification Church; Hare Krishna; Church of God; Scientology; Black Muslims; neopagan satanic, witch, and fairy congregations; and groups known for their apocalyptic denouement: Peoples' Temple (Jonestown, Gayana), Branch Davidians (Waco, Texas), and the Order of the Solar Temple (Quebec and Switzerland).[1] Some movements are not wholly new but have developed within established denominations. These include fundamental, Pentecostal and/or charismatic congregations of Protestants and Roman Catholics, as well as the religious-political movements represented by the Moral Majority and the Christian Broadcasting Network in the United States. Liberation theology has affected Roman Catholic communities, most prominently in Latin America. The century has been active for churches of the former Eastern bloc, which first had to adjust to the severe anticlericalism of Communist regimes and then reasserted themselves as the Soviet Empire collapsed.[2]

The purpose of this chapter is to emphasize the great variety that appears in religion. Even the classic faiths of Judaism, Christianity, and Islam have adapted to a continuing elaboration of pluralities in doctrine and practice that go back to their origins. While many religious organizations attempt a centralized discipline, lapses and flexibility are more common than trials for heresy. Some of the same sources that have issued death decrees against Salman Rushdie and other blasphemers of Islam have also displayed anti-Israeli fanaticism. The fighters of hizbullah, hamas, and Islamic jihad are Muslim fundamentalists, and they receive funding from the revolutionary government of Iran. A group of Islamic believers apparently at odds with this fanaticism gained control of the Israeli-Arab municipality of Um al Fahm and had a tense but pragmatic accommodation with the Israeli establishment.

This chapter will examine the multiple stimuli to political activity that fall under the heading of religion. On the one hand, the prominence of religion as a social force ensures religious issues considerable space on the political agenda. On the other hand, the multiplicity of religious doctrines, even within the same community, and the tendency to dispute among religious leaders moderate the political success that any one religious community can achieve.

Scholars cite many reasons for the allegedly high level of religious creativity. The explanations are eclectic and do not clearly specify causes and effects or linkages between them. The pool of explanations for new religious movements includes the continued development of science, technology, and humanistic education associated with the Enlightenment and increased opportunities in communication and transportation. Together, these features are said to produce greater migration, personal freedom, a breakdown of the family, and a crisis of anomie, all of which direct people to spiritual reflection, religious invention, and affiliation. They are also said to produce increased consciousness about the moral issues of neocolonialism, racism, sexism, and environmental pollution. Greater freedoms in the realms of sex and drugs may lead some people to religion by way of reaction against excessive hedonism, while others are led to religious movements that include sex and drugs in their observances. The year 2000 may see an upsurge of millennialism. The AIDS epidemic and the breakdown of the Soviet Empire have religious implications for those who see cataclysms fashioned by the Almighty.

The analysis of new religions can be as contentious as theological dispute. While some writers decry cults for their brainwashing, others use the same term to depict anticult activities. Researchers opposed to the anticult perspective emphasize the small number of people who actually join NRMs and the smaller number who remain with them more than a year or two.[3]

There is a persistent stereotype that religion appeals more to the lower classes and the less well educated, the passive masses who are fed the opium of faith for a future delivery from their misery. However, research finds that individuals with higher than average incomes are most likely to affiliate with religious bodies.[4]

Religion serves different human needs. Some analysts describe a quest for spiritual satisfaction that has appeared in all cultures. According to Sartre, religious belief fills a "God-shaped hole in the human psyche."[5] Others have written that Homo sapiens is Homo religiosus. "Creating gods is something that human beings have always done. When one religious idea ceases to work, it is simply replaced."[6] Religion often goes along with ethnicity. Doctrines legitimize the distinctiveness of national communities. Individual congregations provide ritual, language, customs, and a meeting place for migrant families who share an ethnic identity in foreign settings. In Communist Poland, the Catholic church stood for national independence and offered a spiritual underpinning for those who opposed the political regime. There are also organizational and intellectual supports for religion: Religious institutions accumulate wealth and bureaucracies, train professional personnel, and provide doctrinaire reasons to distinguish them from competitors.

Why do individuals adhere to one particular faith?[7] Family tradition, personal habit, and convenience are common answers. Most people stay in the faith of their family. Changing religion is commonly a matter of expedience: One wishes to join the faith of one's spouse, to enter into a congregation that is close to one's home, or to find a social outlet in an unfamiliar city. Movement from one religious community to another is most often between those that are similar in doctrine and ritual. Without much soul-searching, Protestants can choose from among several denominations that are close to one another on the theological scale. The Jewish spectrum of modern Orthodox, conservative Conservative, liberal Conservative, and several varieties of Reform likewise facilitate changes in affiliation motivated more by social concerns than by religious conviction.

Social pressure and upbringing also contribute to the large percentage of individuals in many societies who express a belief in God. Sartre's God-shaped hole in our psyches is created and reinforced by environment. It is difficult for some individuals to assert that they do not believe in something that is so widely attested and associated with promises of life after death, numerous holidays, and lots of gifts. Moreover, the varieties of God purveyed by each of the major faiths do not require an explicit choice. One can be attracted to God the creator, God the just, God the moral, God the disciplinarian, God the grantor of worldly wishes or an eternal life, or simply the undefined but powerful word that is God.

Does religion contribute or detract from society and the quality of an individual's life? It depends on one's perspective. Some argue that religion—or at least the Judeo-Christian tradition—enhances democracy by emphasizing the worth of the individual. Others say that sectarian rivalries and an insistence on one view of spiritual truth—also abundant in the Judeo-Christian tradition—add to mean-spirited orthodoxy and an intolerance of anything but the one right way. Some tyrants may be religiously inspired, while others clothe their programs in language chosen for its religious appeal.[8]

Efforts to relate religiosity with indicators for personal health, wealth, and happiness have employed different concepts and tools of research. Overall, the findings are anything but clear. A survey of numerous studies concerned with mental health found that 23 percent reported negative relationships between religion and mental health (i.e., religious people were more likely to suffer mental health disorders), 47 percent positive relationships, and 30 percent no relationship.[9] A study of 3,835 students at U.S. universities found positive relationships between religiosity and emotional maturity, self-esteem, and lack of depression.[10] Another study shows that in the United States adults who affiliate with conservative religious groups tend to be less healthy than others, while those who have a higher than average level of religious practice tend to be healthier than the average. These conclusions take into account variations in levels of income, so it is not the case that the poor are members of conservative religious groups and are less healthy than the average person. A study that sought to link religion and race to physical well-being found that African Americans tend to be more religious and less healthy than white Americans. Among African Americans, however, those who are more religious tend to be healthier.[11] An Israeli study concerned with religiosity and economic productivity found that Orthodox kibbutzim (collective agricultural settlements) score higher than other kibbutzim on net income and savings despite the costs of adhering to ritual norms, higher birthrates, and less industrialization.[12]

Such findings testify more to the hard work and exactitude of social scientists than to the certainty that religion per se is good for the individual.[13] The questions posed in these surveys are specific to time and place as well as to the concepts and measurements of the research. The appeal of religion may rest as much on the basis of perceived truth as on a promise of a tangible reward. The general tendencies found in the individuals studied do not explain the situation of every individual. Now, as in times past, some people find great comfort in their beliefs and prayers, while others struggle with frustrations like those of the biblical Job.

PLURALITY OF DOCTRINES WITHIN THE HEBREW BIBLE

A persuasive view is that the incidence of religious creativity defies measurement and may be more or less constant in history.[14] Even within the monotheistic Hebrew Bible, there are many indications of religious pluralism and innovation. The Bible not only describes numerous cults that competed with that of Israel but provides material for scholars who see several concepts of the Almighty that developed within the Hebrew-Israelite-Judean community. A close reading of biblical passages that appear to be ancient shows an emphasis on God's capability in competition with other deities. These passages describe a God who demonstrated power over competing gods and demons. They suggest the existence and appeals of other gods but assert that they are less powerful than the God of the Israelites. Other early portrayals of God were appropriate to wandering pastoralists like the patriarchs: God promised land and lots of progeny to help with the flocks and the baggage. Some biblical passages, as well as archaeological findings, suggest that the early Israelites conceived of a female consort for their God and worshiped variations of their God from one local shrine to another.[15] Scholars have pondered a phrase in the first chapter of Genesis that uses plural terms: "And God said, let us make man in our image." Does this mean that God had heavenly helpers?[16] The numerous names for God that appear in the Bible may reflect separate deities that developed around localities, tribes, clans, or families and were absorbed into what became the Israelite conception of the Almighty.[17] The covenants described between God and his people also suggest that there were competing gods and that God wanted loyalty to himself rather than to others. God of the Israelites was superior, but not alone. Numerous cases of apostasy were condemned in the Bible, indicating that Israelites were attracted to other gods.

The Bible portrays different faces of God. Especially curious are assertions of his omniscience and omnipotence alongside those of the need to struggle. God's insistence on undivided loyalty appears prominently in the first of the Ten Commandments. The strength of his assertions suggests that he was worried about competitors:

> I am the Lord your God . . .
> You shall have no other god to set against me.
> You shall not make a carved image . . .
> You shall not bow down to them or worship them . . .[18]

The creator of the world could perform many wondrous deeds. The powers ascribed to other gods were no match for him. Yet individuals described in the Bible had free will and thwarted the Almighty's law. Scholars say that God bestowed free will as part of human beings' character to distinguish them from other creatures and to heighten the appreciation of whatever loyalty he received from his people.[19] The loyalty that he received, however, was never enough and never lasted. Could not the Almighty have chosen a better people? A rabbinical interpretation is that God chose a weak people in order to test himself and demonstrate his power.[20]

God wanted to demonstrate the superiority of his power when he worked with Moses to obtain the freedom of the Hebrew slaves.[21] He told Moses how to turn his and Aaron's staffs into serpents and said that the serpent from Aaron's staff would swallow those from the staffs of Egyptian magicians.[22] God took actions that would have been unnecessary if he truly was omnipotent. Some episodes even suggest that the Almighty was a model of Israelite pragmatism. He coped with stressful situations. When the Israelites set out across the desert, he guided them in a roundabout way. He explained that the shortest route would lead the Israelites to encounter the Philistines, whose military power might turn the Israelites back to Egypt.[23]

The biblical passages that seem to be most ancient do not emphasize the notions of justice and righteousness that appear in biblical portions traced to later periods. The God of the desert demanded that the Amalekites be eliminated to the last man, woman, child, camel, and ass.[24] The God associated with later portions of the Book of Isaiah, as well as with the Books of Amos and Nehemiah, wanted righteousness rather than ritual observance:

> When you present your sacrifices and offerings I will not accept them. . . . Spare me the sound of your songs. . . . Let justice roll on like a river and righteousness like an everflowing stream.[25]
>
> Let us give up this taking of persons as pledges for debt. Give back today to your debtors their fields and vineyards, their olive-groves and houses, as well as the income in money, and in corn, new wine, and oil.[26]

Hosea sought an inner knowledge of God more than ritual observance. The God who spoke through the prophet Malachi was different from the God who called for the elimination of the Amalekites. He was concerned about both non-Israelites and the weak among the Israelites. He spoke against "those who wrong the hired laborer, the widow, and the orphan, and who thrust the alien aside."[27]

Sometimes God is portrayed as willing to change decisions. He could be persuaded by individuals who seemed more wise or just than he. Abraham challenged God's intention to destroy the evil city of Sodom, arguing specifically on the nature of justice: "Wilt thou really sweep away good and bad together? . . . Shall not the judge of all the earth do what is just?" When the Israelites made the golden calf and God wanted to destroy them all, Moses reasoned that God must preserve his reputation: "Why let the Egyptians say, 'So he meant evil when he took them out to kill them in the mountains and wipe them off the face of the earth?'"[28]

The Book of Job is prominent in the writings of those who ponder the power and justice of God. The first chapters of the book establish that Job is a blameless, upright, and God-fearing man and that he is the subject of an experiment between God and Satan that tests his faith under conditions of severe deprivation. God's omnipotence and omniscience seem compromised by his willingness to test his certainty about Job.[29] He appears unjust for allowing Job to endure extreme suffering, including the death of his children, for no reason other than to settle a dispute with Satan.

Elsewhere in the Bible, the "dark side of God" is apparent in the cruel testing of Abraham, who was led to the verge of sacrificing his son,[30] and in a passage in the Book of Ezekiel that describes a God who made his people "offer by fire all their first-born, that I might horrify them; I did it that they might know that I am the Lord."[31]

The Hebrew Bible also portrays the different ways in which God views humanity. There is an ethnocentric God, a tribal God who looks after his people, ensures their success in crucial battles, and promises a secure future. There is a God who demands ethnic homogeneity: The Book of Ezra describes a program that required the men who returned from Babylon to divorce themselves from wives whose Jewish roots were suspect. Yet another God of the Hebrew Bible is universalistic: The God of Jonah and Ruth bestowed his blessings even on Ninevah, the capital of the hostile empire Assyria, and welcomed newcomers into the Israelite nation. A God in the Book of Isaiah will bring about a time when all the nations of the world live in peace. The prophets Jeremiah and Ezekiel describe a God who accommodates himself to Jews of the Diaspora.

By one view, Judaic monotheism and universalism developed together and became fully apparent only after the end of the prophetic age.[32] Yet different conceptions of God and other theologically relevant concepts coexisted, and they continue to do so. Religion is a matter of feeling at least as much as rationality. Even those who are inclined to construct clearly ordered systems base them upon principles that defy proof. The Hebrew Bible collects writings of different ages and viewpoints, without ordering them or assigning priorities. While some prophets expressed support for righteousness, justice, and God's concern for all peoples, the ideas of a vengeful and ethnocentric God were also available to those who found greater comfort in them. Writings of subsequent millennia (i.e., the Jerusalem and

Babylonian Talmuds and later rabbinical literature) compile the postures of different sides in the continuing disputes about doctrines and their application.[33] In modern Israel, followers of the late Rabbi Meir Kahane cite Scripture in defense of their demands to exile non-Jews, while opponents describe Kahane's arguments as narrow and tendentious readings of the Holy Book.

Religious Jews have no problem with conflicting biblical passages. There is one God, all powerful and righteous, who is available for us to worship but who is beyond our power to comprehend. A standard explanation offered by religious commentators for difficult materials in the Bible is that they are a sign of God's inscrutability.[34]

RELIGIOUS CREATIVITY BEYOND THE HEBREW BIBLE

The early Christians were no less creative than the Jews. For them, the man-god whose missionaries would accept converts without circumcision was an improvement over what the Jews offered. The different versions of Jesus' life written in the Gospels are no less rich than the different conceptions about God found in the Hebrew Bible. What is written about biblical interpretations attributed to the apostle Paul can apply to many other readings in his generation and later: "The . . . exegeses . . . have an air of freedom. We cannot be sure that if Paul had interpreted the same passage twice he would have interpreted it in the same way."[35]

Later episodes of religious creativity included the rise of Islam and its early schism in the seventh century; the Reformation and its continuing echoes; syncretic amalgams of pagan and Christian traditions in Europe and other places visited by Catholic and Protestant missionaries;[36] the emergence of Christian Science, Jehovah's Witnesses, and Latter-day Saints in nineteenth-century North America; the creation of the Polish National church and other schisms in North American Catholicism by ethnic communities that did not want to be served by Irish or German priests; the emergence of Reform, Conservative, and Reconstructionist Judaism in Europe and North America; and more recent denominational conflicts and spin-offs among Christians and Jews to accommodate feminists, homosexuals, and those who desire innovative or traditional rituals. Black Muslim and Black Christian congregations developed in the shadow of what is called the African spiritual holocaust, when slaves were ripped from their African roots and forced to adopt their masters' view of a proper Christianity.[37] If we do have Sartre's God-shaped hole in our psyches, it is not uniform among us. It appears that a universal quest for spirituality combines with differences of culture and historical experiences to support ever-evolving expressions of faith.

The ethnic cement that binds Jews may facilitate an even greater range of religious creativity than among other religious communities. The ethnic bind works against formal charges of heresy and excommunication directed against Jews who produce variations on traditional religious themes. Jewish mysticism and extreme piety have appeared in several forms since the Middle Ages. Streams of liberal challenge to Orthodoxy developed in nineteenth- and twentieth-century Europe and North America. Their offspring have come to Israel along with Western European and American immigrants, and they challenge the Orthodox monopoly of the official rabbinate. Orthodox rabbis also differ among themselves: in nuances and style of ritual, in doctrines promulgated to deal with new developments in medicine and technology, and in encounters with Jews of suspect antecedents coming to Israel from the former Soviet Union, Ethiopia, and North and South America.

The amorphous character of religion helps to explain its permanent condition of creativity and dispute. None of the monotheistic faiths is monolithic. The intellectual variety rooted in their sacred writings support multiple commentaries and doctrinal invention.[38] Religious doctrines may provide guidance to their congregations, but by themselves they do not determine norms or behaviors. Selective readings of doctrines justify the mores that emerge from the traditions of each community and the preferences of religious leaders. Sophisticated intellectuals and popular writers, as well as Bible-waving preachers, pick and choose among the passages to find legitimacy for positions that they maintain in current disputes about theology, personal morality, or public policy.[39]

I learned a lesson on the selective reading of the Bible during a sabbatical in Salt Lake City, Utah. There I met active Evangelicals whose bookcases held many copies of the Bible, yet they did not recognize the name of our daughter, Tamar. As we became more closely acquainted, I was struck even more that this deeply religious and Bible-connected family did not know the story of either Tamar. Perhaps unpleasant episodes associated with prominent figures were not taught in their church: that of Judah's daughter-in-law who seduced him in order to give birth to a child who would continue his family line[40] or of the daughter of David whose rape by her half-brother is an important incident in the king's troubled history.[41] The Evangelicals' ignorance of Tamar was not a personal failing. While listening to a visiting preacher in their church, I leafed through the Bible that was placed at my pew. Its concordance had no reference to either Tamar. It listed the word *tamar*, but only to indicate that this was the term for the date-producing palm tree, as in Judges 4:5.

After returning to Israel, I encountered a Jewish parallel to Christians who overlook unpleasant biblical episodes. An ultra-Orthodox Jew who seemed well versed in religious doctrines did not know about the Tamar episodes. When I expressed surprise, he said that it was forbidden to read the Bible without the guidance of a rabbi because of the danger of becoming attached to unacceptable interpretations. This same individual took the position that David was a model of piety who did not sin. He said that those who say that David sinned express improper interpretations of biblical episodes.

The appeal of spiritual symbols and values renders religion a factor in the politics of Israel and in other Western democracies. Yet the complexity of religious doctrines, traditions, practices, contemporary commentaries, and preaching multiplies the perspectives of religious constituencies and works against a situation of political dominance by a united religious bloc. The doctrinal dictates of any one religion in modern countries are not so clear as to preclude accommodation of other religious groups or secular interests. Even antireligious activists can find satisfaction in a polity that has a large number of religious issues on its agenda and where religious leaders are kept from implementing their ideas by disagreements among themselves and by other political realities. Some religious and antireligious activists cooperate on issues on which they take similar positions, such as social and environmental policies.

It is as the preacher said: There is nothing new under the sun.[42] Altering the nature of the Almighty and claiming to speak for the Lord in proclaiming truth are practices with ancient roots, apparent in the Hebrew Bible. A reader of the Bible is led to ponder the question of God the creator or God the created. Did God create the world and choose the Jews as his people, or did the Jews devise a concept of God that has served them (and others) well for many years?[43] The multiple facets of God's nature and the several roles he has played suggest that he was shaped by biblical authors and editors for their own purposes. In ancient and modern times, claims about the intentions of this ultimate authority might advance the human fortunes of policy advocates who identify God's purposes with their own. The multiplicity and diversity of those claims work against any one of them being widely accepted as authoritative.

THE POWER OF FAITH

It is too early to bury God. He (or She or It) lives in the minds of many people in countries with sophisticated education and democratic regimes. Faith is a moral force more useful to many people than amoral science.[44] Religion cannot overcome the secular values associated with science and personal freedom, but it guides or legitimizes actions taken in public arenas. In democratic regimes, however, organized religion has ceased to exercise a monopoly of political power.[45] There are trials for heresy and blasphemy, but within congregations rather than in courts of state. Penalties of excommunication and banishment may be severe, but they do not involve state-enforced flogging and burning. Religious leaders influence political followings and occasionally affect the results of an election or the choice of public policy, but they do not command public offices that exercise the power of the state against nonbelievers. Faith in the Almighty may seem anachronistic to nonbelievers, but it has a proven if limited capacity to affect public issues in modern settings.

The tension between religious and secular interests is no less ancient than the phenomenon of religious creativity. Prominent sections of the Hebrew Bible depict conflicts of God and his prophets against secular rulers and economic elites. Moses confronted Pharaoh over the freeing of the Hebrew slaves; Samuel stood against Saul; Nathan against David; Elijah and Micaiah against Ahab; Amos, Hosea, and perhaps several Isaiahs against political and economic elites; Jeremiah against Jehoiakim and Zedekiah; Esther, Mordechai, and Daniel against the regimes portrayed in the Books of Esther and Daniel.[46] The kings usually prevailed. Moses' success with Pharaoh and Nathan's success in persuading David not to build the temple stand out as exceptions. It was more often that prophets criticized and condemned, and the political elites continued their abominable behavior. The authors of the New Testament may have absorbed this lesson after Christ's death at the hands of state authorities. Their expression of subordination was the often quoted "Render therefore unto Caesar the things which are Caesar's; and unto God the things that are God's" (Matthew 22:21).

Explicit anticlericalism may be passé with the waning or aging of revolutions in France, Mexico, and the Soviet Union. Surveys find that less than 10 percent of the U.S. population say explicitly that they do not believe in God.[47] Yet the kulturkampf of God versus the state or the market is no more dead than the Almighty. Churches campaign against the temptations of sex outside of marriage, illicit drugs, abortion, pornography, and other sins. Alliances between religious groups and feminists against pornography exist alongside conflicts between the same groups on issues of abortion. Some religious leaders demand social justice on behalf of the weak, poor, and homeless. Their success is sporadic, but the efforts continue.

Scholars quarrel about the quality of religion that prevails in Western democracies. U.S. president Dwight D. Eisenhower saw religion as fundamental to the American way of life, but he avoided the details of theology: "Our government makes no sense unless it is founded in a deeply felt religious faith, and I don't care what it is."[48] President Ronald Reagan stood with conservative Christians and Jews against abortion and in favor of prayer but allowed his wife to schedule White House events in consultation with a San Francisco astrologer.[49] Daniel Bell describes societies as disjunctive, accommodating different perspectives at the same time. Intellectuals claim to seek order and consistency, while many political leaders, ordinary citizens, and intellectuals mix beliefs and behaviors according to their convenience.[50]

Religions reflect the multifaceted way in which individuals relate to them. Religious doctrines and organizations are Janus-faced and have multiple personalities: exclusive, particularistic, and primordial, as well as inclusive, universalistic, and transcending.[51] We are accustomed to think of the inclusive, universalistic, and transcending as more advanced and humanist. However, each of the major monotheistic faiths also appeal to the fundamental, exclusionary, pedantic, and mean-spirited.

The macro description of religion in Western democracies features a modest standoff between religious and secular interests. The U.S. state of Utah has a large number of Mormons and a strong if not dominant position for church authorities in state politics. Yet the picture is not one of religious homogeneity or clerical dictates to a secular state.[52] Non-Mormons and Mormons with doubts about their faith can be content or miserable in Utah, depending on how seriously they view matters of religion. The situation is more extreme elsewhere: Islamic fundamentalism troubles several countries in the Middle East, and Saddam Hussein, the Muslim leader of Iraq, used religious symbols to justify his invasion of Muslim Kuwait. But standoffs between religious and secular interests in Western democracies are not always moderate. Abortion violence is justified in the name of God. Self-destructive cults like the Peoples' Temple, the Branch Davidians, and the Order of the Solar Temple testify to a seething intensity under the veneer of moderate and reasonable faith. The religious Jew who killed Yitzhak Rabin expressed intense passion and the belief that death is a fitting punishment for any Jew who bargains away part of the Land of Israel.

However, even in explicitly Muslim regimes where fundamentalism seems ascendant, the style of religious leaders shows some influence of modernity. Clerics recruit adherents with the tools of mass communication and the welfare state: cheaply recorded tapes and video cassettes; soup kitchens; clothes and food for poor families; free child care, kindergartens, and schools; and campus programs for university students. Western versions of the same devices may be more slick professionally but appeal to the same needs. In both underdeveloped and advanced societies, religion has recognized the existence of a social market in which it must compete with secular options and alternative preachers. Does this portend a creeping modernism that may eventually secularize even the Islamic Middle East? God knows.

NOTES

1. Geoffrey K. Nelson, *Cults, New Religions and Religious Creativity* (London: Routledge & Kegan Paul, 1987); and Robert Wuthnow, "Religious Movements and Counter-Movements in North America," in James A. Beckford, ed., *New Religious Movements and Rapid Social Change* (London: Sage Publications, 1986), pp. 1–28. For a wide-ranging survey of religious varieties in the United States, see Timothy Miller, ed., *America's Alternative Religions* (Albany: State University of New York Press, 1995).

2. Pedro Ramet, ed., *Religion and Nationalism in Soviet and East European Politics* (Durham, NC: Duke University Press, 1989); and Patrick Michel, *Politics and Religion in Eastern Europe: Catholicism in Hungary, Poland and Czechoslovakia*, trans. Alan Braley (Cambridge: Polity Press, 1991).

3. James A. Beckford, *Cult Controversies: The Societal Response to the New Religious Movements* (London: Tavistock Publications, 1985).

4. Rodney Stark and William Sims Bainbridge, *The Future of Religion: Secularization, Revival, and Cult Formation* (Berkeley: University of California Press, 1985).

5. Quoted in Karen Armstrong, *A History of God: The 4,000-Year Quest of Judaism, Christianity and Islam* (New York: Ballantine Books, 1993), p. 378.

6. Armstrong, *A History of God*, pp. xix, 4.

7. See, for example, Malcolm B. Hamilton, *The Sociology of Religion: Theoretical and Comparative Perspectives* (London: Routledge, 1995); and Thomas Francis O'Dea and Janet O'dea Aviad, *The Sociology of Religion* (Englewood Cliffs, NJ: Prentice-Hall, 1983).

8. Kenneth D. Wald, *Religion and Politics in the United States* (Washington, DC: CQ Press, 1992), chap. 9.

9. A. E. Bergen, "Religiosity and Mental Health: A Critical Reevaluation and Meta-Analysis," *Professional Psychology: Research and Practice* 14 (1983): 170–184.

10. Larry C. Lensen, Janet Jensen, Terrie Wiederhold, "Religiosity,

Denomination, and Mental Health Among Young Men and Women," *Psychological Reports* 72 (1993): 1157–1158.

11. Kenneth F. Ferraro and Jerome R. Koch, "Religion and Health Among American Black and White Adults: Examining Social Support and Consolation," *Journal for the Scientific Study of Religion* 33, no. 4 (1994): 362–375.

12. Aryei Fishman and Yaaqov Goldschmidt, "The Orthodox Kibbutzim and Economic Success," *Journal for the Scientific Study of Religion* 29, no. 4 (1990): 505–511. The study controlled for traits of cultural background of kibbutz members and location in the regions of Israel.

13. Kenneth F. Ferraro and Cynthia M. Albrecht-Jensen, "Does Religion Influence Adult Health?" *Journal for the Scientific Study of Religion* 30, no. 2 (1991): 193–202.

14. Thomas Robbins, *Cults, Converts and Charisma: The Sociology of New Religious Movements* (London: Sage Publications, 1988).

15. P. Kyle McCarter, Jr., "Aspects of the Religion of the Israelite Monarchy: Biblical and Epigraphic Data," in Patrick D. Miller, Jr., Paul D. Hanson, and S. Dean McBride, eds., *Ancient Israelite Religion* (Philadelphia: Fortress Press, 1987), pp. 137–156; David Noel Freedman, "'Who Is Like Thee Among the Gods?' The Religion of Early Israel," in Miller, Hanson, and McBride, *Ancient Israelite Religion*, pp. 315–336; and John Bright, *A History of Israel* (London: SCM Press Ltd., 1980).

16. For commentaries, see Burton L. Visotzky, *Reading the Book: Making the Bible a Timeless Text* (New York: Anchor Books, 1991), chap. 10.

17. See, for example, Walter Beltz, *God and the Gods: Myths of the Bible*, trans. Peter Heinegg (Harmondsworth, England: Penguin Books, 1983); Albrecht Alt, "The God of the Fathers," in his *Essays on Old Testament History and Religion*, trans. R. A. Wilson (Garden City, NY: Doubleday & Company, 1967); and Daniel Jeremy Silver, *A History of Judaism*, vol. 1 (New York: Basic Books, 1974), chap. 1.

18. Exodus 20:1–7.

19. Steven J. Brams, *Political Games: A Strategic Analysis of Stories in the Old Testament* (Cambridge: M.I.T. Press, 1980), p. 34.

20. Silver, *A History of Judaism*, chap. 2.

21. Exodus 4:1–9.

22. Exodus 7:12.

23. Exodus 13:17.

24. I Samuel 15:3.

25. Amos 5: 22–24.

26. Nehemiah 5:10–11.

27. Malachi 3:5.

28. Exodus 32:10–14.

29. See, in particular, Job 2:3.

30. Gunn, pp. 129–131.

31. Ezekiel 20:26. The translation in the King James Bible is less explicit: "And I polluted them in their own gifts, in that they caused to pass through the fire all that openeth the womb, that I might make them desolate, to the end that they might know that I am the Lord." As in many other cases, the original Hebrew is not so clear as to solve the choice between versions.

32. Michael Grant, *The Jews in the Roman World* (New York: Dorset Press, 1973), p. 14. Armstrong, *A History of God*, chaps. 1, 2.

33. Barry W. Holtz, ed., *Back to the Sources: Reading the Classic Jewish Texts* (New York: Summit Books, 1984).

34. John L. McKenzie, S.J., *The Two-Edged Sword: An Interpretation of the Old Testament* (Garden City, NY: Image Books, 1966), p. 104.

35. Robert M. Grant with David Tracy, *A Short History of the Interpretation of the Bible* (Philadelphia: Fortress Press, 1984), p. 28.

36. For example, Edward C. Banfield, *The Moral Basis of a Backward Society* (Glencoe, IL: Free Press, 1958); and Sheila S. Walker, *The Religious Revolution in the Ivory Coast: The Prophet Harris and the Harrist Church* (Chapel Hill: University of North Carolina Press, 1983).

37. Jon Butler, *Awash in a Sea of Faith: Christianizing the American People* (Cambridge: Harvard University Press, 1990).

38. J. Zwi Werblowsky, *Beyond Tradition and Modernity: Changing Religions in a Changing World* (University of London: The Athlone Press, 1976); Northrop Frye, *The Double Vision: Language and Meaning in Religion* (Toronto: University of Toronto Press, 1991); Laurence I. Silberstein, ed., *Jewish Fundamentalism in Comparative Perspective: Religion, Ideology, and the Crisis of Modernity* (New York: New York University Press, 1993); H. Nigel Biggar, Jamie S. Scott, and William Schweiker, eds., *Cities of Gods: Faith, Politics and Pluralism in Judaism, Christianity and Islam* (New York: Greenwood Press, 1986).

39. James Ault, "Family and Fundamentalism: The Shawmut Valley Baptist Church," in Jim Obelkevich, Lyndal Roper, and Raphael Samuel, eds., *Disciplines of Faith: Studies in Religion, Politics and Patriarchy* (London: Routledge & Kegan Paul, 1987), pp. 13–36. See also Abraham Wolfensohn, *From the Bible to the Labor Movement* (in Hebrew) (Tel Aviv: Am Oved, 1975); and William Safire, *The First Dissident: The Book of Job in Today's Politics* (New York: Random House, 1992).

40. Genesis 38.

41. II Samuel 13.

42. Ecclesiastes 1:9.

43. Max I. Dimont, *Jews, God and History* (New York: Signet Books, 1964), chap. 1; and Brams, *Political Games*, p. 176.

44. Langdon Gilkey, *Society and the Sacred: Toward a Theology of Culture in Decline* (New York: Crossroad Publishing Company, 1981).

45. Michael Harrington, *The Politics at God's Funeral: The Spiritual Crisis of Western Civilization* (New York: Penguin Books, 1983).

46. Stuart A. Cohen, *The Three Crowns: Structures of Communal Politics in Early Rabbinic Jewry* (Cambridge: Cambridge University Press, 1990).

47. Barry A. Kosmin and Seymour P. Lachman, *One Nation Under God: Religion in Contemporary American Society* (New York: Crown Publishers, 1993).

48. Kosmin and Lachman, *One Nation Under God*, p. 25.

49. Butler, *Awash in a Sea of Faith*, p. 1.

50. Daniel Bell, "The Return of the Sacred? The Argument on the Future of Religion," *British Journal of Sociology* 28, no. 4 (December 1977): 419–449.

51. José Casanova, *Public Religions in the Modern World* (Chicago: University of Chicago Press, 1994).

52. See, for example, J. D. Williams "The Separation of Church and State in Mormon Theory and Practice," *Dialogue: A Journal of Mormon Thought* 1, no. 2 (Summer 1996): 30–54; Frank H. Jonas, "Utah: Crossroads of the West,"

in Jonas, ed., *Western Politics* (Salt Lake City: University of Utah Press, 1961); and Q. Michael Croft, "The Influence of the L.D.S. Church on Utah Politics, 1945–1984" (Ph.D. diss., University of Utah, 1985).

3

JUDAISM(S)

The only possible interpretation of Torah and Talmud is mystical interpretation.[1]

The essence of Judaism is the affirmation that the Jews are the chosen people; all else is commentary.[2]

The mixture of ethnicity, culture, and doctrine is especially pronounced in the case of the Jews, and it adds to the problem of defining Judaism. The doctrines are many, accumulated over a period of 3,000 years. During most of those years, widespread literacy in Jewish communities added to the creativity. Jewish culture permits and even encourages dispute. And for the better part of 2,000 years, there has not been a central authority to rule in cases of dispute. For the vast majority of the world's Jews, membership in the community is determined not by acceptance of principles but by inheritance. Jews have eschewed proselytizing since the Romans ruled Judea. For many years Christian and Muslim rulers of the Jews forbid conversion to Judaism. The result of all this is that Judaism comes in many varieties and recognizes as Jews those individuals who insist that they subscribe to none of them.

One is tempted to conclude that Judaism is what Jews believe or do, but the formulation raises more questions than it answers. How, for example, should we view individuals born as Jews who renounce the Jewish faith, choose another, and claim that they are not Jews? Hapless individuals with those traits were killed as Jews by the Nazis. And what about individuals with no apparent Jewish background who announce that they are Jews and claim migration rights to Israel? Several thousand such people have managed to enter Israel, and uncounted others have sought entry. The lack of finite answers to questions like these creates a puzzle of Judaism that begs answers from scholars and from Israeli officials charged with designating individuals as Jews or administering laws pertaining to immigration and marriage that depend on an individual's designation as a Jew or something else.

Prominent in raising the issues of what should be considered Jewish and how to describe Jews' activities over the ages is Norman F. Cantor's *The Sacred Chain*, which challenges conventional interpretations, from the biblical patriarchs to modern Diasporas and Israel.[3] With respect to fifteenth-century Spain, Cantor asserts that many Jews converted to Christianity and did not wish to secretly practice Judaism. He sees some truth in the anti-Semitic stereotypes that helped to motivate anti-Jewish edicts and mobs and writes that Jews were skillful survivors of chaotic periods when Gentiles and Jews, peasants and town dwellers, suffered from poverty and depredations. Cantor pokes his barbs both at U.S. academics who describe Jewish history so as to provide comfort to what he terms the local billionaires who support their institutes and at Israeli academics who concentrate on the importance of Zionism while most Jews enjoy the wealth and culture of the Diasporas.

This chapter describes the diversity in Jewish doctrines and practices, and it is meant to prepare the reader for a discussion of religion and politics in Israel. Variety in theme is a hallmark of Judaism and Jewish culture. The long-standing variety within Judaism suggests a capacity to accommodate different perspectives.[4] It points to a lack of monopoly of any Jewish Orthodoxy, despite the fact that several groups claim to represent all of Judaism. The many voices that come from the Jews of Israel on matters relating to the Jewish character of the state ensure a limited influence by any one perspective.

POLITICAL REPRESENTATIVES OF ISRAELI ORTHODOXIES

A list of Orthodox political parties and movements provides insight into the plurality of Jewish Orthodoxies in Israel.[5] Members of these groups insist that they are strictly religious, and they occasionally accuse one another of being lax on an item of importance. Agudat Israel has been an umbrella organization of ultra-Orthodox congregations in Palestine and Israel since the second decade of the twentieth century. Its structure and politics derives from the congregations formed around the religious academies (yeshivot) whose own roots are in Central and Eastern Europe. The most prominent heads of congregations sit on the governing body of Agudat Israel, the Council of Torah Sages. Members of the congregations dress distinctively and tend to live in separate neighborhoods, mainly in Jerusalem and Bnei Brak. They have large families; education is almost exclusively religious and may continue long into adulthood for males; the sexes are strictly separated in education and social contacts; and members exclude themselves from secular Israeli society by using Yiddish as the mother tongue and by avoiding military service, secular newspapers, television, secular higher education, and occupations that demand advanced secular training. This separation renders the ultra-Orthodox marginal but at the same time prominent. They do not encourage social scientific inquiries into their lifestyles.[6] In congregations that are politically active, a strong sense of communal identity and an acceptance of rabbinical leadership facilitate high turnout and bloc voting. Yet some religious leaders are indifferent or even opposed to matters of the Israeli state, and their followers have low levels of turnout.

As a political party, Agudat Israel has elected representatives to every session of the Knesset, yet it has not been free of factions. Most prominent in recent years was the splitting off of the Association of Sephardi Observants of the Torah (known by the acronym SHAS) prior to the election of 1984. The founders of SHAS charged that Agudat Israel provided only limited opportunities for ultra-Orthodox Jews of North African and Asian communities. Degel Hatorah is a division among the Ashkenazim (Europeans) who are dominant in Agudat Israel. Its roots are among the congregations termed Mitnagdim (i.e., opposed to Hasidism) or Lithuanian, after the location of their major academies prior to the Holocaust. Agudat Israel, Degel Hatorah, and a small faction of Sephardi Jews opposed to SHAS combined for the 1992 election under the label of Torah Judaism.

Scholars quarrel as to whether SHAS is a religious party whose appeal is largely ethnic (to Jews of North African and Asian origins, i.e., Sephardim or Oriental) or a movement that differs from other ultra-Orthodox religious parties on matters of religious doctrine. Curiously, there are indications that the leadership of SHAS is more willing than that of other religious parties to give up part of the Land of Israel for the sake of peace, while the voters of SHAS are more stridently nationalist than the followers of other ultra-Orthodox parties and are not inclined to territorial concessions.

The Chabad or Lubavitcher community also has European roots but has recruited Jews from both non-European and non-Orthodox backgrounds. It has moved in and out of political alliances with other ultra-Orthodox groups, a result of differences regarding the proselytizing of Jews and the status to be accorded its late rebbe (spiritual leader), Rabbi Menachem Mendel Schneerson. Many Lubavitcher expected the rebbe to declare himself the Messiah. When he died without making such a declaration, some followers repeated a traditional explanation for the failure of the Messiah to appear: The Jews were still not ready; they were not sufficiently pious. Other Lubavitcher spoke about their leader's life after death in ways that other ultra-Orthodox ridiculed as un-Jewish.

The National Religious Party (NRP) ascribes to Orthodox Judaism but distinguishes itself from the ultra-Orthodox by virtue of its Zionism. Its followers tend to wear knitted skullcaps rather than the black skullcaps of the ultra-Orthodox. NRP founders supported the development of modern institutions in the Land of Israel and saw the creation of the state as a sign of God's participation. NRP's young men typically serve in the Israeli military. They are prominent in units that combine religious studies with military duties and have made a credible record in battle. Gush Emunim (Group of the Faithful) is allied with the NRP as a movement primarily concerned with maintaining Israeli control over all parts of the Land of Israel taken in the Six Day War. By some views, Gush supporters are religious fanatics who want to force the future in the belief that this is a messianic age and that God will intervene again as he did in the wars of 1948 and 1967. By other views, the messianic language is a rhetorical screen to cover skillful and pragmatic politicking by Israelis who are nationalistic and suspicious of Arab intentions.[7]

Edah Ha-Haredit and Neturei Karta are ultra-Orthodox groups that take extreme positions with respect to Israeli state authorities. Attitudes of their members range from active opposition to the Zionists for having created a Jewish state without clear signs from the Almighty to an aloof indifference to secular issues. When the Palestine Liberation Organization was outlawed by Israeli authorities as terrorist and Jordan was officially an enemy of Israel, leaders of Neturei Karta occasionally made dramatic overtures to Yasir Arafat and King Hussein, asking them to take control of Palestine. When Israel's Central Bureau of Statistics was preparing the national census in 1995, the rabbinical tribunal of Edah Ha-Haredit ruled that counting Jews was against religious law and would cause a plague, as did a census taken by King David (II Samuel 24). The rabbis of other ultra-Orthodox communities also opposed the census but accepted a proposal by the bureau to remove a question of religious affiliation from the questionnaire. This would turn the census into a counting of Israelis and not a counting of Jews. For the rabbis of Edah Ha-Haredit, the measure was not sufficient, and they continued to oppose the census. As in years past, it was likely that the census would undercount the number of ultra-Orthodox Israelis, some of whom worried about the catastrophe that had followed the census of King David.[8] A former chief rabbi opposed a question on the census form about marital status that he interpreted as endorsing homosexual unions, and nationalist and religious settlers in the occupied territories urged their followers to boycott the census to express their opposition to the government in power and its policy of making concessions to the Palestinians.[9]

Kach is a political party that was created by Rabbi Meir Kahane with the purpose of eliminating the rights of non-Jews in Israel or expelling non-Jews altogether. After the party was outlawed for racist incitement and Kahane was assassinated by an Arab in New York City, the party divided into a number of fluid, competitive, and partly underground movements. A member of one of these groups, Dr. Baruch Goldstein, came to world attention in February 1994 when he killed some thirty Muslims in a mosque at Hebron's Cave of the Forefathers. By 1995, the faction called Kahane Lives had emerged as the most prominent. A handful of young members were occasionally shown on the nightly news celebrating their hero Baruch Goldstein, demonstrating with the raised fist that Kahane had adapted from other fascist movements, or struggling as they were being dragged away by the police. Another faction called the Sword of David published a statement that recalled the struggle waged by the Maccabees against the Greek regime and Jews who accepted Greek culture:

> Awake awake sons of Zion and arouse the heroes of Judea about the abominable evil that occurs before our eyes as wicked men who have become like Greeks persecute pious Jews who walk in the true way of the Torah and continue the sacred work of Meir David Kahane, of blessed memory, may the Lord revenge his blood.

This group has threatened retaliation against Jewish security officials, including the head of the General Security Service, who is said to have persecuted the organization. Until now, the organization has claimed responsibility only for violence against Arabs: three workers gunned down as they traveled home and a resident of a Jerusalem Arab neighborhood.[10]

ORTHODOXIES AND OTHER JUDAISMS

Judaism is a religion with several faces and numerous themes in its doctrines. One side of Judaism is the theme of strict monotheism and other doctrines that brook no compromise with revealed truth. The Ten Commandments give expression to this side of Judaism in their insistence on the primacy of the Israelites' God ("You shall have no other god to set against me").[11] Other elements of this theme are the doctrine of the chosen people and prohibitions against marriage with foreigners. Another side of Judaic doctrine are those themes that express a desire that peace will prevail for all the nations, a concern for the proper treatment of foreigners, and an openness to converts into the Jewish fold. The biblical roots of these elements appear in the laws that provide rights to non-Jews,[12] the story of the convert Ruth, and the often-quoted ode to international peace in the Book of Isaiah: "They shall beat their swords into plowshares, and their spears into pruning hooks: nation shall not lift up sword against nation, neither shall they learn war any more."[13] Some contemporary Israelis identify with the monopolistic, jealous, and exclusionary elements in Judaism. They are condemned by those who identify with the more open and cosmopolitan elements.

Religious Jews are outnumbered in Israel, but they claim for themselves the advantage of preserving what is pure in an ancient community. The labels of Orthodox and ultra-Orthodox imply the legitimacy of what has always been. Only somewhat less advantaged in this verbal one-upmanship are those called traditional in Israeli parlance. Although these traditional Jews have modified some points of Jewish doctrines and practice, their label identifies them with established traditions, as in the case of the Orthodox and the nearly Orthodox. Some secular Israelis are sensitive to these nuances and argue whether the terms nonreligious, secular, liberal, free-thinking, cosmopolitan, or humanist are more or less suitable to their own concerns for legitimacy.

Judaisms labeled Reform, Conservative, and Reconstructionist dominate North American Jewry. Given the autonomy of individual rabbis and congregations, it is no simple task to describe the differences among them. Each abbreviate the Orthodox prayer book, the Reform more so than the Conservative or the Reconstructionist. The prayers of a Reform congregation also use more English and less Hebrew than the others. The kitchen of a Reform congregation and the members' individual practices are less likely to be kosher, and the congregants are less likely to cover their heads during prayers or wear prayer shawls. Men and women sit together in Reform and Reconstructionist and almost all Conservative congregations, and women are likely to take part in the services and even serve as rabbis in each of these denominations. There are a few such congregations in Israel. They differ from their North American counterparts in their extensive or exclusive use of Hebrew, but it is Hebrew likely to be spoken with an American accent.

Activists in each of these denominations specify the cardinal distinctions between them and Orthodoxy. No less impressive, however, are the nuances apparent in the expressions of individual rabbis. The differences are not clear points on a spectrum from more to less observant but overlap parts of the spectrum. The divisions are blurred by ideas that do not clearly distinguish the groups of Reform, Conservative, or Reconstructionist rabbis from one another or from rabbis on the liberal edge of the Orthodox spectrum.

Some years ago the editors of *Commentary* magazine produced an anthology of articles in which rabbis addressed the concepts of the chosen people, Jewish law, and the interface between Judaism and politics.[14] The rabbis' contributions display more diversity than unity of opinion.

One topic of disagreement was the concept of the chosen people. According to one Conservative rabbi "the revision of the ethnocentric impetus in our tradition should be the first item on the agenda."[15] The founder of Reconstructionism stated, "The best way . . . to answer the charge that the chosen-people doctrine has been 'the model' for theories of national and racial superiority is to eliminate that doctrine from the Jewish liturgy."[16] Others ascribed to an assertion by a Conservative rabbi that "the essence of Judaism is the affirmation that the Jews are the chosen people; all else is commentary."[17]

Several rabbis believed that a number of the biblical commandments are anachronistic and that individuals learned in the Torah are entitled to decide how to observe them or whether to observe them at all. A number of Orthodox rabbis asserted that they accepted every word of the Torah (i.e., the Pentateuch, or Genesis through Deuteronomy) as revealed from God. However, one Orthodox rabbi made a significant point about the importance of doubt or skepticism:

> I do teach that Judaism encourages doubt even as it enjoins faith and commitment. A Jew dare not live with absolute certainty, not only because certainty is the hallmark of the fanatic and Judaism abhors fanaticism, but also because doubt is good for the human soul, its humility, and consequently its greater potential ultimately to discover its Creator.[18]

A well-known Conservative rabbi wrote that although Jews await the Messiah, they should remember the Jewish experience with false messiahs, "from Jesus to Shabbethai Zevi to Karl Marx and Leon Trotsky," and view skeptically the claim that the true Messiah has arrived.[19]

Some rabbis stressed that Judaism was not so diverse as to be open to all perspectives. They believed that it was necessary to rely on those who are learned in the Torah in order to discern the Jewish approach to an issue, yet the Torah provides a basis of different and even contrasting opinions. There is no monopoly of wisdom. Orthodox rabbis concede the different schools in rabbinical tradition. A classical rabbinical view encourages consultation in order to seek God's will and not one's own.[20]

Rabbinical consultation can be contentious. The work of an Orthodox rabbi previously quoted was described by another rabbi as an example of modern Orthodoxy. The critic referred to the treatment of Jewish law by this school as "dangerous and even ludicrous . . . crude misunderstandings of the . . . material . . . glaring misuses of . . . generalities . . . semantic legerdemain."[21] Some rabbis of Orthodoxy's right wing describe rabbis affiliated with Conservative, Reform, and Reconstructionist movements as not deserving of the title of rabbi or as beneath contempt for the corruption that they have introduced into Judaism.

Jewish humanism also deserves mention in a survey of Judaisms with political relevance. The phenomenon begs definition. It has no prominent organizations or rabbis, although there are secular rebbes with substantial followings. At times, Jewish humanism appears to be antireligious, although it often expresses itself in traditional Jewish terms. Given the amorphous nature of Judaism, it may be best to describe humanism as sometimes anticlerical (i.e., antirabbinical) rather than antireligious.

The Israeli author Amos Oz is one rebbe of Jewish humanism. Among his books is a diary he kept while traveling throughout the country and speaking with many individuals who articulated humanism's range of opinions.[22] Oz attacked what he perceived as the close-minded religiosity of settlers in the West Bank and asserted in traditionally Jewish terms that his own secular humanism is integral to the Jewish tradition.

> The Jewish people have a great skill of creating destruction. We are perhaps the world champions of destruction. Of course, people can assert that all the destruction that they impose on themselves comes as a decree from heaven, and justify the decree. . . . "Because we sinned we were expelled from our land." . . . But our skill at destruction is not a decree from heaven. . . . Our characteristic demand for thoroughness, totality, to invent an ideal to accomplish fully, or to break our heads against the wall in failure. All or nothing. . . . Similar to the demand of Gush Emunim. Redemption Now.[23]

There are no simple, unambiguous boundaries to the various streams of Judaism.[24] It is possible to use such indicators as membership in synagogues that affiliate formally with one or another movement or to ask individual Jews how they define themselves or if they observe various commandments. Sociologists who work in this field identify commandments related to dietary practices and Sabbath observance as critical indicators that discriminate between the Orthodox and the non-Orthodox.[25] For scholars of the ultra-Orthodox, however, these indicators only begin to distinguish the truly observant Jews from the wayward. And like the biblical prophets, modern Jewish commentators lament individuals who observe the letter of many commandments but do not behave in ways that are just or righteous.

LEGITIMATE CRITICISM IN THE HEBREW BIBLE

The disputatious character of Judaism has ancient roots. The Hebrew Bible was composed in a period marked by autocratic government and limited concern for individual rights. What is notable to a modern political scientist is the Bible's sensitivity to the faults in political leaders and to the reverence it bestows on prophets who severely criticized political and economic elites and prevailing policy.[26] The following readings of the biblical text would likely be viewed as severely flawed by some rabbis who ascribe to what they view as conventional interpretations. In reading the Bible, as in many other things, Judaism is plural. This section of the chapter describes certain cultural roots from the Hebrew Bible that may shed light on how the Jews of modern Israel deal with issues of political and religious controversy. It provides the reader with many views rather than a simple biblical orthodoxy, a skepticism with respect to authorities, and a capacity to bestow reverence on prophets who were, among other things, severe critics of elites.

A Revered and Flawed King

David's story shows the willingness of the Bible's authors and editors to recognize that a great national hero may have traits that are less than desirable. David was tested and ultimately worn down by the problems of seizing power, maintaining control, managing subordinates, and then passing on authority to the next generation. His immoral personal behavior was matched by flaws in his public activities.

The young David was a chivalrous innocent who spent his time in song, battle with Philistines for the sake of the Israelites, and foregoing opportunities to harm his mad king. But he also gathered around him a force numbered at one point as 400 and at another as 600.[27] "Every one that was in distress, and every one that was in debt, and everyone that was discontented."[28] One episode depicts David and this gang of desperadoes selling protection. Nabal's wife Abigail pleaded with David not to take revenge on her husband for refusing to pay. By the end of the story, Nabal was dead and Abigail was David's wife.[29] The incident reinforces the image of Saul's weakness and his inability to protect the countryside from David and his ilk.

The mature David had problems as a military commander and monarch. Early in the Bathsheba story, before the adultery and killing, it is apparent that the once brave warrior was at home in the palace while Joab, Uriah, and other troops were fighting in Ammon. David's use of Joab to implement the death of Uriah depicts his dependence on his military commander, a dependence that resurfaces on several occasions. At times, it is difficult to tell who is superior and who subordinate.

The problematic relationship between David and Joab began with their victory over the forces of Saul's son, Ishbosheth. There was a falling out between Ishbosheth and his commander Abner, and Abner offered to bring all of Saul's realm with him to David.[30] David granted Abner safe passage, but Joab killed him in revenge; Abner had killed Joab's brother during the conflict between Ishbosheth and David. David protested his own innocence in the death of Abner and cursed Joab, yet the only punishment he imposed on Joab was an order to attend Abner's funeral.[31]

Sometime later, Joab chastised his king for failing to lead his troops in battle and threatened him with an ultimatum: "You had better muster the rest of the army yourself, lay siege to the city and take it, lest I take it and name it after myself."[32]

David's flight during the rebellion of his son Absalom also shows less than heroic behavior. The king organized a defense but acceded to the troops' call that he not endanger himself by taking part in battle.[33] The rebellion ended with Joab's killing of Absalom, contrary to David's explicit order.[34] Not only did Joab escape censure, but when David mourned his son, Joab rebuked him severely and issued another ultimatum:

> You have put to shame this day all your servants, who have saved you and your sons and daughters, your wives and your concubines. You love those who hate you and hate those that love you. . . . Now go at once and give your servants some encouragement; if you

refuse, I swear by the Lord that not a man will stay with you tonight, and that would be a worse disaster than any you have suffered since your earliest days.

David responded to this dressing down with quiet compliance.[35]

Perhaps to put Joab in his place and to obtain the support of those who had sided with Absalom, David chose Absalom's general Amasa as the commander of his army. However, David again did not punish Joab when he killed Amasa during the rebellion of Sheba.[36]

David's weakness reached its lowest point in his final days, during a messy transition to Solomon's reign. While David was still alive, his oldest surviving son, Adonijah, allied himself with Joab and took steps to have himself proclaimed king. A counterplot by Nathan the prophet and Bathsheba stopped Adonijah and put Bathsheba's son Solomon on the throne.[37] The procedure that David followed in crowning Solomon suggests an old man's insensitivity to tensions in his regime, and it may have contributed to the regional problems that eventually split the kingdom. David had acquired his own reign over Judah and Israel in stages, with at least the nominal consent of elites in both regions. However, he ordered that Solomon be mounted on the royal mule and anointed by the priest Zadok and the prophet Nathan. David proclaimed that Solomon was king over both Israel and Judah, without asking the consent of leaders in either region.[38]

The Bible offers two versions of David's final actions. A saintly version appears in II Samuel, when David praises the justice, glory, and reliability of God.[39] In contrast is a settling of accounts by a bitter old man in I Kings, in which David advises Solomon to do away with the problem of Joab: "Let not his hoar head go down to the grave in peace."[40] The key to this version may be Joab's lapse of judgment. He had chosen to support the monarchical aspirations of the unsuccessful Adonijah.

A Prophet with Power and Tenure

Nathan's censure of David's adultery with Bathsheba and involvement in the death of her husband ("Thou art the man")[41] included a prophecy for both the private and public sides of David's monarchy: His child would die and there would be bloodshed within the royal family.[42] Later, Nathan dissuaded David from building the temple and was instrumental in the selection of Solomon as David's successor. In these cases, we see something that may be described as persuasion, a strong adviser, or perhaps even the wielding of a veto by a prophet who is able to stand against the king.[43]

The story of David's and Nathan's roles in building the temple is one of those puzzling biblical issues because of its different versions. In II Samuel God is presented as modest and satisfied to be identified with a tent and tabernacle:

> Did I ever ask any of the judges whom I appointed shepherds of my people Israel why they had not built me a house of cedar?[44]

In I Chronicles the explanation concerns David's military record.

> The word of the Lord came to me, saying: thou hast shed blood abundantly, and hast made great wars; thou shalt not build a house unto my name, because thou has shed much blood upon the earth in my sight.[45]

A creative inference by modern scholars is that David decided not to build the temple on account of popular opposition to a census he had taken prior to recruiting forced labor. By this interpretation, the disagreement about the temple was an early expression of the Israelites' antipathy to taxation and work levies, which led eventually to rebellion and division of the kingdom.[46]

The Most Extreme and Critical Prophet

Jeremiah was extreme in both the style and the substance of his prophecy. He threatened kings, priests, and competing prophets with the end of their regime, death, or great personal suffering and urged capitulation in the face of a foreign army. He confronted the emissaries of foreign kings dressed in an ox's yoke to symbolize his prophecy that they and Judah must accept the rule of Babylon. He was beset with intense adversaries on several occasions and hounded almost to death. Yet he also had well-placed supporters. There is no indication that he ever succeeded in changing the behaviors of the targets of his prophecies. However, over his long career, he persisted in his intense public criticism of political leaders. During national emergencies, he surpassed the boundaries that modern democracies under stress have imposed on critics.

How could such a misfit in politics win such a venerated place in the Bible? A reader of Jeremiah sees the ancient roots of modern Israelis who scream their criticisms of one another on such issues as who is a Jew, the sale of nonkosher meat, the proper observance of the Sabbath, and which concessions should be made to the Palestinians.

The books of II Kings and Jeremiah describe in some detail the problems of the prophet's lifetime. His country was subject even more than usual to the actions of great powers. Egyptian and Mesopotamian regimes competed for dominance. Assyria had recently collapsed, but Judah had few advantages in the power vacuum that resulted. During Jeremiah's youth there had been a spurt of religious revival and a hope for national autonomy and expansion. The Bible praises Josiah's reign (639–609 B.C.E.) for religious observances in contrast to previous reigns of Manasseh (696–642) and Amon (641–640). As the Assyrian empire weakened, Josiah encroached on the population and the territory that had been the northern kingdom of Israel until the Assyrian conquest of 722. However, Egypt also coveted the spoils of the Assyrian empire, and Josiah was killed at Megiddo in what II Chronicles describes as an ill-advised military campaign against the Egyptians.[47] The Egyptians then displaced the Judaic king who had been selected to replace Josiah and chose another royal brother as Judah's king.[48]

Jeremiah called shame on King Jehoiakim and prophesied his destruction for social injustice, forcing his people to work on the expansion of his palace without compensation, and the shedding of innocent blood.[49] Jeremiah's prophecies against the next king, Zedekiah, were no less harsh. The prophet proclaimed that not a single honest and just man could be found in Jerusalem and that each generation was more evil than the last.[50] For its sins, the Lord would wreak great destruction.

> [Jerusalem will be] an astonishment, and a hissing; every one that passeth thereby shall be astonished and hiss because of all the plagues thereof . . . [the city's residents will] eat the flesh of their sons.[51] . . . [The Lord] will give all Judah into the hand of the king of Babylon, and he shall carry them captive to Babylon, and shall slay them with the sword. . . . all the treasures of the kings of Judah . . . [they] shall . . . carry them to Babylon.[52]

The prophet seems to have been a chronic disputant, impelled to conflict regardless of his adversaries' postures or motives. There is no indication that he ever responded to the arguments of others or that he accommodated criticism or advice. He proclaimed his own positions and cursed opponents. On one occasion, Jeremiah was said to be a madman posing as a prophet of the Lord.[53] Jeremiah did not mention prominent prophets whose periods overlapped with his (Zephaniah, Nahum, Habakkuk, and Ezekiel).[54] He had no praise for

Uriah, who was killed by Jehoiakim for uttering prophecies similar to his own.[55] Jeremiah grouped other prophets together with priests and scribes as liars, frauds, adulterers, and hypocrites.[56] Perhaps his claim of being a prophet and hearing the words of the Lord saved him from the need to converse, discuss, and adjust in the manner of ordinary mortals. He expressed doubts about his capacity to carry the Lord's word and to stand up to his adversaries, but not about the substance of what he presented as the Lord's message.

Jeremiah was in and out of trouble several times during Zedekiah's reign. Once he was arrested as a traitor, flogged, and imprisoned, when he tried to leave the city.[57] During the final siege of Jerusalem in 586 he was charged with treason for urging the surrender of the soldiers and the population.[58] The king initially ordered that he be executed; then the king responded to the request of another official that Jeremiah be saved. Zedekiah provided refuge to the prophet and sought his counsel, but the king did not change his policy.[59]

The Book of Jeremiah portrays features of an ancient regime that a modern democrat might admire. The prophet's success in getting away with direct criticism of the regime's policy compares well with the record of dissidents in modern democracies during World War I and II and the Cold War.

A Problematic Monarchy

Among the prominent topics of Jewish lore that are variously viewed in biblical episodes is the value of the Israelite monarchy. The topic has obvious political implications insofar as it deals with the supreme human ruler. Religious implications rest in its source in Holy Scripture, especially those portions found in the Torah said to be given by God to Moses.

Deuteronomy calls on the Israelites to appoint as king the man chosen by God.[60] However, the final passage in Judges is a classic expression of individual freedom unfettered by loyalty to a human ruler: "In those days there was no king in Israel, and every man did what was right in his own eyes."[61]

The prophet Samuel discouraged the Israelites when they asked for a king.

> This will be the manner of the king that shall reign over you: He will take your sons. . . . And he will take your daughters. . . . And he will take your fields, and your vineyards, and your olive yards, even the best of them. . . . And he will take your menservants, and your

maidservants, and your goodliest young men, and your asses, and put them to his work. . . . And ye shall cry out in that day because of your king which ye shall have chosen you; and the Lord will not hear you in that day.[62]

As if to assert the credibility of this warning, the first king anointed by Samuel turned out to be a poor ruler. There were early hints of Saul's problems: "An evil spirit from the Lord troubled him," and the king's aides sought to bring comfort by asking the young David to play the harp.[63] A more substantial sign of the king's instability occurred when the people shouted greater praise for David than Saul as a warrior. Saul alternately pursued David and then swore he would do him no harm.[64]

Saul's madness may have derived from shoddy treatment by the prophet Samuel. One story begins with the Israelites in one of their usual difficult situations. In what may be a case of biblical hyperbole, the Philistines are said to have amassed against them 30,000 chariots, 6,000 horsemen, and as many men as there are grains of sand at the seashore. Wisely, the Israelites scattered, saving themselves for a more promising battle. Some went across the Jordan, and others hid in caves, thickets, rocks, high places, and pits.[65]

Before Saul could engage the enemy, it was necessary to perform a sacrifice to the Lord. Samuel was to perform the sacrifice but did not arrive. Saul waited seven days for the prophet while the military situation continued to deteriorate. Finally, Saul performed the sacrifice himself; then the prophet appeared, denouncing the king for acting against the commandments of the Lord and proclaiming the end of his monarchy.

A simple reading of the text reveals that because Samuel was late, Saul had to perform the sacrifice in order to go to battle and preserve his nation against a strong enemy. If Saul did violate God's commandments, it seemed to be for a good cause. For this action, however, Samuel proclaimed that Saul and his family must lose the Lord's blessing.[66] Another episode that contributed to Saul's loss of the monarchy occurred after a battle against the Amalekites. Saul did not destroy all of the enemy and their possessions as instructed, but spared the king and the best of the livestock—"everything worth keeping." When challenged by Samuel, Saul insisted that he had taken the livestock in order to sacrifice to the Lord. Saul's defense led Samuel to rage that the Lord desired not sacrifice but obedience. The prophet then renounced Saul and killed the Amalekite king with his own hands.[67]

The Bible does not explain why two different episodes are described as the cause for the end of Saul's rule. Neither does it assign more weight to either story. Religious commentators assert that Saul's downfall reflects the severity of his faults and his lack of suitability as king.[68] To a believer in God's justice, Saul's harsh punishment signifies the severity of his sin. On the face of things, however, Saul's sin seems less severe than that committed by Aaron in the story of the golden calf—a sin for which there appears to have been no commensurate punishment. ("They gave me their gold, I threw it into the fire, and out came this bull calf.")[69] Perhaps Saul's greatest problem was that he preceded David. Whatever Saul did, those who finally compiled the Book of Samuel, perhaps half a millennium or more after its events are supposed to have occurred, had to justify the end of his kingdom in order to make way for David.[70]

We have already seen the Bible's treatment of David. He was the centerpiece of the Israelite monarchy but was severely flawed. Later kings were no better and generally much worse. Solomon was praised for the lavish character of his court and the construction of the temple but was condemned for paying homage to foreign gods. After Solomon, the stories are typically somber. With few exceptions, most kings are cited for social injustice and the worship of foreign gods.

STRESS, AMBIVALENCE, AND COPING IN THE HEBREW BIBLE

Related to the biblical theme of problematic kings and shrill critics are biblical episodes that recount the problems of individuals who face great stress, wrestle with ambivalence, and cope by making decisions that are manifestly imperfect. These episodes contradict the caricature of the Hebrew Bible as a source of absolute and fundamental truths. It also foretells the practice of modern Israelis who cope with the contrary pressures of religious and antireligious Jews by not granting to either what they demand.

The familiarity with stress and ambivalence seems endemic to the Hebrews-Israelites-Judeans-Jews of the Bible and subsequent generations, a weak people with a strong sense of national identity. During the generations of the Bible, they were fated to occupy a subordinate position to others who were generally more powerful. Later, they were displaced to a number of Diasporas and had varying degrees of prosperity, poverty, security, and uncertainty. A learned capacity to cope may have helped the Jews survive their numerous encounters with conditions of severe stress. Modern Israelis cope with extreme and competing demands that come from religious and antireligious activists. For some, coping consists of enjoying the political theater that surrounds them. For those in authority, it can mean waiting out one crisis until another takes its place in the media or trying to provide partial appeasement to one group of extremists while not igniting their competitors.

Modern psychologists characterize coping as a way of dealing with stress.[71] Research into patterns of responding to personal stresses has developed categories of coping, clusters of behaviors that some term *active* and *passive* coping are similar to what others call *hardiness* and *helplessness,* or *engagement* and *avoidance.* Engagement (active coping or hardiness) includes efforts to salvage something from a difficult situation and an adjustment of expectations in the face of conditions that are not likely to change in the short range. Avoidance (passive coping or helplessness) includes pointless emoting that involves loss of control and direction for oneself and allies; refusing to consider new options; distorting reality; making quixotic choices in an effort to do something without taking account of likely costs and benefits; and wasting resources in efforts that do not produce significant accomplishments.

Researchers find that ambivalence is associated with stress, and they make the point that coping is unlikely to be elegant or to fit neatly into crisply defined categories. The figures of the Bible, as well as modern Israelis, exhibit more than one type of coping. Engagement and avoidance are useful categories, but individuals in stress are likely to exhibit more of one than another rather than wholly one or the other.

A Fearful Moses

Moses' encounter with the Almighty shows ambivalence in the face of an awesome boss and a difficult task. The assignment was no less than to free the Israelite slaves from their bondage, which would require Moses to overcome his fear of receiving a sentence of death for having killed an Egyptian,[72] to make a direct approach to Pharaoh, and to remove sizable human assets from the Pharaoh's economy. Slaves were likely to be a passive lot, and Moses was unsure that he could convince them that he would lead them to a better life: "And Moses said unto God, Who am I, that I should go unto Pharaoh, and that I should bring forth the children of Israel out of Egypt?"[73]

God sought to strengthen Moses' resolve with training in magic that would demonstrate the power that he represented and by telling

Moses that he would go to Pharaoh accompanied by the elders of Israel. Moses continued to doubt himself ("I am slow of speech, and of a slow tongue").[74] The Lord showed his temper when Moses persisted in questioning his own ability and that of God to help him. God finally instructed Moses to take his smooth-talking brother Aaron with him, assuring Moses that he "will be with thy mouth, and teach thee what thou shalt say." And he reminded Moses to bring his staff in order to perform magic.[75]

The portrayal of coping in this story is less strong than that of Moses' ambivalence. Yet it also shows that Moses used engagement coping rather than avoidance coping and that he was successful in dealing with God. Moses' expressions of doubt may have been his way of coping with the difficult assignment by asking for help, and God strengthened his hand. After Moses expressed more doubts, God promised to provide the words that Moses must speak to Pharaoh.

God Also Was Insecure

This episode involving God, Moses, and Pharaoh also reveals ambivalence and coping in the behavior of the Almighty. Both God and Moses appeared to suffer stress in anticipation of persuading Pharaoh to give up his slaves. They coped by lying: God instructed Moses to ask not for the slaves' freedom but only for a holiday so the slaves could go to the wilderness for a religious feast.

Should this be condemned as the kind of lie the Lord's emissary should not tell? Or accepted as the dissembling appropriate to one who would free the slaves of a powerful state? God made no secret of his plans among the Israelites: He told Moses to encourage the Israelites by saying that God would release them from slavery and deliver them to the land that he promised their forefathers.[76] An element that complicates the analysis is God's wish to make the task difficult. God told Moses that he would harden Pharaoh's heart so that Pharaoh would not let the Israelites go readily. God usually said that he had made Moses' task more difficult in order to demonstrate his greater power for the benefit of the Egyptians.[77] Occasionally, however, God said it was meant to convince the Israelites that he was powerful and a fitting object of loyalty.

If God is all powerful, why did he not simply change Pharaoh's heart in order to facilitate the liberation of the slaves and lessen the damage that must be done to the Egyptians? It is commonly explained that God limited his own power in order to provide humans with free will. Yet if God was responsible for hardening Pharaoh's heart, did he not deprive Pharaoh of free will? There are no convincing answers. The variety of questions shows the Bible as a text that raises more questions than it answers. It portrays a God with several characteristics, not all of which indicate omnipotence or a commitment to simple views of truth and justice. Perhaps the various faces of God reflect the circumstances experienced by the authors and compilers of biblical episodes. Life was difficult. Their history did not lend itself to a God who was powerful and consistent in providing care to his people.

The lie attributed to God and Moses is a kind still found in politics, and it fits the model of engagement coping: God and Moses recognized the power of their adversary and sought to neutralize it with dissimulation. But the lie was also a cunning maneuver with an eye toward what was possible. Should not the value of freeing a nation justify telling something other than the complete truth to the powerful autocrat who is enslaving that nation? The Hebrew Bible is not a collection of absolutes. "Thou shalt not bear false witness against thy neighbor"[78] does not mean "Never tell a lie." This episode indicates that even the Almighty may at times have to demonstrate a sly mode of coping rather than outright power.

David's Plight

The Hebrew Bible is at its literary richest in the story of David, who is not the stereotype of a hero or a villain but a complex individual who shows strength and weakness in the presence of temptation and stress. Early in his story, David was pursued by the mad King Saul. (This followed the time when the prophet Samuel renounced his blessing of Saul as king and anointed David and preceded the time David assumed the monarchies of Judah and Israel.) David coped in several ways during this period. In general, he avoided a deadly encounter with Saul, reserving his resources for the time when he would assume leadership. Such behavior fits the model of engagement coping: David recognized his weakness and sought to build his strength with the opportunities available. (At one point, he assembled a band of what may have been outlaws who sold protection to landowners, as portrayed in the story of Nabal and Abigail.)[79]

During this period of weakness, David subordinated himself to Achish, the son of a Philistine king, and for his services received the town of Ziklag.[80] When Achish asked David to join him in a campaign against the Israelites, David agreed, as would be expected from a vassal who had been awarded a town.[81] Before the battle could be joined, however, other Philistine commanders refused to fight alongside an Israelite.[82] David protested his loyalty to Achish: "But what have I done? and what hast thou found in thy servant so long as I have been with thee unto this day, that I may not go fight against the enemies of my Lord the king?"[83] Achish asserted his trust in David but said nonetheless that he could not overcome the opposition of his Philistine colleagues.[84] Did this make David a traitor to the Israelite people? Perhaps an offer to change alliances was necessary for an up-and-coming leader who was dependent on a Philistine lord.

David engaged in avoidance coping at the end of this period in his life. His victory over the forces of Saul's son came after a falling-out between Saul's son and his commander Abner, who offered to bring all of Israel with him to David.[85] Then, despite having been given safe passage by David, Ishbosheth's turncoat commander was killed by David's commander Joab.[86] This was an early instance in a long series of tense encounters between David and Joab, each of which ended with David's inability or refusal to discipline Joab. Prominent in the series were Joab's killing of Absalom against the instructions of David,[87] and Joab's killing of David's general Amasa during the rebellion of Sheba.[88] These cases suggest that the subordinate was not without power over the superior, and they portray David's coping via avoidance instead of confrontation. The series ends only with David's death and his final instructions to Solomon that he "let not [Joab's] hoar head go down to the grave in peace."[89]

The Weakness of a Pious King

After the death of Solomon, Josiah was one of the few Israelite kings that the Bible praised. Yet he also had a flaw that proved deadly: He failed to recognize the nature of a stressful situation and to cope properly. The stress was that of opportunity on the one hand and risk on the other. The episode is set in 609 or 608 B.C.E. The Assyrian Empire that had conquered the northern kingdom of Israel in 722 was weakened. In 612 it lost its own capital of Nineveh to an attack by the Babylonians, and Assyria's territory of Israel seemed to be available for any ruler who could take it. Josiah had done well as the king of Judah. He was credited with leading a period of religious revival and earned the most fulsome praise received by any king after Solomon: "And like unto him was there no king before him, that turned to the Lord with all his heart, and with all his soul, and with all his might, according to all the law of Moses; neither after him arose there any like him."[90]

Josiah aspired to take back the territory that had been lost to the Assyrians. Yet the area was also prized by the Egyptians. II Chronicles indicates that Josiah was warned of the folly involved in going against the army of the powerful country, then describes his mortal wounding in the northern valley of Megiddo.[91] "Josiah hearkened not unto the words . . . from the mouth of God, and came to fight in the valley of Megiddo."[92] The situation had called for concession or avoidance of conflict in the face of a stronger rival. Josiah had unwisely chosen to act as a hero instead of recognizing his limited power. After Josiah's death, Judah deteriorated further until the country's destruction by the Babylonians.

Another King Torn Between Conflicting Pressures

The prophet Jeremiah is the hero of the book that carries his name. In this section, however, we will focus on the stresses on Zedekiah, one of Jeremiah's adversaries. They are a continuation of the pressures that resulted in the death of Josiah.

About a decade after Josiah's death, in 598 or 597, King Zedekiah became head of a government that had chosen to be a vassal of Egypt as opposed to Babylon. The choice is roundly criticized in the Book of Jeremiah, but it was not without merit. Egypt was closer to Judea; moreover, Egypt had shown its concern by intervening in Judea. Egyptian troops had killed Josiah in a battle over the spoils of the Assyrian Empire, and Egypt had removed one Judean king, replaced him with another, and imposed a substantial payment on the Judean court.[93]

Babylon was also powerful and interested in asserting its domination over Judea. In 605 its troops defeated Egyptian forces at Charchemish (northeast of Judea on the upper Euphrates near the modern Turkish-Syrian border) and in 604 sacked Ashkelon (on the Mediterranean coast between Judea and Egypt). Babylon had put Zedekiah on the Judean throne after a military intervention, yet the weight of opinion in his court was in favor of an Egyptian alliance. Moreover, Egypt had intervened and caused Babylon to retreat when Babylon laid siege to Jerusalem in 588. The Egyptian assistance proved to be only temporary; Babylon returned and destroyed the city in 586.

The stresses on Zedekiah included the prophecy of Jeremiah, who shrilly criticized the corruption of the elite and their submission to Egypt rather than Babylon. For these sins, the Lord would employ the Babylonians to wreak a destruction that would be complete and ugly.[94] During the final siege of Jerusalem by the Babylonian forces, the prophet urged the soldiers and people of Jerusalem to surrender.[95] Not surprisingly, members of Zedekiah's court accused the prophet of treason.

Chapter 38 of Jeremiah describes the king's ambivalence and his efforts to cope. He first acceded to demands that Jeremiah be killed. Three princes threw the prophet into a muddy pit, without food and water, where he seemed likely to drown or starve. Then the king responded to the plea of a court official that Jeremiah be saved. He had Jeremiah brought before him and listened to his prophecy as to what the king must do and what would happen if he refused. (The king did not change his policy.) Zedekiah expressed a fear for his own future[96] and bound Jeremiah to a promise not to reveal that he had given him an audience: "Let no man know of these words, and thou shalt not die."[97] In exchange, he allowed Jeremiah to live in the palace, where he remained until the city was destroyed.

It is tempting to label Zedekiah's coping as avoidance insofar as he did not take account of the greater power of Babylon and its insistence on asserting its control over Judah. To be fair to the king, however, the situation that he faced was not clear. Reality, as he assessed it, included the considerable power of Egypt and the support in his court for an alliance with that country. Zedekiah's ambivalence is apparent, but what is less certain is the nature of his decision process and whether his coping should be labeled avoidance or engagement. Perhaps Zedekiah coped by engaging with reality as he saw it. If so, the disastrous outcome may be attributed to the failure of Egypt to provide the support it may have promised or to Zedekiah's error in judging Egypt's power to be greater than Babylon's. The end of Zedekiah's story is a classic lesson for a vassal that betrays the more powerful of the countries that demands its subordination. Babylonian troops broke the defenses of Jerusalem and seized the king. "And they slew the sons of Zedekiah before his eyes, and put out the eyes of Zedekiah, and bound him with fetters of brass, and carried him to Babylon."[98]

The Doubts of Ecclesiastes

There is no more prominent expression of ambivalence in the Hebrew Bible than in the Book of Ecclesiastes. According to the preacher who is identified as the author of the book, everything is ephemeral. Wisdom is preferred to foolishness and is better than money or possessions. However, the pursuit of too much wisdom—or too much of anything—is like chasing the wind. One should not be overly righteous or overly wise. Why make a fool of oneself? It is best to enjoy what can be attained and to live the best life possible.[99]

> Everything has its season . . . a time to be born and a time to die; a time to plant and a time to uproot; a time to kill and a time to heal . . . a time to love and a time to hate; a time for war and a time for peace.[100]

Scholarship is unreliable. By one reading of a difficult passage, the preacher urges his readers not to use a surplus of words.[101] More certain are the oft-quoted lines from the concluding chapter: "The use of books is endless, and much study is wearisome."[102]

God is not to be denied, but God is also a subject of the preacher's ambivalence. Those scholars who see piety as the preacher's major point cannot be ignored. Man has a sense of time past and future but no comprehension of God's work from beginning to end.[103] The vanity, meaninglessness, or impermanence that the preacher describes relates most clearly to the things of human existence. Earth, the heavens, and the Lord are everlasting.[104] It will be well with those who fear God and obey his commands.[105] God knows all our secrets and brings everything we do to judgment.[106] Yet God is inscrutable, and one should not be overly righteous. The preacher repeats that death is the end of the just as well as the unjust.[107] The prime of life is to be enjoyed, but it will pass and seem in retrospect to be emptiness.[108]

At different points the book seems both to express the theme of Job ("there is a just man that perisheth in his righteousness, and there is a wicked man that prolongeth his life in his wickedness")[109] and to repeat the argument of Job's friends ("Whoso keepeth the commandment shall feel no evil thing.")[110] The epilogue of Ecclesiastes is not helpful to the reader who wishes to know just what are the most important values of the preacher. It says that the speaker turned over many maxims in order to teach; that he chose his words carefully in order to give pleasure, even while he taught the truth. The third verse from the end is the classic remark against too much study. The last two verses urge the reader to fear God and obey his commands.

The contribution of Ecclesiastes to this argument is to emphasize the ambivalence that appears in the Hebrew Bible. Ecclesiastes has no detailed portrayal of coping. Indeed, the book is distinctive in that it ponders issues with pervasive ambivalence and no outcome. Robert Gordis offers some conclusions about the preacher on the basis of what is not in the text. The book's lack of social commentary distinguishes it from the books of the prophets and suggests that the writer led a sheltered life in court circles. The book has no clear historical setting. The preacher's concern was not a particular community in a given situation but the fate of individuals facing a universal problem. According to Gordis, the problem is that of individuals (including, perhaps, the preacher) who had striven for ideals or personal accomplishment in their younger years and then encountered the frustrations of old age and the emptiness of what lies beyond.[111] There is one passage that suggests coping by engaging with reality. To the holder of a government position, the preacher advises against resignation if a ruler expresses anger. It is possible to overcome great transgressions with passive acceptance of momentary stress. (The Hebrew leaves the preacher's words quite vague. In the King James translation, the passage is rendered, "If the spirit of the ruler rise up against thee, leave not thy place; for yielding pacifieth great offenses.")[112] Then the author returns to the more prominent theme of the transitory and temporary nature of glory. Perhaps the larger message is that life will pass. Individuals are advised to cope with opportunities in the realization that there are no lasting rewards.

The Suffering of Job

The story of Job is one of intolerable stress, pained expressions of ambivalence, and efforts at coping whose results are perplexing. At the same time it is a portrayal of injustice and an honest admission that even the Almighty may be flawed. A culture that produced Job and Ecclesiastes could tolerate difficult questions about its central values.

The first chapters of Job establish that Job is a blameless, upright, and God-fearing man and that he is subject to an experiment between God and Satan that tests his faith under conditions of severe deprivation: "And the Lord said unto Satan, Behold, all that he hath is in thy power; only upon himself put not forth thine hand."[113] The introductory chapters define the truth of Job's persistent claim that he is innocent of wrongdoing. God's omnipotence, omniscience, and justice are compromised by what seems to be his insecurity and his desire to test his certainty about Job against the allegations of Satan.[114] God allows Job to suffer greatly on account of his dispute with Satan. The death of Job's children presents a problem for God's reputation as a source of justice, perhaps even more severe than Job's suffering.[115]

There are two experiments to test Job's faith. The first is the loss of his children and his possessions, which does not shake his faith.

The second experiment touches Job even more directly. It leaves him with miserable sores, sitting on a pile of ashes and scratching himself with a piece of broken pottery. A neutral umpire of the dispute between God and Satan might conclude that this experiment brought Job to question his faith, if not to renounce it.

The three participants in Job's dialogues are the challengers and foils of Job's claims of innocence and his outbursts against God's injustice. To the three friends, Job expresses despair and rages at God in a way that belies the traditional assertion that Job is a model of resolute patience.[116] Job demands to know what he has done to deserve his punishment.[117] He challenges God to tell him why he has become a target.[118] Job will not be silenced and speaks his mind.[119]

Ultimately, God does speak to Job, but the divine performance is disappointing for those who expect a settling of accounts. There is a great wind and much noise, but the words are beside the point. God asserts his status and puts man in his lower place. It is God who will ask questions and man who will answer. The questions attributed to God are tendentious and bombastic: Who are you to speak to me as you do? Where were you when I created the earth? Did you determine the laws of nature? Do you know where the darkness dwells? Do you know when the mountain goats are born?[120]

On the surface, God's speech is a forthright proclamation of his power. However, a reader might wonder if the author meant to ridicule the Lord by emphasizing his loud evasion of Job's plight. The ambiguity continues in Job's response to God's questions: "What can I say. . . . I already spoke, and will not speak again."[121] Does Job surrender, or does he assert that he has said his piece and cannot penetrate God's self-righteousness? A commentary on the Book of Job assembles the following epithets that scholars have used to describe God as they perceive him in that book: "blustering, buffoon, bully, childish, evil, inscrutable, insecure, irrelevant, irresponsible gambler, less clever than Satan, less than average human being with a great deal of power, majestic, petulant, small-minded king that everyone has to humor, thundering, wantonly cruel, weak."[122]

BEYOND THE BIBLE

Jews appear to be at least as creative with respect to religious thought and practice as any other group. Since biblical times there has been no Jewish regime with the power to enforce religious orthodoxy on the Jews, in the style of historic linkages between states and Christian churches. Further, because of the ethnic element in Jewry, individuals continue to be Jews despite their profession of a deviant religious perspective or even no religious convictions. Widespread literacy has undoubtedly added to the numerous varieties of Judaism, Jewish humanism, and secular Jewish culture. The interpretations of biblical episodes offered earlier are not likely to be accepted by many Orthodox Jews. Some take the position that an individual should not study the Bible without the guidance of learned rabbis. Rather than assessments of tensions, coping, and individuals who are flawed, religious Jews may see only pious observance of God's commandments in figures like Moses, David, and Job.[123] For anyone wishing to parse the distinctions between Judaisms, the subtleties and nuances are infinite. It is no easier for an outsider to define the distinctions among and between Hasidic and anti-Hasidic ultra-Orthodox congregations than to distinguish between Baptists, Pentecostals, and Evangelicals.

The discussion of postbiblical Judaisms may begin with communities that Hellenized. As in other ancient periods, we cannot be sure of the true and complete record. Some scholars see Greek influence in the biblical books of Ecclesiastes, Daniel, Proverbs, and Song of Songs.[124] And those who Hellenized beyond a certain degree (perhaps having themselves uncircumcised) might have ceased being Jews. The Books of Maccabees (not accepted into the Hebrew Bible) provide the most graphic description of the conflict between Hellenized Jews and those who opposed Hellenic influences. The picture resembles that which Josephus later describes of the clash between Jews attracted to the culture of Rome and those who violently rejected Rome and Romanized Jews. Modern Israelis see these episodes as civil wars between zealous, ethnocentric Jews and those willing to accept the cultures of dominant Gentile powers. Some fear a repeat of the old violence, now between zealous Jews who insist on holding on to all of the Land of Israel that was taken in the 1967 war and those who are willing to concede territory in order to accommodate Palestinian demands.

The origins of what became Christianity (what some call "Paul's Reform Judaism")[125] and its separation from Judaism are lost in the uncertainty surrounding the composition of the Gospels.[126] What is clear is that many of the earliest Christians had been Jews or were Jews and Christians simultaneously. The period that produced Jesus was one of both religious and political turmoil. The categories of Sadducees, Pharisees, Essenes, and Christians only begin to record the groups, sects, or schisms that appeared in Judea.[127] Political chaos and religious creativity served each other. The pressures of Rome led some Jews to messianism and zealotry, and the turmoil caused by new religious movements led religious and secular authorities to crack down on dissidents and troublemakers, as in the case of Jesus' crucifixion. The increased pressure from the regime seems likely to have produced even more zealotry and messianism, and so on in a vicious circle.

The products of the increased tension included two prominent Judean revolts against Rome, in 66–73 and 132–135 C.E. For the Jews the results were severe repression, economic catastrophe, and forced and voluntary dispersion. Jewish communities and religious academies formed outside of Jerusalem and Judea. Over the next several hundred years, rabbis adjusted doctrines and rituals to the destruction of the Temple and the end of sacrifices at its alter and produced the elaboration and codification of oral law (i.e., the Mishnah and the Talmuds of Babylon and Jerusalem) that continue as the basis of Rabbinic Judaism. There were also uprisings against the Gentile authorities in Alexandria and other Jewish centers of the Diaspora in 114–117 C.E. The uprisings resulted in repression by the authorities as well as popular violence and pillage against Jews and their property that was encouraged or permitted by the authorities. The followers of one Jewish troublemaker, Simeon ben Koseva (Bar Kokhba), described him as the messiah. Unlike the case of Jesus, however, Bar Kokhba's death at the hands of the Romans in 135 C.E. did not produce a new religious movement that lasted.

Dispersion had been a prominent feature of Judaism since the expulsion carried out by the Babylonian conquerors of Jerusalem in 586 B.C.E. Perhaps less than half of the Jews living in Babylon returned to Judea when that was allowed in 537, and a only minority of the world's Jews lived in the Land of Israel from that time onward. Most of the remainder lived in Mesopotamia, the Arabian peninsula, Syria, North Africa, and Asia Minor until Europe and then North America became the principal Jewish homelands. Individuals adopted the language, dress, and other practices of their host cultures. Rabbinic education and correspondence between religious academies provided a degree of uniformity in Judaism that existed alongside regional differences.

Crises, population movement, and religious creativity continued in Jewish history. Prominent among the crises were the depredations associated with the movement of Crusaders from the Rhineland to the Middle East in the eleventh century; expulsions from the Iberian peninsula in the fifteenth century; massacres in the Ukraine in the seventeenth century; pogroms that marked Russia from the 1880s; and later the Holocaust and the Israeli wars of 1948, 1967, and 1973.

Points of creativity included the work of Maimonides in the twelfth century; the development of Kabbalah, especially after the expulsion from Spain; the schisms surrounding Shabbetai Zevi and Jacob Frank in the seventh and eighteenth centuries; the development of Hasidic congregations from the eighteenth century; the flowering of secular education among Jews; the development of Reform and Conservative Judaism associated with the European Enlightenment from the end of the eighteenth century and massive population movements from Eastern Europe to Western Europe and North America; and a flowering of Jewish nationalism in Israel and its appearance in the Diaspora.

Jewish communities in the United States invite attention even in a book concerned with religion, politics, and public policy in Israel. American Jews represent the largest national Jewish community. There were five to six million Jews in the United States in the mid-1990s, depending on one's definition and the estimate used, whereas there were four to five million in Israel. American Jews affect the Israeli scene by virtue of their creativity in religion, arts, science, and economics and their influence in U.S. culture and politics.[128]

A consideration of religion and politics in Israel would be parochial in the extreme if it did not consider the financial and political support for various modes of Israeli Judaism that come from North American congregations. And there may be as much spiritual influence from Israel to the United States as the reverse. Both national communities contribute to the development of Judaism. The international community has become bipolar, with centers in Jerusalem, Tel Aviv, and Bnei Brak on the one hand and in New York and several other U.S. cities on the other hand.

Assimilation was a theme of American Jewry by the beginning of the nineteenth century. An early leader of Reform Judaism proclaimed that "America is our Zion and Washington is our Jerusalem."[129] The descendants of only one of the twenty-three Jews who settled in New Amsterdam in 1654 were still Jewish in the mid-1950s. Jews are now close to the top of U.S. religious groups on traits of education and income and are found increasingly in high status occupations where they were once excluded. Intermarriage occurs in some 50 percent of newly formed couples. A Christmaslike Hanukkah has greater prominence than Succoth and Shavuot, which traditionally were more important. There has been a decline of attendance in programs of supplementary Jewish training (Hebrew school and Sunday school) among Jews who attend public schools.[130]

Alongside fears that the Jews of the United States will disappear through intermarriage and other forms of assimilation is the old concern that Jewish security can never be ensured. An Israeli undergraduate in a seminar at Hebrew University asked, "When will the American Holocaust occur?" Sophisticated American Jews put the issue more delicately. Rabbi Shalom Carmy, a teacher at Yeshiva University, writes about a "conviction that 'America is different,' if not forever, at least for the time being."[131] On the first page of his book on American Jewry, Alan M. Dershowitz of Harvard Law School asks, "Are American Jews truly first-class citizens of this nation to which we have contributed so much? Or have we merely managed to achieve a greater degree of toleration than Jews have been accorded by other 'host nations' throughout history?"[132]

Religiosity is more prominent in the United States than religious content. Will Herberg describes "pervasive secularism and mounting religiosity." Henry Commager writes that "religion prospered while theology went bankrupt."[133] A Protestantization of religious norms and rituals, or an absorption into an American amalgam, affects both Catholic and Jewish communities. Substantial numbers of American Catholics take positions at odds with official church positions on the ordination of women, clerical celibacy, birth control, abortion, and the use of condoms to prevent the spread of AIDS.

The blending of some Judaisms into an American amalgam exists alongside findings that in the United States Jews are more likely than any other group to admit a lack of religious affiliation.[134] And not to be forgotten are the growing American Orthodox and ultra-Orthodox congregations. Since World War II Jewish day schools in the United States have increased from 30 to 570, and the number of pupils from fewer than 6,000 to over 160,000. Orthodox and ultra-Orthodox congregations in the United States have adapted some doctrines and practices to modern society, even while their observance of certain features of religious law and practice have been described as more strict than those of their parents and grandparents.[135] What suggests that moderation has the upper hand in the United States is a pragmatic cooperation that links Jewish Orthodox activists, fundamentalist Protestants, and Catholics on issues like abortion and public support for religious education. Also suggesting the greater weight of moderate religion in the United States is the failure of these efforts to achieve their most important legislative goals. Multidenominational campaigns in favor of public support for religious education and an end to abortion manage to gain publicity every once in a while but have not changed public policy in any basic manner.

One of the intriguing features of American Jewry is the persistence of Democratic Party loyalty.[136] This contrasts with generally strong relationships between socioeconomic traits and voting behavior. Well-to-do and well-educated Americans usually vote Republican. Groups such as European Catholic ethnics who were once poor and were attracted to Democratic promises of social benefits changed parties as they climbed the ladder of success. Jews, however, continue to vote Democratic—in presidential elections sometimes more than 80 percent—despite their material success. The anomaly has deepened with the emergence of African American anti-Semitism. African Americans are the one social group even more likely than Jews to vote Democratic, and Jews remain allied with them in the party despite anti-Semitic and anti-Israel postures taken by prominent African Americans. The Democratic loyalties of American Jews also survived the tendency of Democratic president Jimmy Carter to be less supportive of Israel than his predecessors, and they were not altered appreciably by the records of Republican presidents Richard Nixon and Ronald Reagan as especially generous supporters of Israel. Jewish voters may have punished individual Democratic candidates by voting for their opponents, but the group as a whole has remained strongly Democratic.

Political scientists have several explanations for this anomaly. One is that the social values associated with Judaism produce left-wing loyalties. However, this explanation runs afoul, because numerous surveys find that Orthodox Jews, who presumably would be most affected by traditional Jewish values, are less likely than other Jews to vote Democratic. Somewhat more persuasive is the explanation that indicators of Jews' social and economic success do not measure their sense of really having made it in the United States. By this reasoning, a persistent feeling of insecurity reinforces Jewish identification with the underprivileged and translates itself into support for left-wing candidates. Heavy Democratic voting among American Jews testifies to their lack of assimilation, despite education, wealth, occupational status, and intermarriage. Most Jews still vote like the poor immigrants they once were. Conservative and Reform Jews may not be exposed to a great deal of traditional Jewish learning, but they have learned enough Jewish history to fear that their comforts might be temporary.

The relatively weak Democratic tendencies among Orthodox Jews is a puzzle. Perhaps some Orthodox Jewish Americans are offended by the postures taken by Democratic candidates on issues like abortion and homosexuality. Or the Orthodox may be more cognizant than other American Jews of the significance of African American Democrats who are anti-Zionist and anti-Semitic.

* * *

What elements of Judaism can be said to be distinctive after three millennia of wandering and writing? To be sure, there are distinctive points of doctrine, rules, and ritual. The editor of a widely used college text on Jewish thought emphasized Jewish ethnicity and a short list of doctrinal points:

> The convictions that there is only one God who created the universe and who guides history, that He commands justice and mercy, and that Israel is His people provide the starting points and focus of Jewish religious thought throughout most of history and affect secular Jewishness in the modern world as well.[137]

It is a reflection of Judaism's influence in world history that the principles of monotheism, justice, and mercy also characterize Christianity and Islam. In order to proceed with an analysis that distinguishes Judaism from these other faiths, it is necessary to return to the themes of this chapter. The truth is that Jewish writers can appear anywhere on several intellectual spectra and still be considered to be within Jewish traditions.

> The Jewish past has a dialectical character. . . . it contains many internal tensions and polarities: messianism and halakhah, rationalism and mysticism, folk tradition and intellectual elitism, holy land and Diaspora, internal and external causation, and so on.[138]

Whether the quotations come from a professor of Jewish history at a secular U.S. university or distinguished rabbis, the message is similar: The doctrines and practices of Judaism are diffuse and diverse and lend themselves to ever-evolving interpretation.[139] The Jews of modern Israel are no less creative than those of the past or contemporary Diasporas in reinterpreting their traditions. They are on a developing and dangerous frontier. Their society is challenged by migrations that bring diverse cultures, by the threats of Palestinians and other Arabs, by the building of the institutions of a new state, and by socialism, privatization, and other governmental fashions that have touched Israel.

This discussion of general principles of Judaism should not overlook the detailed differences in doctrine and practice that distinguish Jewish congregations. Later chapters describe the angry words that flow between the Jews of Israel who are secular and even antireligious and those who are non-Orthodox, Orthodox, and ultra-Orthodox.

Observers may wonder about the nature of Judaism that unites a majority of Israelis who are secular with a minority who appear to be fanatically attached to ideas long out of date. They may wonder even more about those ultra-Orthodox politicians who insist that the exemption of ultra-Orthodox men from military service is justified by their service as students of the Torah yet who refuse to respect Israeli holidays that commemorate victims of the Holocaust, those who died in the military service of the country, or Israeli Independence Day. Along with these political frictions are the personal frictions, apparent when religious children are forbidden by their parents to play with secular children or when religious men spit at women who have entered a religious neighborhood while wearing short sleeves.

There may be no other answer to the question of what unites Jews than Judaic ethnicity. The sharing of a history that has featured persecution culminating in the Holocaust, terrorist attacks, and one-sided condemnations of Israel by the United Nations seems to have welded Israeli Jews into a national unity that is stronger than the internal strains.

Judaic ethnicity is something of its own mystery. The Jewish population of Israel ranges in color and racial types from blondes with Slavic faces to blacks and browns from Ethiopia, Yemen, and India. Among the topics of Israeli quarrels are the credentials to demand from someone claiming to be a Jew, and how to treat individuals converted to Judaism by non-Orthodox rabbis and the children of those converts.

The diversities portrayed in this chapter should make clear to the reader that the opinions and arguments heard from religious and secular Israelis preclude clear victories or losses that can be assigned to religious or secular camps. Competing stereotypes of religious and antireligious power and domination do not stand up to detailed inquiry.

Intellectual variety is also apparent among Christians and Muslims. An impressive number of modern Christian writers make the point that the story of Christ's miraculous birth and resurrection are metaphorical. A Christian who takes this view is left with a compendium of moral postures that Jesus articulated from the Hebrew Bible. From such a viewpoint, Christianity truly is a first cousin of Judaism, but with a claim of universalism as opposed to the ethnicity of Judaism.[140]

Given the diversity that ranges between such Christian liberals and fundamentalists, and the varieties of language and ritual that mark churches with national roots, it is hardly surprising that the religious-political landscape throughout Western democracies resembles that of Israel. The continued vitality of religion affects the political agenda, but a lack of unity among religious interests explains why they fall short of dominating modern polities.

NOTES

1. Gershom Scholem, *Sabbatei Sevi: The Mystical Messiah*, trans. R. J. Zwi Werblowsky (Princeton: Princeton University Press, 1973), p. 117. Jonathan Z. Smith makes a similar point when he writes that a preacher's interpretation of sacred text resembles a pagan witch doctor divining meaning from the arrangement of sacred objects. See his *Imagining Religion: From Babylon to Jonestown* (Chicago: University of Chicago Press, 1982), p. 51.
2. Arthur Hertzberg, *The Condition of Jewish Belief: A Symposium Compiled by the Editors of Commentary Magazine* (New York: Macmillan, 1966), p. 90.
3. Norman F. Cantor, *The Sacred Chain: The History of the Jews* (New York: Harper Collins, 1994).
4. See Ira Sharkansky, *Ancient and Modern Israel: Explorations in Political Parallels* (Albany: State University of New York Press, 1991).
5. Charles S. Liebman and Eliezer Don-Yehiya, *Civil Religion in Israel: Traditional Judaism and Political Culture* (Berkeley: University of California Press, 1984).
6. Exceptions include Menachem Friedman, *Haredi Society: Sources, Goals, and Procedures* (in Hebrew) (Jerusalem: Jerusalem Institute for Israel Studies, 1991); and Tamar El-Or, *Educated and Ignorant: On Ultra-Orthodox Women and Their World* (in Hebrew) (Tel Aviv: Am Oved, 1992).
7. Janet Aviad, "The Messianism of Gush Emunim," in Jonathan Frankel, ed., *Jews and Messianism in the Modern Era: Metaphor and Meaning. Studies in Contemporary Jewry: An Annual* (Jerusalem and New York: Institute of Contemporary Jewry, Hebrew University and Oxford University Press, 1991), pp. 197–213; and Ehud Sprinzak, *The Ascendance of Israel's Radical Right* (New York: Oxford University Press, 1991).
8. *Ha'aretz* (in Hebrew), October 11, 1995, p. 5.
9. *Ha'aretz* (in Hebrew), October 20, 1995, p. 6.
10. *Ha'aretz* (in Hebrew), April 20, 1995, p. 1.
11. Exodus 20:3.
12. For example, Deuteronomy 10:18.
13. Isaiah 2:4.
14. *The Condition of Jewish Belief*.
15. Jacob B. Agus, *The Condition of Jewish Belief*, p. 12.
16. Mordecai M. Kaplan, *The Condition of Jewish Belief*, p. 121.
17. Hertzberg, *The Condition of Jewish Belief*, p. 90.
18. Emanuel Rackman, *The Condition of Jewish Belief*, p. 179.
19. Hertzberg, *The Condition of Jewish Belief*, pp. 90–97.
20. Rackman, *The Condition of Jewish Belief*, p. 181.
21. Chaim Dov Keller, "Modern Orthodoxy: An Analysis and a Response," in Reuven P. Bulka, ed., *Dimensions of Orthodox Judaism* (New York: KTAV Publishing House, 1983), pp. 253–271.
22. Amos Oz, *A Journey in Israel: Autumn 1982* (in Hebrew) (Tel Aviv: Am Oved, 1986).
23. Oz, *A Journey in Israel*, pp. 111–112.
24. Charles S. Liebman and Steven M. Cohen, *Two Worlds of Judaism: The Israeli and American Experiences* (New Haven: Yale University Press, 1990).
25. Even in biblical times there were no absolute demarcations around the concept of *Jew*. See Smith, *Imagining Religion*, chap. 1.
26. Some of the material in this chapter comes from Ira Sharkansky,

Israel and Its Bible: A Political Analysis (New York: Garland Publishing Company, 1996).
  27. I Samuel 22:2; 23:13.
  28. I Samuel 22:2.
  29. I Samuel 25:2–44.
  30. II Samuel 3.
  31. II Samuel 3:26–33.
  32. II Samuel 12:28.
  33. II Samuel 2–4.
  34. II Samuel 18:14.
  35. II Samuel 19:5–8.
  36. II Samuel 20:10.
  37. For a description of this as a coup d'état, see Tryggve N. D. Mettinger, *Solomonic State Officials: A Study of the Civil Government Officials of the Israelite Monarchy* (Lund, Sweden: CWK Gleerup, 1971), p. 121.
  38. I Kings 1:32–40.
  39. II Samuel 23:1–7.
  40. I Kings 2:6.
  41. II Samuel 12:7.
  42. II Samuel 12.
  43. I Kings 1; and Mettinger, *Solomonic State Officials*.
  44. II Samuel 7:7.
  45. I Chronicles 22:8.
  46. Carol Meyers, "David as Temple Builder," in Patrick D. Miller, Jr., Paul D. Hanson, and S. Dean McBride, eds., *Ancient Israelite Religion* (Philadelphia: Fortress Press, 1987), pp. 357–376.
  47. II Chronicles 35:20–25.
  48. II Kings 23–33.
  49. Jeremiah 22:13–17.
  50. Jeremiah 7:25–27.
  51. Jeremiah 19:8–9.
  52. Jeremiah 20:4–5.
  53. Jeremiah 29:26–27.
  54. John Bright, *Jeremiah: The Anchor Bible* (Garden City, NY: Doubleday & Company, 1965), introduction.
  55. Jeremiah 26:20–24.
  56. Jeremiah 23:14; 28:15–16.
  57. Jeremiah 37:11–16.
  58. Jeremiah 38:2–4.
  59. Jeremiah 38:14–28.
  60. Deuteronomy 17:14–20.
  61. Judges 21:25.
  62. I Samuel 8:11–18.
  63. I Samuel 16.
  64. I Samuel 24–26.
  65. I Samuel 13:5–7.
  66. I Samuel 13:5–14.
  67. I Samuel 15.
  68. Adin Steinsaltz, *Biblical Images: Men and Women of the Book* (New York: Basic Books, 1984).
  69. Exodus 32:24.

70. David M. Gunn, *The Fate of King Saul: An Interpretation of a Biblical Story*, Journal for the Study of the Old Testament Supplement Series, no. 14 (Sheffield: Sheffield Academic Press, 1984); Meir Shalev, *The Bible Now* (in Hebrew) (Jerusalem: Schocken, 1985), pp. 65–73; John A. Sanford, *King Saul, The Tragic Hero: A Study in Individuation* (New York: Paulist Press, 1985); and Steinsaltz, *Biblical Images*, chap. 16.

71. For contemporary discussions of coping, see George V. Coelho, David A. Hamburg, and John E. Adams, eds., *Coping and Adaptation* (New York: Basic Books, 1974); S. Folkman et al., "Dynamics of a Stressful Encounter: Cognitive Appraisal, Coping, and Encounter Outcomes," *Journal of Personality and Social Psychology* 50, no. 5 (1986): 992–1003; Susan Folkman, "Personal Control and Stress and Coping Processes: A Theoretical Analysis," *Journal of Personality and Social Psychology* 46, no. 4 (1984): 839–852; Rudolf H. Moos and Jeanne A. Schaefer, "Life Transitions and Crises: A Conceptual Overview," in Moos in collaboration with Schaefer, eds., *Coping with Life Crises: An Integrated Approach* (New York: Plenum Press, 1986); A. A. Stone and J. M. Neale, "New Measure of Daily Coping: Development and Preliminary Results," *Journal of Personality and Social Psychology* 46, no. 4 (1984): 892–906. This literature is related to political concepts in Ira Sharkansky, "Coping Strategies of Engagement and Avoidance: The Case of Jerusalem," *Policy and Politics* 23, no. 2 (April 1995).

72. Exodus 2
73. Exodus 3:11.
74. Exodus 4:10.
75. Exodus 4:11–17.
76. Exodus 6:2–8.
77. Exodus 7:3–6.
78. Exodus 20:16.
79. I Samuel 25:2–44.
80. I Samuel 27:6.
81. I Samuel 28:1–2.
82. I Samuel 29:1–5.
83. I Samuel 29:8.
84. I Samuel 29:9.
85. II Samuel 3.
86. II Samuel 3:26–33.
87. II Samuel 18:14.
88. II Samuel 20:10.
89. I Kings 2:6.
90. II Kings 23–25.
91. II Chronicles 35:23–24.
92. II Chronicles 35:20–22.
93. II Kings 23.
94. Jeremiah 9:10; 19:8–9; 20:4–5.
95. Jeremiah 38:2–4.
96. Jeremiah 38:19.
97. Jeremiah 38:24.
98. II Kings 25:7.
99. Ecclesiastes 2:13; 7:16.
100. Ecclesiastes 3:1–8.
101. Ecclesiastes 6:11. The Hebrew of this passage employs a word that

can be rendered as *thing* or *word*. The King James translation is, "Seeing there be many things that increase vanity, what is man the better?" The New English Bible translation is, "The more words one uses the greater is the emptiness of it all; and where is the advantage to a man?"

102. Ecclesiastes 12:12.
103. Ecclesiastes 3:11.
104. Ecclesiastes 1:4.
105. Ecclesiastes 8:13.
106. Ecclesiastes 12:13–14.
107. Ecclesiastes 7:16–17; i:14–17; 9:2–6.
108. Ecclesiastes 11:9–10.
109. Ecclesiastes 7:15.
110. Ecclesiastes 8:5.
111. Robert Gordis, *Koheleth: The Man and His Work: A Study of Ecclesiastes* (New York: Schocken Books, 1968), chap. 10.
112. Ecclesiastes 10:4.
113. Job 1:12.
114. Job 2:3.
115. David Penchansky, *The Betrayal of God: Ideological Conflict in Job* (Louisville, KY: Westminster/John Knox Press, 1990).
116. James 5:11.
117. Job 6:24.
118. Job 7:21.
119. Job 7:11.
120. Job 38–41.
121. Job 40:4–5.
122. Penchansky, *The Betrayal of God*.
123. For a politically relevant discussion of Rabbinic Judaism, see Stuart A. Cohen, *The Three Crowns: Structures of Communal Politics in Early Rabbinic Jewry* (Cambridge: Cambridge University Press, 1990).
124. Gordis, *Koheleth*, p. 68.
125. Karen Armstrong, *A History of God: The 4,000-Year Quest of Judaism, Christianity and Islam* (New York: Ballantine Books, 1993), p. 90.
126. See, for example, Herman C. Waetjen, *A Reordering of Power: A Sociopolitical Reading of Mark's Gospel* (Minneapolis: Fortress Press, 1989); John Dart, *The Jesus of Heresy and History: The Discovery and Meaning of the Nag Hammadi Gnostic Library* (San Francisco: Harper and Row, 1988).
127. Robert A. Kraft and George W. E. Nickelsburg, eds., *Early Judaism and Its Modern Interpreters* (Philadelphia: Fortress Press, 1986).
128. Peter Y. Medding, ed., *A New Jewry? America Since the Second World War. Studies in Contemporary Jewry: An Annual* (Jerusalem and New York: Institute of Contemporary Jewry, Hebrew University and Oxford University Press, 1992); Shalom Carmy, "A View from the Fleshpots: Exploratory Remarks on Gilded Galut Existence," in Chaim I. Waxman, ed., *Israel as a Religious Reality* (Northvale, NJ: Jason Aronson Inc., 1994), pp. 1–42; Eliezer Don-Yehiya, "Does Place Make a Difference? Jewish Orthodoxy in Israel and the Diaspora," in Waxman, *Israel as a Religious Reality*, pp. 43–74; Sam Lehman-Wilzig and Bernard Susser, eds., *Public Life in Israel and the Diaspora* (Ramat Gan: Bar-Ilan University Press, 1981); Chaim I. Waxman, *America's Jews in Transition* (Philadelphia: Temple University Press, 1983); Liebman and Cohen, *Two Worlds of Judaism;* and Paul L. Wilkes, *And They Shall Be My*

People: An American Rabbi and His Congregation (New York: Ballantine Books, 1995).

129. Barry A. Kosmin and Seymour P. Lachman, *One Nation Under God: Religion in Contemporary American Society* (New York: Crown Publishers, 1993), p. 25.

130. Kosmin and Lachman, *One Nation Under God.*

131. Carmy, "A View from the Fleshpots," p. 11.

132. Alan M. Dershowitz, *Chutzpah* (New York: Touchstone, 1991), p. 3.

133. Kosmin and Lachman, *One Nation Under God*, pp. 25, 46, 47.

134. Kosmin and Lachman, *One Nation Under God*, pp. 76, 121.

135. On recent changes in Orthodoxy as practiced in the United States and Israel, see Haym Soloveitchick, "Rupture and Reconstruction: The Transformation of Contemporary Orthodoxy," *Tradition* 28, no. 4 (1994): 64–131.

136. Kenneth D. Wald, *Religion and Politics in the United States* (Washington, DC: CQ Press, 1992), pp. 321f.

137. Robert M. Seltzer, *Jewish People, Jewish Thought: The Jewish Experience in History* (New York: Macmillan, 1980), p. xi.

138. Seltzer, *The Jewish Experience in History*, p. 718.

139. Abba Hillel Silver, *Where Judaism Differs: An Inquiry into the Distinctiveness of Judaism* (New York: Collier Books, 1989), introduction.

140. Dart, *The Jesus of Heresy and History;* Brad H. Young, *Jesus and His Jewish Parables: Rediscovering the Roots of Jesus' Teaching* (New York: Paulist Press, 1989); Herman C. Waetjen, *A Reordering of Power;* and Frederick C. Grant, *Ancient Judaism and the New Testament* (Westport, CT: Greenwood Press, 1959).

4
ISRAELI POLITICS

Israel's Declaration of Independence proclaims it a Jewish state. The declaration also contains a commitment that Israel will not discriminate on the basis of race, religion, national origin, or sex.

Not the least of the problems that the document raises is determining the meaning of *Jewish state*. It does not mean a state only for Jews: Some 17 percent of the population is not Jewish. It does not mean a state to be governed by Jewish religious law (halaka) or ruled by rabbis. Jewish religious law is used as the basis of marriages and divorces among Jews, yet the Jews who object to this aspect of Israeli life can avoid it by well-known procedures. Religious parties generally do not exceed 10–15 percent of the vote in national elections, although they gained almost 20 percent in 1996. Most Israelis define themselves as secular, many of them speak out in opposition to the Orthodox rabbinate and to religion more generally.

One aspect of Israel as a Jewish state is that Jewish history, holidays, and religious symbols are adopted by the state and are central themes in education. Another is that the Jewish majority favors itself in the distribution of political appointments and policy benefits. Yet another meaning of Israel's Jewish character is that its citizens spend a great deal of effort arguing about Jewish issues. Ethnicity, religion, and politics are chronically on the political agenda. The diversity of the society has stood in the way of a clear selection of a governing party by majority vote. Individual disputes can be settled or pushed aside to be settled later. However, basic questions of Israel's Jewish character are unsettled, returning time and again in a constellation of demands by a religious or secular faction.

This chapter surveys Israeli politics with an emphasis on those traits that are relevant to the competition between religious and secular interests. It describes the character of Israeli democracy and identifies issues that may be endemic to a Jewish state. (These issues appeared on the agenda of the ancient Judeans and seemed to be awaiting the birth of modern Israel after 2,000 years of Jewish statelessness.) The chapter describes the results of surveys into the religiosity of Israeli Jews and the political views that tend to be associated with various degrees of religiosity. It concludes by noting that coping with difficulties, as opposed to solving problems once and for all, is a style of policymaking that suits the Jews of Israel. Most likely, it was learned and sharpened in their long and stressful history.

ISRAELI SOCIETY AND GOVERNMENT

In describing Israeli politics social scientists have emphasized the coexistence of sharp dispute and social cohesion among the Jewish majority. The elements that produce this strange combination include the ideological cleavages of socialism versus capitalism and religiosity versus secularism, a structure of government that hinders the development of clear majorities on either side of current disputes, and a shared history of Jews having to stand together against non-Jewish adversaries. Compromises improvised by leading figures have acquired the status of precedents. Israel's founding prime minister, David Ben-Gurion, defined key parameters when he agreed to the provision of serving only kosher food in state institutions and the exemption of women and students of religious academies from compulsory military service.[1]

Israel earns its place in the list of democratic regimes because of its free and open elections and the peaceful transfer of power from incumbents who lose elections.[2] Typically, about twenty parties compete in national elections based upon proportional representation, and about ten pass the minimum electoral requirements for gaining a seat in the Knesset. The ideological spectrum represented in the Knesset has ranged from Communists and Arab-dominated parties on the left to free-enterprise, Jewish religious, and nationalist parties on the right. Islamic religious parties have won places in local councils. Both Jews and non-Jews have credible records of voter turnout at about 80 percent in national elections. The largest parties now employ primaries open to all dues-paying members to select nominees for major offices.

Severe problems distinguish Israel from other Western democracies: war, terror attacks, heavy immigration, unsettled boundaries, economic burdens, and the scars of the Holocaust and other persecutions. Some 14,000 Israelis have died as a result of military engagements since 1948, not counting civilians killed in terrorist raids.[3] To compare that number to the U.S. population, it would be as if 900,000 Americans had died in combat during the same years. (Actually, about 90,000 U.S. military personnel died in the Korean and Vietnam wars together.)[4] Three hundred thousand Americans died in World War II (0.2 percent of the national population). During that war, the Nazis and their allies killed 40 percent of all the Jews in the world. A large number of Israelis are Holocaust survivors or their descendants. Many others came as refugees from persecution in Arab lands. Family losses add poignancy to discussions of what Israelis are willing to risk by way of physical security for treaties with enemies who only a short while ago called for the country's complete destruction. Israel's 1979 treaty of peace with Egypt was its first with a neighboring country. The second agreement occurred in 1994 with Jordan. Still pending are negotiations with Syria, Lebanon, and the Palestinians.

As a percentage of gross national product, Israel's annual financial outlays on security are five to ten times greater than other democracies. Outlays for security combine with the socialism that is joined to Zionism to produce a major role for government ministries in economic management. In some years the expenditures of government and quasi-governmental bodies have exceeded gross national product.[5] Overseas purchases of military equipment contribute to a high international debt and a chronic imbalance between imports and exports. Israel's inflation reflects the pressures on its economy. Price increases were above 100 percent annually from 1979 through the middle of 1985 and since 1992 have been considered modest in the range of 8–15 percent. Inflation in other Western democracies is generally below 4 percent annually.

A history of violence against the state and its citizens is cited to explain security procedures—censorship and other legal provisions—that are severe compared with those of other democracies. Israel has secretly arrested, tried, and sentenced spies, terrorists, and other violators of its security laws, never revealing the details of the cases to the public or to the attorneys for the accused. Under some conditions, Israeli security forces are allowed to use "moderate physical pressure" in interrogations.[6]

Criticisms of Israel's shortfalls from democratic ideals are well known and will be reviewed here briefly.[7] More attention will be devoted to the tantalizing question of how Israel has come to be as democratic as it is. Most of Israel's population came only a generation or two ago from Central and Eastern Europe or the Middle East, where democracy was weakly established if it existed at all. The first years of the state's existence were marked by a difficult war and mass immigration. Almost all of the immigrants were desperately poor and in need of housing and social services. Such conditions are typically used to explain coups d'état and other cancellations of democratic procedures. Few countries that entered the world's scene in the decade after World War II came close to fulfilling their proclamations of democracy with the success that Israel achieved.

Israeli politics are contentious. There is a broad spectrum of print media in Israel and no lack of controversial material on government-operated radio and television. Comparative research finds that Israelis are more likely than residents of other Western democracies to express their dissatisfaction by mass demonstrations as opposed to individual letters of complaint. Activists from all points of the spectrum criticize their adversaries in shrill terms,[8] and is not uncommon to hear threats of violence. However, a study of political killings in Israeli history concludes that its incidence has been low in relation to other national experiences.[9] In the case of protests having a religious theme, religious Israelis and especially the ultra-Orthodox are more likely to be involved in protests than secular Israelis. This may reflect the number of students who assemble daily in religious academies and are readily bused to wherever their rabbis want to demonstrate. According to one scholar who studies this phenomenon, ultra-Orthodox Israeli rabbis learned their protest techniques from U.S. rabbis who demonstrated against threats from African Americans to their congregations in Brooklyn.[10]

An explanation for the generally high level of protest in Israel is a blockage in conventional opportunities for policy innovations. The multiplicity of political parties and an electoral system of proportional representation both reflects and reinforces a tendency toward a diversity of options without a clear choice among them. No party has ever won a majority at an Israeli national election. All cabinets have been coalitions between parties whose leaders continue to quarrel even while they govern. The Israeli version of what Americans call governmental gridlock is made up of coalition governments in which several parties possess an informal power of veto against policy changes they consider to be undesirable. One study of twenty-eight long-term protest campaigns in the 1980s discovered that the success ratio was 38 percent. By one observation, this was a "paltry" record, but there was no international comparison to support the adjective.[11]

The most sensitive questions concerning Israel's democracy concern the balance of opportunities between the Jewish majority and non-Jews. No democracy is truly egalitarian, but Israel departs from that standard explicitly by labeling itself a Jewish state. Israeli intellectuals (Jews and non-Jews) and governmental reports concede that Jews receive a major portion of political opportunities and policy benefits. Israelis argue various sides of the question as to whether or not those distributions are justified by threats of security, the small size of the non-Jewish minority, or Arab disinclination to recognize the legitimacy of the Israeli regime. A subset of these arguments focuses on the territories occupied as a result of the 1967 war, where non-Jews have had a minimum of civil rights. Large parts of those territories are currently being transferred to Palestinian authorities, with the future of the remainder yet to be negotiated.

Civil libertarians criticize the Israeli regime for giving religious authorities (Jewish, Muslim, Christian, and Druze) a near monopoly to deal with the marriages and divorces in their communities according to their religious laws. These laws are inconvenient to members of religious communities who are anticlerical. They preclude the performance of a marriage ceremony between members of different religious communities or between individuals with other traits whom religious law disqualify as marriage partners. For Jews, this means that a *mamzer* (a bastard as defined by religious law) cannot marry a Jew, that males with the surname of Cohen cannot marry a woman who has been divorced, and that a childless widow cannot remarry without the consent of her late husband's brother. All of these prohibitions can be avoided if the individuals concerned are willing to marry outside of Israel and register themselves as married with the Ministry of Interior. Likewise, Israelis can divorce outside of Israel and have their status registered with the Ministry of Interior. Israeli civil courts will enforce the rights and obligations of married or divorced persons according to their registered status. The courts will also enforce the rights of spouses and children where no formal marriage has occurred.

Israel's capacity for self-criticism is prominent among the traits that grant it status as a democracy. Harsh critics of the regime are widely heard and occasionally honored. The late Yehoshafat Harkabi was head of military intelligence and became a professor of international relations at Hebrew University in Jerusalem. Harkabi used a historical analysis to argue a point of contemporary policy. He opposed those Israelis who revere the heroic nationalism of the Bar Kokhba rebellion against the Romans in 131–135 C.E. According to Harkabi, Bar Kokhba was guilty of irrational warfare that was bound to end in disaster. He wrote that the modern crazies are those who insist that the West Bank should be Israel's possession and predicted disaster, perhaps even the destruction of the Jewish people, if the zealots did not stop or were not stopped by more reasonable Israelis. Harkabi was among the first prominent Israelis who urged the government to deal openly with the Palestine Liberation Organization at a time when that organization was conventionally viewed as terrorist and beyond the pale of political discourse.[12]

Meron Benvenisti was a ranking member of the Jerusalem municipal council soon after the Six Day War and worked unsuccessfully to create boroughs to give political expression to the city's ethnic and religious communities. He earned a doctorate at Harvard's Kennedy School, returned to Israel, and dedicated himself to the West Bank Data Project, which investigated Jewish settlements in the occupied territories. Benvenisti referred to Israelis as conquerors and parasites and compared them to medieval autocrats who plundered the lands they occupied. Like Harkabi, Benvenisti predicted national disaster if his warnings were not heeded.[13]

The late Yeshayahu Leibowitz was a religious Jew and an emeritus professor of chemistry at Hebrew University. He appeared frequently on Israeli television, usually in rumpled clothes, with his eyeglasses and skullcap askew. Shortly after the end of the Six Day War in June 1967, Leibowitz began to warn Israelis about the moral costs of military occupation. He believed it was impossible to realize Jewish values in a binational state, and he predicted a scenario of brutalization by those Israelis who achieved an upper hand by force and who would put people like him in concentration camps.[14]

Each of these critics was prominent in Israel's mass media. Harkabi and Leibowitz were designated recipients of prestigious Israel Prizes for 1993 by the Ministry of Education and Culture. The public accepted Harkabi's award routinely, but Leibowitz's evoked both condemnation and praise. Much of the censure was directed at his use of the term *Nazi* to describe Israel's actions. For a society built on the ashes of the Holocaust, that defined a criticism that was beyond public honor. Leibowitz resolved the issue after a few days of controversy by declining the award.

An aggressive state comptroller (the supreme auditor, responsible to the Knesset) is a prominent source of moral reflection and self-criticism. The laws empowering Israel's state comptroller are unusually broad in comparison to those of parallel bodies in other countries. Israel's auditor is authorized to review government activities for their moral integrity and for the more conventional standards of legality, economy, efficiency, and effectiveness. Israel's state comptroller was among the first government auditors to criticize not only the implementation of policy but the choice of major policy goals. Its reports have covered such important issues as military research and development, a major restructuring of Israel's banks, police responses to terrorist episodes, and the allocation of resources for Arab education.[15]

Recently there has been a further extension of the state comptroller's responsibilities. Political auditing focuses on the activities of officials and citizen activists that are concerned directly with political advantage.[16] It involves the auditor in the thick of political conflict and exposes the auditor to the anger of elected officials. Several audit reports have criticized government ministers for selecting unqualified cronies for appointive positions, ordering that units under their control purchase equipment from companies owned by party supporters, and distributing public funds to programs run by their party colleagues. The auditor has listed citizens who contribute money to two or more political parties; the contributions violate no law or regulation but are contrary to the auditor's view of proper democracy. The prophetic tone in some audit reports is reflected in the comptroller's comments on legislation that seemed contrary to the principles of good government: "This legislation cut off the law from its moral basis and left it with only formal validity."[17] This recalls the language used by the prophet Amos, who demanded righteousness rather than narrow compliance with religious law.

> Though ye offer me burnt offerings and your meat offerings, I will not accept them: neither will I regard the peace offerings of your fat beasts. Take thou away from me the noise of thy songs; for I will not hear the melody of thy viols. But let judgment run down as waters, and righteousness as a mighty stream.[18]

EXPLAINING ISRAEL'S DEMOCRACY

The tolerance of disputatious criticism in Israel's polity suggests that we look backward in history to determine the source of the numerous factions that have long been a hallmark of Jewish culture. Factionalism may be a cultural trait of Jews and may answer at least part of the question about democracy. That is, Israel is democratic because Jews have acquired a tolerance for numerous perspectives.[19]

From where comes the capacity to live with numerous perspectives? Part of the answer may be the high level of literacy that has characterized Jews (or at least Jewish men) for centuries and even millennia. Jewish communities have not relied on small groups of learned elites. This capacity may also lie in the fact that Israel's population has come from many lands that have different ways of dealing with public issues, including the fundamental question of how Jews should relate with Gentiles. European Jews in the nineteenth century, who provided the source of the first Israeli leaders, had multiple intellectual and political options, as they left the isolation of closed religious communities for the experience of the Enlightenment. Organizations sprang up to advocate different and contradictory ways of managing the new opportunities and residual problems of European Jewry. They encouraged Jews to learn Gentile languages and pursue a greater integration into a European homeland; to learn Hebrew and prepare for migration to Palestine; or to promote Yiddish and form a distinct community that would pursue its interests within the framework of a European nation. Many Jews became enthusiastic socialists, and some became explicitly humanistic, agnostic, atheistic, or anticlerical. Others were attracted to liberalism or remained religious and aloof from secular issues. Among the religious, there were choices from Hasidic and anti-Hasidic congregations. Especially in Western Europe and North America, there were also Jewish religious variations from Orthodoxy.

The first generation of Israeli politicians may not have come from democratic societies. However, they came from countries where political movements that aspired to democracy seethed on or beneath the surface. David Ben-Gurion, Israel's first prime minister, was an archetype of the Eastern European Jews who lived through Jewish youth movements prior to migration, activity in a kibbutz, the Labor Federation (Histadrut) and Jewish Agency during the late Ottoman period, and the British Mandate in Palestine. Like many others of his generation, Ben-Gurion had limited formal academic training, yet he engaged the leading scientists and scholars of Israel in disputes about philosophy and science. Many of the controversies he provoked concerned state building: the appropriate limits of government authority, the nature of democracy, and the contributions to be expected from intellectuals in creating a new country. He encouraged and participated in biblical scholarship and polemics. The distinguished scholar Ephraim Urbach was present on one occasion when the prime minister perceived support in the prophets for his political vision. Urbach reminded Ben-Gurion that the prophets criticized the political elites of their time.[20]

Some insights about the style of Israeli politics come from the Hebrew Bible. This is not an effort to judge the politics in modern Israel by virtue of what is sanctioned by the Bible. Israelis view the Bible as part of their history, however, and it can offer clues as to Israelis' political perspectives. We saw in Chapter 3 that the Hebrew Bible describes a culture that was critical of its leaders. Beyond this, the diversity of politically relevant themes in the Bible suggests that authors or compilers of the Holy Book were open to numerous viewpoints. The candid telling of heroes' stories suggests that the Bible's writers were not purists in maintaining strict ideas about acceptable behavior. David was an adulterer and killer yet also a penitent, a cunning plotter who became a venerated king but could not keep his own family from fratricide and civil war. Not even the Almighty is beyond reproach. Both Abraham and Moses questioned his justice and persuaded him to moderate punishments decreed against sinners. God's reputation of omnipotence and omniscience did not protect him from an unreliable people. And none of the leaders God chose for his people were without blemish. Dissonance is a prominent trait of the Bible, especially in Job, where God appears as insecure and unjust.[21]

It is tempting to abandon the Hebrew Bible as a source of political insight on account of its lack of clear doctrine. For the argument of this book, however, a lack of doctrinal clarity is less a problem than a virtue. It suggests a capacity to accommodate different outlooks.[22]

ETHNOCENTRIC VERSUS UNIVERSALISTIC PERSPECTIVES IN THE BIBLE AND MODERN ISRAEL

A consideration of biblical politics is relevant not only because Jewish familiarity with divergent perspectives from the creation of the Hebrew Bible can partially explain Israel's style of democracy. On Israel's agenda is a dispute that has been unresolved in Jewish traditions since biblical times. On the one hand are those who emphasize the Jewish character of the state and claim special privileges for Jews. Some assert that they are God's chosen people given ownership of the Promised Land. They bolster their claim to the land by citing the historical suffering of the Jews, the beleaguered nature of modern Israel, and the need of Jews for a national refuge that is controlled by Jews. On the other hand are those Israelis who emphasize biblical norms of universal justice and egalitarian rights. Some Israelis who ponder the historical suffering of the Jews conclude that it supports compromise on territorial issues.

The Israelites' status as God's chosen people and numerous episodes indicating their special treatment support the assertion that the Bible is ethnocentric. A notable example is the curses heaped on the Amalekites, who were among the peoples who did not want to share land with the Israelites and who time and again served as the symbols of hostile foreigners. God demanded that the Amalekites be destroyed completely, along with all their possessions.[23] The Books of Ezra and Nehemiah relate to a later time in Judaic history and take strong postures in behalf of Judaic purity.

> The land which you are entering and will possess is a polluted land, polluted by the foreign population with their abominable practices,

which have made it unclean from end to end. Therefore, do not give your daughters in marriage to their sons, and do not marry your sons to their daughters, and never seek their welfare or prosperity.[24]

In contrast is the story of the Moabite Ruth that emphasizes the openness of Judaism to newcomers. According to some, the Book of Ruth was composed at about the same time as the Books of Ezra and Nehemiah for the purpose of expressing a universal humanist perspective in contrast to the ethnocentricism of those books.[25] Not only was Ruth welcomed into a Judaic family, but she was the great-grandmother of no less than King David.[26] The Book of Jonah may also have been written at about the same time. It expresses a universal perspective in describing God's mercy for the Assyrian enemies of Israel.

For those who seek complexity in the Bible, the Book of Isaiah offers numerous examples of the contrasting perspectives of ethnocentrism and universalism. Some passages express the Lord's concern for all nations: "Nation shall not lift up sword against nation, neither shall they learn war any more."[27] Other sections of Isaiah are ethnocentric: "Israel will prevail over the nations"[28]; "For that nation and kingdom that will not serve thee shall perish; Yea, those nations shall be utterly wasted."[29]

The tensions between universality and ethnocentrism continue to trouble Israelis. A secular newspaper reported in 1995 that an examination for rabbinical candidates asked if it was permitted to violate the Sabbath in order to save the life of someone who appeared to be an Arab. The article referred to one religious precedent that permitted such a violation but only to save a Jew, but the report indicated that such a view was not accepted by contemporary rabbis. It also quoted the chief Sephardi rabbi of Israel as demanding an inquiry into the examination, which he viewed as not sufficiently sensitive to current realities. Other participants in the dispute argued that a proper phrasing of the question would have referred to goyim (Gentiles) and not Arabs per se and that it is established practice for Orthodox Jewish physicians to treat Jews and non-Jews equally.[30]

The late rabbi Meir Kahane was the most outspoken ethnocentric in modern Israel. He often quoted passages from Ezra and Nehemiah in order to justify proposals to forbid sexual relations between Jews and non-Jews, to deprive non-Jews of all civil rights, and to expel them from Israel.[31] Kahane's opponents compared his demands to the Nuremberg Laws that the Nazis legislated against the Jews. They led a campaign to outlaw political parties that incite racism and employed this law to prevent Kahane and his successors from offering their candidacy to the Knesset in the elections of 1988 and 1992.

VIOLENCE AMONG JEWS

The manner in which Jews have carried on their disputes is important to this analysis of the Israeli polity. The incidence of political violence is one measure of a country's capacity to deal with conflict. However, the issue is clouded by problems of concept and method: which incidents of violence are political and which are the activities of unstable individuals or ordinary criminals that may have been directed against a politician or been given a patina of a political cause?[32]

Nachman Ben-Yehuda extensively reviewed political killings by Jews and analyzed the phenomenon from a sociological perspective. He admits the difficulty in classifying cases as political and reports the public controversies that have erupted over whether incidents were politically motivated, whether they were justified, or whether the perpetrators were dealt with appropriately. His data show eighty-three cases of assassinations and attempted assassinations, including killings of Jews by Jews for political reasons, from the prestate period in Palestine through more than four decades of the Israeli regime. According to his reckoning, from 1948 to 1993, there was only one case of Jews killing a Jew for political reasons. Ben-Yehuda concluded that once Israel was established, Israeli Jews came to rely on the institutions of the state to achieve justice among themselves. He concedes a lack of reliable comparative data but surmises that the incidence of political violence in Jewish history has been low in relation to other national experiences.[33]

A comparative indicator that supports Ben-Yehuda's conclusion is the incidence of murder reported in the official *Statistical Abstracts* of Israel and the United States. During 1991, the Israeli murder rate was 1.97 per 100,000 population, while that of the United States overall was 9.8, with rates of 80.1 in Washington, D.C., 68.9 in New Orleans, 65.0 in St. Louis, and 59.3 in Detroit.[34]

Israelis of various political and religious persuasions pondered the implications of the assassination of Prime Minister Yitzhak Rabin by a religious Jew in November 1995. They recalled the bloodshed of ancient civil wars among the Jews in the periods when they were ruled by the Greeks and Romans and repeated rabbinical admonitions against sectarian conflict. Some perceived the first signs of widespread civil violence, and others stressed the small number of individuals who seemed to be involved in a conspiracy to kill the prime minister. The Jews of Israel had become like other democracies, without the luxury of overlooking the possibility of political violence.

RELIGIOUS AND SECULAR ISRAELIS AND THEIR POLITICAL INSTITUTIONS

There is no simple way of counting the proportion of Israel's Jewish population that is secular or religious, ultra-Orthodox, simply Orthodox, or traditional. The Central Bureau of Statistics records the numbers of Jews and non-Jews in Israel but does not measure the religiosity of the residents. In the election of 1992, Israel's citizens gave 8 percent of their votes to ultra-Orthodox parties and 5 percent to the Orthodox National Religious Party (NRP). However, some of the votes received by these parties come from outside their religious congregations, some from non-Jews, and many religious Jews voted for the secular parties.[35]

Several surveys have sought to measure the proportions of Israeli Jews according to their religiosity. One survey of 1,287 Israeli Jews was conducted by Tel Aviv University sociology professor Yohanan Peres. The sample excluded members of kibbutzim, soldiers in army camps, new immigrants who did not speak Hebrew, and settlers in the occupied territories. Respondents identified themselves on a religious-secular spectrum as ultra-Orthodox, 10 percent; Orthodox, 10 percent; traditional, 29 percent; and secular, 51 percent. (In the Israeli context, *traditional* means identifying with some but not all of the practices of Orthodox Judaism.) Another survey of Israeli Jews employed a continuum from "strictly observant" to "totally nonobservant." Fourteen percent of the respondents defined themselves as "strictly observant," 24 percent as "observant to a great extent," 41 percent as "somewhat observant," and 21 percent as "totally nonobservant." Yet another survey asked the respondents to identify themselves as Orthodox, Conservative, or Reform. It found 76 percent not identifying with any of these options; of the remainder, 12 percent identified themselves as Orthodox, 9 percent Reform, and 3 percent Conservative. (A critic of this survey wonders if its terms of reference were well chosen for an Israeli sample. For example, does "Orthodox" include the "ultra-Orthodox"? Does "Conservative" convey the U.S. movement that has a few congregations in Israel, or does it mean something in the general sense of the word, perhaps "to the right of Orthodox"?) Yet another survey found 20 percent religious, 41 percent traditional, and 37 percent secular. The same survey found that 18 percent of the sample said that they "observe most of the commandments," 40 percent "observe some of the commandments," and 32 percent "do not observe any of the commandments."[36]

Peres found differences of political views that corresponded to religious identification. Sixty-eight to 70 percent of the ultra-Orthodox and Orthodox identified themselves as right or moderate right, while only 6 percent of both groups identified themselves as left or moderate left. In contrast, 28 percent of secular Israeli Jews identified themselves as right or moderate right, and 31 percent as left or moderate left. Traditional Jews were closer to the Orthodox than to secular Jews in their political identification: 53 percent called themselves right or moderate right, and only 11 percent left or moderate left.[37]

Scholars who seek to differentiate the various groups of religious Israelis by political traits distinguish between the Orthodox (also termed religious, Religious Zionist, Modern Orthodox, or Neo-Orthodox) on the one hand and the ultra-Orthodox on the other. The Orthodox, identified with the NRP, support the state and its purposes. Their children tend to study in state religious schools. Orthodox men generally serve in the military, frequently in special units that combine opportunities for religious study with periods of military service. Many Orthodox young women take advantage of the exemption granted from military conscription for religious women but volunteer for national service in schools, hospitals, or other social institutions. Ultra-Orthodox families are more likely to live in self-segregated neighborhoods. Their children study in independent schools that are financed by the state but operated by religious congregations. Ultra-Orthodox men and women generally abstain from military service or national service. Many of the men continue as full-time students in religious academies well into adulthood.

Groups at different points on the religious-secular spectrum tend to be socially isolated and express antagonistic stereotypes of one another. The separation is voluntary but is reinforced by separate schools for the ultra-Orthodox, Orthodox, and secular Israeli Jews; opportunities for separate military service for the Orthodox and total exemption for the ultra-Orthodox; and newspapers that serve the Orthodox and ultra-Orthodox communities. The inner roads of ultra-Orthodox neighborhoods are closed to vehicles on Shabbat and religious holidays, there is social pressure against listening to the radio or television, and kiosk owners may fear selling secular newspapers. Ultra-Orthodox neighborhoods in Jerusalem gave upwards of 70 percent of their vote to ultra-Orthodox parties in the 1988 national election.[38]

Research shows social separation reinforced by stereotypes that prevail even among religious and secular individuals who work together or live close to one another. However, in some research, the reality of each community's attitudes toward the other appears to be less extreme than the stereotypes portray. The stereotypes expressed by religious and secular Israelis indicate that members of one community are aggressively antagonistic toward the other. Nevertheless, when questioned directly, members of each community express understanding of the other.[39] It is also the case that the emergence of the Association of Sephardi Observants of the Torah (SHAS) in the mid-1980s has shaken up what were neat divisions of Orthodox and ultra-Orthodox. SHAS's voters come from both sectors and from Jews of North African and Asian backgrounds generally described as traditional. More than other religious parties, SHAS shows inner tension between the tendencies to be active in state institutions like the NRP and to withdraw into apolitical religiosity like some ultra-Orthodox Jews of European origin.

The Politics of Religion

The politics of religion revolves around the activities of several government ministries and political parties. During the period 1992–1996, three of the parties represented in the Knesset were religious, and one was outspokenly secular and sometimes antireligious.

The Ministry of Religious Affairs distributes state funds to synagogues, churches, mosques, schools, ritual baths, and other religious programs in the Jewish, Christian, Muslim, and Druze sectors. Israeli reformers who want to rationalize the distribution of government funds according to objective criteria like numbers of clients in each program or decisions by broadly representative commissions have not succeeded in dealing with the Ministry of Religious Affairs. Audits have revealed that the ministry has paid money to religious organizations on the basis of inflated lists of students or other false reports.[40] The ministry is one of the honey pots of Israeli government patronage, and the appointment of its minister is a prize sought by Jewish religious parties. In early 1995, after the Sephardi ultra-Orthodox party SHAS had been outside of the Rabin coalition for some time and was unable to agree on any offer to entice it back, Prime Minister Rabin assigned as head of the ministry a secular member of the Labor Party. One newspaper article mentioned the opportunity the new minister had to appoint many members of local religious councils and thus ensure himself supporters in the primaries that would select Labor Party candidates for the next national election.[41] Subsequent stories covered the minister's efforts to ease the plight of Israelis affected by religious laws concerning marriage and burial and the problems of the minister in implementing his reforms against the opposition of religious activists.

The Ministry of Interior is another prize sought by religious parties. It distributes funds to local authorities, some of which are earmarked for religious activities. It also contains the population registry, which controls the designation of Israelis as Jews or something else. This designation is an issue of considerable doctrinal importance to religious Jews. Among its sensitive points are the recognition of conversions to Judaism by non-Orthodox rabbis and the status of individuals who claim to be Jews but whose family backgrounds are unclear. Like the Ministry of Religious Affairs, the Ministry of Interior did not have an active minister while SHAS vacillated between participation and opposition during the Rabin government. The prime minister appointed Ehud Barak as its minister in the summer of 1995. Barak had just retired as military chief of staff and was seen as politically astute and a potential future prime minister. Perhaps to protect his status among religious as well as secular politicians, Barak did not move prominently on issues of religious significance during his few months in the interior ministry. When Shimon Peres became prime minister after the death of Yitzhak Rabin, he promoted Barak to the position of foreign minister.

The Ministry of Education is important not only for the funds it distributes but for its influence on the content of schooling in the state secular and the state religious (i.e., Orthodox) schools. The ministry is also a conduit of funds to ultra-Orthodox schools, designated formally as Independent education because of the capacity of individual congregations to determine program content. Ultra-Orthodox schools are marked by a segregation of the sexes and a heavy concentration on traditional religious education. In some of these schools, there are minimum lessons in modern Hebrew and arithmetic, and no science, secular history, or humanities.

Units of the Ministry of Education that deal with state religious schools have traditionally been the province of Orthodox Jewry represented by the NRP. On occasion, this party has been sufficiently important in the governing coalition to win the appointment of the minister of education and have the potential for affecting the treatment of Jewish history, doctrine, and holidays in the state secular schools. The problems of the education ministry are meager resources and extensive demands. Class sizes tend to be large by Western standards, averaging twenty-eight students in the Hebrew sector and thirty-one in the Arab sector in 1991–1992. (A comparable figure for the United States was seventeen pupils per classroom teacher.)[42] Groups demanding special programs are those concerned with education for the handicapped and the gifted and those who wish to expand opportunities in poor neighborhoods and small towns. Jewish congregations that are non-Orthodox have had some success in establishing their own schools and receiving Israeli government funds to go along with the money collected from Reform and Conservative congregations in the Diaspora.

When the Ministry of Education has functioned as the Ministry of Education and Culture, it has had a role in financing, appointing personnel, awarding prizes, and affecting the content of programs in Israeli broadcasting and state-supported museums, theater, and community centers. Ministerial units concerned with culture have felt the contrasting pressures of religious and antireligious Israelis regarding the allocation of public resources and the imposition of censorship (or its lack) on the content of cultural programs.

A number of other ministries are important to religious interests by virtue of the funds they control. Decisions of the Ministry of Housing and Construction affect housing units, schools, and other public facilities. The Ministry can decide how much housing will be designed for typically large religious families or smaller secular families, or sold in bulk to religious congregations for resale to member families. The Ministry of Welfare has funds for the social programs of religious organizations, including the community centers and old age homes affiliated with them.

Israel's official rabbinate is headed by two chief rabbis, one each for the Ashkenazi and Sephardi communities. It is associated with the Ministry of Religious Affairs and has a role in the appointment of local religious councils, community rabbis, inspectors of kashruth (Jewish food laws), and the governing of cemeteries and burial societies.

The chief rabbinate is another playing field for religious politics rather than a supreme religious authority. With respect to the weight given its religious rulings, a scholar who identifies with the Orthodox has written, "Secularists and *haredim* [ultra-Orthodox] largely ignore it, while the non-Orthodox [i.e., Reform and Conservative Jews] actively fight it."[43] Traditionally, the positions of chief rabbi were in the control of the religious Zionists in the NRP. With the emergence of SHAS as a political force in the mid-1980s, however, that party has competed aggressively for control over the size and share of state resources devoted to religious institutions in the Sephardi community and the selection of the chief Sephardi rabbi.

SHAS is a relatively new player in the ultra-Orthodox sector that was long dominated by Agudat Israel. SHAS emerged as a protest against what its founders felt was the anti-Sephardi discrimination by leaders of Agudat Israel. SHAS also appealed to Sephardi voters who had supported the NRP. In the first national election in which it campaigned (1984), SHAS won four seats in the Knesset, Agudat Israel's number dropped from four to two and the NRP's from six to four. SHAS has developed a school system that covers prekindergarten through eighth grade. According to a 1993 report, there are 6,000 children in SHAS elementary schools, 10,000 in its kindergartens, and an additional number in its prekindergartens. The system appeals to parents by offering a long school day, a hot meal, and transportation. One estimate is that a third of the families sending their children to the SHAS schools are not overtly religious.[44] SHAS won six seats in the Knesset election of 1992, and ten seats in 1996.

SHAS is not known for the subtlety of its political tactics. It used its swing position in coalition politics to acquire government money for its school system, its leaders justifying their tactics as making up for years of deprivation at the hands of the Ashkenazim (Europeans) who dominate the Israeli establishment. SHAS stands for the Israeli version of corrective discrimination.[45] As of this writing, one former parliamentarian has served a prison term, and another is on trial for charges of financial irregularities and improper property transactions. SHAS's patronage tactics resemble those used in the past by other Israeli parties. By one view, it is the party's bad luck to come on the scene after a change in the game's informal rules. Once routine techniques of patronage in allocating public resources are now grounds for prosecution and incarceration. Some SHAS supporters believe that the change in norms has been directed against SHAS and that the indictment of party leaders reflects jealousy of the movement's success.

SHAS's willingness to compete for resources in state forums has brought other ultra-Orthodox congregations closer to Israeli government institutions. Traditionally, the ultra-Orthodox, represented by Agudat Israel and a variety of independent congregations, have sought to distance themselves from the Zionist enterprise. Many of their rabbis opposed the Zionist movement in pre-Holocaust Europe, and some of them continue to oppose the existence of the Israeli state. An exotic few declare the state unholy insofar as it came into existence without the clear blessing of the Lord or the arrival of the Messiah. Others more modestly oppose policies of the state that they do not see as operating according to Jewish law. They view the state as flawed in Sabbath observance, the content of education, food regulation, the regulation of modesty in dress and public entertainments, the implementation of marriage and divorce law, abortion, and other medical practices.

SHAS's success shook up the organization of Agudat Israel. Agudat Israel is now a component of Torah Judaism, a party that won four Knesset seats in the 1992 election and again in 1996. Torah Judaism is a tense coalition among ultra-Orthodox communities whose animosities toward one another have European origins, and its principal components are Agudat Israel and Degel Hatorah. Congregations that support Degel Hatorah are alternatively termed Mitnagdim (opposed to Hasidism) or Lithuanian (the location of their pre-Holocaust religious centers in Europe). Torah Judaism has had only partial success in attracting the Lubavitcher (Chabad) movement and ultra-Orthodox Sephardim who oppose the leadership of SHAS.

The NRP served in every governing coalition from the founding of Israel until the Rabin government created after the election of 1992. It is the representative of religious Zionists, Orthodox Jews who support the Israeli state. Its founding rabbis saw the country's emergence as a sign of the messianic age. In their view, the role of religious Jews is to seek their redemption by building their own state in the land given to Israel by the Almighty.

The Six Day War of 1967 created immediate opportunities and eventual problems for the NRP. On the one hand, stunning victories gave control of the West Bank and all of Jerusalem to Israel. The heart of the biblical Land of Israel was in Jewish hands for the first time in two millennia. This seemed further proof that the Lord was on the side of Israel. Individuals associated with the NRP created Gush Emunim (the bloc of the faithful) and took as their cause the promotion of Jewish settlement throughout the newly occupied territories. Their settlement program began modestly under Labor governments that served until 1977 and thrived under Likud governments from 1977 to 1992.

The problems for Gush Emunim and the NRP developed along with the prospects for Israeli-Arab peace. Jewish settlements established by earlier governments had become stumbling blocks on the road to peace. The NRP responded to the peace initiatives of the 1990s by moving to the right, supporting continued settlement and opposing territorial compromise. This political isolation of the party followed other events that had weakened it among the electorate. For some years, the moderate Orthodoxy that was the basis of the NRP had been losing individuals to a resurgence of ultra-Orthodoxy. When SHAS developed as a Sephardi religious alternative, many Sephardim who had voted NRP left the Ashkenazi-dominated party. NRP's share of the vote fell from 10 to 5 percent between the elections of 1969 and 1992, while that of ultra-Orthodox parties (including

SHAS) increased from 6 to 8 percent. For the first time in Israeli history, the government formed after the 1992 election had no ministers affiliated with the NRP. The NRP's representation in the Knesset increased from six to nine seats with the election of 1996, and its leaders served as ministers in the Cabinet of Prime Minister Benjamin Netanyahu.

Meretz formed in the run-up to the 1992 election as a combination of three parties to the left of the Israeli center. Its name is both an acronym formed from the names of its constituent parties and a Hebrew word meaning energy or vigor. Meretz won twelve seats in the Knesset and became the second party in the coalition formed by Yitzhak Rabin. Rabin's own Labor Party contributed forty-four seats to the coalition. One of the components that united to form Meretz was the Citizens' Rights Party, which had been prominent on the left of Israeli politics and had been represented in most sessions of the Knesset since the election of 1973. It had staked out a position against the religious parties and the monopoly of the rabbinate in Jewish marriages and divorce. The head of the Citizens' Rights Party, Shulamit Aloni, became head of Meretz. In Rabin's cabinet, she became Minister of Education and Culture.

The story of Shulamit Aloni is an example of the problems involved in sorting out religious and other influences in Israeli politics. SHAS joined Meretz, then threatened to leave in response to what it viewed as Aloni's antireligious statements and behavior. The prime minister responded by rebuking Aloni. Her public remarks, the protests of SHAS, and the prime minister's rebukes were repeated several times until Rabin took the sensitive education portfolio away from Aloni, demoting her to minister of culture and communication and appointing a less colorful and less outspoken parliamentarian of Meretz to serve as minister of education. None of what Rabin did kept SHAS in his coalition. SHAS representatives described its departure as motivated by considerations of policy toward religion, but the real motivation may have been the indictment on criminal charges of SHAS's parliamentary leader.

There is no permanent alliance or enmity among religious and secular parties. Certain lines of cooperation prevail in given political constellations, but cooperation or hostility has varied with issues and personalities. After Likud formed a government for the first time in 1977, its nationalism took on a flavor of religiosity that may have appealed to the NRP, Agudat Israel, and SHAS. On the other hand, those parties may have joined the coalition not so much for the willingness of Prime Minister Menachem Begin to express his affinity for Jewish themes as for the mutual benefits that Likud and the religious parties could offer one another. Likud gathered support for its coalition, and the religious parties gained money for their institutions and some mostly symbolic policy enactments.

With the change in political strengths in the election of 1992, SHAS initially joined the parliamentary bloc of Labor and Meretz and then alternately distanced itself and reapproached the coalition. Agudat Israel (now an element in Torah Judaism) sat on the fence while offering veiled support to the coalition, and the NRP was on the outside. Yet from time to time, representatives of Labor and the NRP talked about what it would take to bring them together.

Although it appeared that Likud was the more natural ally of the religious parties if it could win enough seats to lead a coalition, the religious parties had some problems with Likud. Don Meridor was a leading figure in Likud and had been justice minister prior to the 1992 election. He was a known supporter of civil rights and advocated legislation that would give civil procedures advantages over the dictates of rabbinical courts. This led a parliamentarian of Torah Judaism to mix some metaphors and distinguish his party from the traditions of Catholicism: "We are not linked to Likud in a Catholic marriage. We join Likud because of its feelings toward religious issues. If Meridor's movement toward a legal revolution grows, he can find himself with his legal revolution sitting in the Opposition."[46] A columnist wrote in the newspaper of Agudat Israel that the difference between the Labor and Likud parties was like the difference between a cow and a donkey. Both of those parties would render the religious interests handicapped: One would offer crutches and the other a wheelchair. He said that leaders of Likud remembered the ultra-Orthodox with great intensity during election campaigns, but once in government they ignored and insulted Torah sages.[47]

The religious parties also have problems with a right-wing party that appears to be a natural ally of Likud in a government coalition. Tsomet (Junction) is in some ways a right-wing Meretz. It has taken strong stands against issues on the religious parties' platforms, such as the exemptions from military service granted automatically to students at religious academies. The young secular Israelis who supported Tsomet in the 1992 election would not look kindly on religious legislation that closed their places of entertainment on Friday evenings. Some believe that Tsomet is a short-lived star in Israeli politics. It is more strongly identified with the gruff personality of a former chief of the military general staff than with a coherent program that could outlive the career of its leader. Tsomet won 2 percent of the vote in the 1988 election and 6 percent in the 1992 election. Its eight seats made it the fourth largest party after Labor, Likud, and Meretz. Midway through the 1992–1996 period, however, three of Tsomet's Knesset members left the party in what seemed to be a protest against its leader. Tsomet affiliated with Likud in the 1996 election and at least for the time being gave up its separate existence.

The multiplicity in parties that claim to speak for religious and antireligious Israelis (Torah Judaism, SHAS, the NRP, Meretz, and Tsomet) made up some 29 percent of the Israelis who voted in the 1992 Knesset election and accounted for 36 of the 120 Knesset members. Neither Labor, with 44 members, nor Likud, with 32, could form a government without shopping for partners among the religious and antireligious parties. The basic divisions of the electorate were not new to Israeli politics, even though the particulars reflected conditions of the 1990s. The tensions of coalition government have often included religious and antireligious parties sharing seats around the cabinet table. It is not a condition that provides a clear victory to one side or another. Rather, it reinforces a standoff in particular disputes and ensures that the underlying tensions will return to the agenda in another form.

ON THE STYLE OF ISRAELI POLITICS: COPING WITH MULTIPLE ADVERSITIES

In several of my previous writings about Israel, I have emphasized the pressures on citizens and policymakers and the importance of coping as a style of governing.[48] The pressures result in part from the conflicts between religious and secular Jews that I examine in this book. Another pressure is the external threat that has been with Israel since its inception. The economic weight of defense generates the pressure of scarce resources, which is sharpened by the ideological commitment of Israel's major parties to maintain extensive social services. Economic and military pressures have also rendered Israel dependent on the good will of overseas Jewish communities and foreign governments to provide funds, political support, and military equipment. The personnel demands of the military also pressure the society, insofar as most Jewish males must allocate three years after high school and then upwards of thirty days per year to military service until their late forties. For many, the reserve duty is unpleasant and dangerous patrolling, in contrast to the weekend soldiering of reserve militaries in other Western countries.

Immigration was a major source of pressure on Israel from 1948 through the mid-1950s, when the population more than doubled. The issue returned in the late 1980s with the collapse of the Soviet Union and a spurt of immigration that added more than 10 percent to the national population in 1988–1995. In both periods, the immigrants imposed heavy demands on social services. In the early period, especially, the influx of impoverished refugees fleeing the persecutions of Europe and Arab lands and the poverty of a small and undeveloped economy produced intense hardships. The immigrants of both periods have unmet aspirations and have used their electoral clout to punish the parties that they blame for their inadequate treatment.

Coping is a style of policymaking that appears in many polities under conditions of stress. It may also be among those traits—along with a capacity to argue among themselves as to what is best for the Jews, severe criticism of ruling powers, and self-deprecating humor—that Jews developed during their long and often unpleasant history. The discussion of Judaism in the Chapter 3 describes some coping behaviors apparent in the Hebrew Bible. In those episodes and in modern Israel, coping implies something less than devising solutions.[49] It is conveyed with the terms *adapting, managing, dealing with* and *satisfying*,[50] which imply decisions that are "good enough," even if they are not what any of the participants really want. One mode of coping calls for engagement with one's difficulties. It responds to stress by trying to salvage something from a difficult situation; keeping a process going in the expectation of greater opportunities or holding off great losses; surveying options and recruiting support; maintaining the integrity and political assets of oneself and one's organization; and ranking priorities in order to achieve the more important at the expense of the less important. Another mode of coping displays avoidance, passivity, or even flight. It responds to stress with a lack of control, hopelessness, confusion, rigidity, distortion, disorganization, randomness, disorder, distress, depression, anxiety, or submission.[51] Israeli authorities generally cope by engaging with their problems. And several thousand individuals each year leave the country for greener and/or more peaceful pastures. For them, avoidance is the best way to cope with Israel's problems.

* * *

The chronic tension between religious and secular Jews has been especially sharp since the onset of the Enlightenment prompted most Jews to leave the culture of the shtetl or urban ghetto, exclusively religious education, and pious observance. Similar tensions appeared in the periods of Greek and Roman domination of Judea, when there was bloodshed between those Jews attracted to the cultures of the ruling empires and zealots who insisted on Judaic piety closed to outside influences. The modern response to the conflict has not been mass bloodshed, but chronic tension at a low level, with an occasional flare-up that usually produces a hyperbole of accusations and demands, mass demonstrations, and the use of nondeadly weapons. Both religious and antireligious interests express dissatisfaction with the status quo and what they see as their opponents' successes. That the outcome is a standoff rather than a victory of either party seems to reflect the efforts of the authorities to cope with the demands of religious and antireligious interests. The success of these efforts is reflected in the low level of violence that generally marks the continued conflict. But the success has been only partial: There are frustrations over the incomplete treatment of chronic problems. The assassination of Prime Minister Rabin by a religious Jew signifies the danger of greater violence.

NOTES

1. See, for example, Peter Y. Medding, *The Founding of Israeli Democracy 1948–1967* (New York: Oxford University Press, 1990); Daniel Shimshoni, *Israeli Democracy: The Middle of the Journey* (New York: Free Press, 1982); and Dan Horowitz and Moshe Lissak, *Trouble in Utopia: The Overburdened Polity of Israel* (Albany: State University of New York Press: 1989).
2. On the designation of Israel as a democracy, see Arend Lijphart, *Democracies: Patterns of Majoritarian and Consensus Government in Twenty-one Countries* (New Haven: Yale University Press, 1984); G. Bingham Powell, Jr., *Contemporary Democracies: Participation, Stability, and Violence* (Cambridge: Harvard University Press, 1982); and Medding, *The Founding of Israeli Democracy*.
3. *Jerusalem Post*, September 30, 1994, p. 5.
4. *World Almanac and Book of Facts, 1992* (Microsoft Multimedia Viewer Version 1.00a.358).
5. See Ira Sharkansky, *The Political Economy of Israel* (New Brunswick, NJ: Transaction Books, 1987).
6. For descriptions and discussions of these issues, see *Israel Law Review* 23, nos. 2–3 (Spring–Summer 1989); and Menachem Hofnung, *Israel— State Security Against the Rule of Law 1948–1991* (in Hebrew) (Jerusalem: Nevo Publisher, 1991).
7. For criticisms of Israeli democracy, see Gregg Barak, "Toward a Criminology of State Criminality," in Barak, ed., *Crimes by the Capitalist State: An Introduction to State Criminality* (Albany: State University of New York

Press, 1991), pp. 3–16; Daniel E. Georges-Abeyie, "Piracy, Air Piracy, and Recurrent U.S. and Israeli Civilian Aircraft Interceptions" in Barak, *Crimes by the Capitalist State*, pp. 129–144; Avner Yaniv, ed., *National Security and Democracy in Israel* (Boulder, CO: Lynne Rienner Publishers, 1993); Horowitz and Lissak, *Trouble in Utopia*; and *Israel Law Review*. 23, nos. 2–3 (Spring–Summer 1989).

8. Gadi Wolfsfeld, *The Politics of Provocation* (Albany: State University of New York Press, 1988); and Sam Lehman-Wilzig, *Stiff-necked People, Bottle-necked System: The Evolution and Roots of Israeli Public Protest, 1949–1986* (Bloomington: Indiana University Press, 1991).

9. Nachman Ben-Yehuda, *Political Assassinations by Jews: A Rhetorical Device for Justice* (Albany: State University Press of New York, 1993). Ben-Yehuda offers an extensive review of political assassinations by Jews and concedes that a lack of reliable comparative data precludes anything stronger than a surmise about its relative incidence.

10. Lehman-Wilzig, *The Evolution and Roots of Israeli Public Protest*. See *Jerusalem Post*, April 4, 1991, magazine, p. 18.

11. *Jerusalem Post*, April 4, 1991, p. 18.

12. See Yehoshafat Harkabi, *The Bar Kokhba Syndrome: Risk and Realism in International Relations*, trans. Max D. Ticktin, ed. David Altshuler (Chappaqua, NY: Rossel Books, 1983); and Yehoshafat Harkabi, *Israel's Fateful Hour*, trans. Lenn Schramm (New York: Harper & Row, 1988).

13. Meron Benvenisti, *The West Bank Data Project: A Survey of Israel's Policies* (Washington, DC: American Enterprise Institute for Policy Research, 1984), p. 34; Meron Benvenisti, *The Sling and the Club: Territories, Jews and Arabs* (in Hebrew) (Jerusalem: Keter Publishing House, Ltd., 1988); and Meron Benvenisti, *The Shepherds' War: Collected Essays (1981–1989)* (Jerusalem: Jerusalem Post, 1989).

14. Yeshayahu Leibowitz, *On Just About Everything: Talks with Michael Shashar* (in Hebrew) (Jerusalem: Keter Publishing House, Ltd., 1988).

15. Ira Sharkansky, "Israel's Auditor as Policy-maker," *Public Administration*, 66, no. 1 (Spring 1988); and Ira Sharkansky and James J. Gosling, "The Limits of Government Auditing: The Case of Higher Education," *Politeia* 11, no. 2 (1992): 2–15.

16. Ira Sharkansky, "Pushing the Frontiers of State Audit: Political Auditing by Israel's State Comptroller," *International Journal of Public Administration*, 18, no. 12 (1995): 1841–1858.

17. *Annual and Special Reports: Selected Chapters* (Jerusalem: State Comptroller, 1992), pp. 312–316.

18. Amos 5:22–24.

19. Ezra Mendelsohn, *On Modern Jewish Politics* (New York: Oxford University Press, 1993); Jonathan Frankel, *Prophecy and Politics: Socialism, Nationalism, and the Russian Jews, 1862–1917* (Cambridge: Cambridge University Press, 1981); Zvi Gitelman, ed., *The Quest for Utopia: Jewish Political Ideas and Institutions Through the Ages* (Armonk, NY: M. E. Sharpe, Inc., 1992); and Eli Lederhandler, *The Road to Modern Jewish Politics: Political Tradition and Political Reconstruction in the Jewish Community of Tsarist Russia* (New York: Oxford University Press, 1989).

20. Michael Keren, *Ben Gurion and the Intellectuals: Power, Knowledge, and Charisma* (Dekalb: Northern Illinois University Press, 1983).

21. William Safire, *The First Dissident: The Book of Job in Today's Politics*

(New York: Random House, 1992); David Penchansky, *The Betrayal of God: Ideological Conflict in Job* (Louisville, KY: Westminster/John Knox Press, 1990).

22. For a fuller development of this idea, see Ira Sharkansky, *Israel's Bible: A Political Perspective* (New York: Garland Press).

23. I Samuel 15:3.

24. Ezra 9:11–12.

25. Harry M. Orlinsky, "Nationalism-Universalism and Internationalism in Ancient Israel," in Orlinsky, *Essays in Biblical Culture and Bible Translation* (New York: KTAV Publishing House, Inc., 1974), pp. 78–116; see also Fibal Melzar on the Book of Ruth in *The Five Scrolls* (in Hebrew) (Jerusalem: Mossad Harav Kook, 1973), p. 3.

26. Ruth 4:13–22.

27. Isaiah 2:4.

28. Isaiah 54:3–4.

29. Isaiah 60:12.

30. *Ha'aretz* (in Hebrew), July 11, 1996, p. 12.

31. Rabbi Meir Kahane, "Forty Years" (Brooklyn, NY: The Institute of the Jewish Idea, 1983).

32. On the related issue of state crime, see Jeffrey Ian Ross, ed., *Controlling State Crime* (New York: Garland Press, 1995), including the chapter by Ira Sharkansky, "A State Action May Be Nasty but Is Not Likely to Be a Crime."

33. Ben-Yehuda, *Political Assassinations by Jews*. See also Ehud Sprinzak, *Between Extra-Parliamentary Protest and Terror: Political Violence in Israel* (in Hebrew) (Jerusalem: Jerusalem Institute for Israeli Research, 1995); and Ehud Sprinzak, *The Ascendance of Israel's Radical Right* (New York: Oxford University Press, 1991).

34. *Statistical Abstract of Israel, 1992* (Jerusalem: Central Bureau of Statistics, 1993), Table 21.14; *Statistical Abstract of the United States 1993* (Washington, DC: U.S. Government Printing Office, 1994), Tables 300, 303.

35. Menachem Friedman, *The Ultra-Orthodox Society: Sources, Goals and Processes* (in Hebrew) (Jerusalem: Jerusalem Institute for Israeli Research, 1991).

36. *Jerusalem Post*, January 7, 1994, p. 4B. For a discussion of nuances among categories of Israeli Jews, see pp. 1–42; Eliezer Don-Yehiya, "Does Place Make a Difference? Jewish Orthodoxy in Israel and the Diaspora," in Chaim I. Waxman, ed., *Israel as a Religious Reality* (Northvale, NJ: Jason Aronson Inc., 1994), pp. 43–74.

37. *Jerusalem Post*, January 17, 1992, p. 1B.

38. Maya Choshen, "The Elections to the Knesset in Jerusalem: Statistical Outlook" (in Hebrew) (Jerusalem: Jerusalem Institute for Israel Studies, 1990).

39. Ephraim Tabory, "Avoidance and Conflict: Perceptions Regarding Contact Between Religious and Nonreligious Jewish Youth in Israel," *Journal for the Scientific Study of Religion* 31, no. 2 (1992): 148–162.

40. *Kal Ha'Ir* (in Hebrew), July 11, 1996, p. 29.

41. *Kal Ha'ir* (in Hebrew), July 11, 1996, p. 79.

42. *Statistical Abstract of Israel, 1992*, Table 22.16; *Statistical Abstract of the United States 1993*, Table 223.

43. Aharon Lichtenstein, "The Israeli Chief Rabbinate: A Current Halakhic Perspective," in Waxman, *Israel as a Religious Reality*, p. 131.

44. *Jerusalem Post*, June 25, 1993, p. 5.

45. *Audit Report on the Provision of Support to Institutions by Local Authorities* (in Hebrew) (Jerusalem: State Comptroller, 1991).

46. *Ha'aretz* (in Hebrew), July 11, 1996, p. 7.

47. *Ha'aretz* (in Hebrew), April 2, 1995, p. 7.

48. Ira Sharkansky, "Coping Strategies of Engagement and Avoidance: The Case of Jerusalem," *Policy and Politics* 23, no. 2 (1995).

49. George V. Coelho, David A. Hamburg, and John E. Adams, eds., *Coping and Adaptation* (New York: Basic Books, 1974).

50. Herbert Simon, *Administrative Behavior* (New York: Free Press, 1976).

51. Jack T. Tapp, "Multisystems Holistic Model of Health, Stress and Coping," in Tiffany M. Field, Philip M. McCabe, and Neil Schneiderman, eds., *Stress and Coping* (Hillsdale, NJ: Lawrence Erlbaum Associates, Publishers, 1985), pp. 285–304. Some writers perceive engagement coping as leading to more effective adaptations to situations of crisis. See Rudolf H. Moos and Jeanne A. Schaefer, "Life Transitions and Crises: A Conceptual Overview," in Moos in collaboration with Schaefer, eds., *Coping with Life Crises: An Integrated Approach* (New York: Plenum Press, 1986), pp. 3–28. Other researchers make the point that the literature has yet to confirm any strong linkage between types of coping and the outcomes of stressful situations. See Susan Folkman, "Personal Control and Stress and Coping Processes: A Theoretical Analysis," *Journal of Personality and Social Psychology* 46 (1984): 839–852.

5

THE INTENSITY OF RELIGIOUS POLITICS

Religion remains a vital force in economically developed Western democracies two centuries after the Enlightenment that was supposed to mark its decline. Secular intellectuals have proclaimed God's death and express wonder at the continued capacity of those who claim to represent the Almighty to attract the faithful and elevate their concerns to the center of political discourse. Those who perceive religion as dominant are no more accurate than those who view religion as a withering relic; a stalemate between the secular and the religious is a more accurate description.

Several of Israel's traits make it likely that religious issues will be prominent in politics: It proclaims a religious identity as a Jewish state; it gives control over sensitive personal matters to the religious authorities of Jewish and other communities; and much of its population is only a generation or two removed from pre-Enlightenment conditions or is still immersed in them. Even more than Israel as a whole, Jerusalem provides a setting for the intense expression of religious interests on account of its history, holy sites, and a population that has a higher number of religious Jews, Muslims, and Christians than other Israeli cities.

In the Holy City and elsewhere in Israel, religious and secular interests exist in a condition of chronic tension, where neither dominates the other. Religious and secular (including antireligious) activists are responsible for putting religious issues on the political agenda, but they cannot dictate how controversies will end. The ambiguous status of religion with respect to marriage and divorce is only one field where public policy touches issues of religion. Jewish, Christian, Muslim, and Druze functionaries have a formal monopoly of these services in Israel, according to the religious law of each community. Nonetheless, the Ministry of Interior records citizens as married or divorced if they have acquired those statuses from secular authorities overseas (sometimes by mail, without leaving Israel) even if their personal situation would not permit them to achieve a religious marriage or divorce in Israel. When a secular member of

Knesset was appointed as minister of religious affairs in 1995, he sought to formalize the criteria by which the rabbinate decided that certain individuals would not qualify for Jewish marriages in Israel, and he proposed a system of financial aid for those individuals who would be forced to travel abroad in order to marry.[1]

RELIGIOUS ISSUES OF HIGH EMOTIONAL AND POLITICAL CONTENT

There is no doubting the prominence of religious issues on Israel's political agenda. On one day in March 1995 the following items appeared on the inner pages of the daily newspaper *Ha'aretz*.[2] They had been matters of public interest for some time, but their location in the paper indicated that they were not the major issues of the day. The individual issues were resolved, but the quarrels underlying them seemed likely to return again.

- Three hundred male and female rabbis of Reform Judaism, mostly visitors from overseas, were about to pray together near the Western Wall. They were expected to provoke Orthodox and ultra-Orthodox Israelis, who object to mixed prayer sessions of men and women and deny that either Reform Jewish men or women qualify for the designation of rabbi.
- The Civil Service Commission began disciplinary proceedings against a religious official of the Justice Ministry who was responsible for giving advice on the interpretation of Hebrew law. He had publicly made a politically incorrect comparison between homosexuals and men who have sex with animals. Among the sources that provided the basis of his comparison was the following passage from the Book of Leviticus:

> If a man also lie with mankind, as he lieth with a woman, both of them have committed an abomination: they shall surely be put to death; their blood shall be upon them. . . . And if a man lie with a beast, he shall surely be put to death: and ye shall slay the beast.[3]

The recently empowered homosexual lobby protested the official's statement, and the civil service commissioner complained that the adviser was not authorized to express such an opinion. A week later, the commissioner backed down under a backlash from the free-expressionist minister of justice and others who said that the adviser was, after all, paid to advise on Hebrew law.

- Prison authorities were preparing for a demonstration by the followers of a Yemenite rabbi who had been incarcerated with several of his adherents after violent protests concerning Yemenite children who allegedly were taken from their parents by state authorities in the 1940s.
- The court of an ultra-Orthodox congregation proclaimed that anyone aiding a construction project in Jaffa that was said to be desecrating Jewish graves would be struck with cancer, mental illness, and bankruptcy. Ultra-Orthodox rabbis declared a boycott against Bank Hapoalim for financing the Jaffa project, and the police apprehended three yeshiva students setting fire to two of the bank's cash machines.

Newspaper archives are an efficient way of learning Israel's religious disputes, the participants' own words showing the heat of their feelings. In reviewing the press, however, there is the problem of deciding which issues are Jewish and which issues simply concern Jews. The problem recalls a comment made some years ago by an Israeli friend visiting me in Madison, Wisconsin. After reading the local newspaper for several days, he snorted that the Israeli press was more cosmopolitan. Years later, I decided that he was correct. Israeli newspapers are filled with stories about Jews in Buenos Aires, New York, London, and Moscow, as well as Israel.

The character of Jews and Judaism confounds the determination of which items concern religion, which are ethnic, and which reflect universal interests but trouble Jews in their Israeli manifestations. The following sections portray the religious tensions among Israelis in a number of sensitive areas: relations between Jews and Gentiles; competition between ultra-Orthodox, Orthodox, and other forms of Judaism; issues concerning the Land of Israel; Jewish issues associated with Jerusalem; and some expressions of moderation and exasperation by Teddy Kollek, who served as Jerusalem's mayor from 1966 to 1993. The categories overlap, and some incidents could be presented under more than one heading. The location of individual reports is less important than the total picture they create: one of extensive commotion about issues with a religious component that keep coming to the agenda and cannot be solved.

Jews and Gentiles

The holy sites of three faiths, as well as the sensitivities of Christians, Muslims, and Jews in Israel and abroad, provide countless points of friction. The international side of Israel's religious issues appeared in an exchange of letters among a group of U.S. Christian clerics, the White House, and U.S. Jewish leaders. The Christians complained to the White House about the continued construction of Jewish neighborhoods around Jerusalem. Leaders of U.S. Jewish organizations complained about the tone of the Christians' letter, prompting clarification from the Christians. According to the revised letter, it was not the Christians' intention to threaten Israel's status in Jerusalem or to increase the status of the Vatican in the city. They wanted only to ensure the future of their coreligionists in Israel and to facilitate the Israeli-Arab peace process.[4]

The Latin patriarch of Jerusalem, who is an ethnic Palestinian, had a larger agenda for the Israelis. He called on them to give non-Jewish religious leaders a say in city government and to free 10,500 Palestinian prisoners as a sign that Israel was sincere about making peace. On his list of prisoners to be freed was Sheikh Ahmed Yassin, a leader of an Islamic fundamentalist group identified with acts of violence against Israelis.[5]

The complications in Jewish-Christian relations were apparent in the response of a Greek Orthodox cleric to the Latin patriarch. (As usual, Christians were worrying about one another's advantages.) The Greek cleric wrote, "If the Christians shared in the [municipal] administration, the Vatican would set the tone."[6] At the time, Israel and the Vatican were negotiating the Vatican's formal recognition of Israel and an exchange of ambassadors, and the negotiations had aroused the concern of the Greek Orthodox church about its status with respect to Christian holy sites.

The same negotiations also raised suspicions among the Jews. In April 1995 Agudat Israel's supreme forum, the Council of Torah Sages, published a condemnation of what it saw as the initiative of Foreign Minister Shimon Peres to grant the Vatican spiritual authority over the Old City of Jerusalem. It called on all Jews to resist such an action. The foreign minister replied formally to the Council of Torah Sages that he had made no such initiative.[7]

Contention between faiths also includes new religious movements. A visit by Hawk Ja Han Moon, the wife of the Reverend Sun Myung Moon, brought protest from an antimissionary organization, causing the cancellation of public appearances of Hawk Ja Han Moon and representatives of the (Jewish) Battered Women's Shelter in Herzliya and the Acre Home of the Arab Child.[8]

An incident at the end of 1992 reflected both a Jewish mistrust of Christian clerics and friction between religious and secular Jews. Minister of Education and Culture Shulamit Aloni was challenged in the Knesset to defend her invitation to Father Marcel Dubois, a lecturer in the philosophy department of Hebrew University, to discuss "Religion in Jerusalem" at a conference of school principals. (Aloni was a frequent target of religious parties and was eventually forced to give up the education portfolio.) She was attacked by members of Knesset Menahem Porush (Torah Judaism), who claimed that there was strong opposition to the presentation by school principals and asked if there was no Jew who could speak on the subject.[9]

When some Jews moved into an empty building near the Church of the Holy Sepulcher just before Easter in 1990, they were condemned by Greek Orthodox clergy, who recalled the historic Christian practices of permitting no Jews to live in Jerusalem when the Crusaders controlled the city and throwing stones at Jews who wandered near the Church of the Holy Sepulcher when Muslims were in charge of the city. The issue put Mayor Teddy Kollek in the delicate position of chastising Jews who chose Easter as the season to become neighbors of the Holy Sepulcher while defending the right of Jews to live anywhere they could legally secure residence in Jerusalem. Among the interchanges was a public letter to the Greek Orthodox church from Israel's president Chaim Herzog. Excerpts from the letter reflect the strength of feeling between religious groups with a long history of antagonism:

> I do not propose to go into the rights or wrongs of the action taken by those claiming a right to residence in the building. . . . I am, however, very disturbed by the behavior of the Greek Orthodox Church on this issue and by the very unpleasant innuendoes which have been publicized abroad by the officials of the Church. . . . I must say that the sight of a priest in clerical garments, standing on a ladder, ripping down a Star of David from a Jewish residence, cheered on by an enraged mob, is a horrible reminder of what our people lived through in history on many sad and tragic occasions. . . . I have been horrified to receive organized mail from the United States, in which it alleged that the Greek Orthodox Patriarch has been subject to physical assault by Israelis. This is a blatant lie which is being published abroad without any basis whatsoever. The issue centers on a dispute in a real-estate deal which is being contested in the courts of law in Israel and in respect of which over $5 million changed hands. For a Church to turn such a real-estate transaction, to which it is privy and a party, into a defamatory anti-Jewish campaign, is nothing short of disgraceful and despicable.[10]

Jews have no monopoly of feeling offense at the insensitivity of others. A Jerusalem Christian wrote to the *Jerusalem Post* objecting to an editorial that had stated: "Local Christian church leaders, under Arab pressure, raise bogus issues of alleged Israeli disregard for

Christian sites." The writer felt that the discovery of bones that might be those of Saint Stephen was not given proper weight by the editorial writer or the Israeli Antiquities Authority: "Would the bones of a great Jewish tzadik have been removed if they had been discovered at the same site?"[11]

A larger bone problem generated a squabble between the Ministry of Religious Affairs on one side and the Greek Orthodox church and the Israeli Antiquities Authority on the other. The issue concerned the remains of several thousand persons unearthed by a construction project near the Old City of Jerusalem. The antiquities authority concluded that they were the bones of Christians slaughtered during a sixth-century Persian invasion and recommended that they be transferred to the Greek Orthodox patriarchate for reburial. However, the religious affairs ministry claimed that some might be the remains of Jews. According to its policy, such a possibility required a Jewish burial for all the bones.[12]

The Druze have protested government involvement in their communal affairs, particularly in what appears to be a struggle between extended families. Opponents of one candidate for the leadership of the Druze community protested the planned visit of Prime Minister Rabin to that candidate's home during a Druze religious celebration. To the protesters, the prime minister's selection of a site to honor the Druze community was evidence of the government's involvement in what should be a solely Druze task of selecting a communal leader.[13] In response to Druze protests, the prime minister announced that he would observe their holiday at a neutral site: a community center erected in honor of Druze soldiers who gave their lives in the service of the Israeli army.[14]

Holocaust Remembrance Day in 1995 provided another occasion of conflict. Cardinal Jean-Marie (né Aaron) Lustiger was born a Jew but was baptized into the Catholic church at the age of fourteen during the Holocaust. His mother and other members of his family were killed as Jews by the Nazis. The chief Ashkenazi rabbi, a Knesset member for Degel Hatorah, and the head of the Yad Vashem memorial joined in criticizing Tel Aviv University for inviting the cardinal to lecture as part of its Holocaust observances. According to the chief rabbi, the cardinal represented to Jews a model that threatened them spiritually. Lustiger had abandoned his people in their time of greatest distress and had chosen a path that has tempted many Jews over the centuries. The chair of Yad Vashem's international board of directors, a former leading member of the National Religious Party (NRP), explained the refusal to invite the cardinal to Yad Vashem's Holocaust memorial ceremony: "Baptism represents a crossing of a border. One who baptizes no longer is part of the Jewish people, and has no place in an official observance."[15]

At the same time, two Knesset members of Likud criticized a planned Holocaust program in a Tel Aviv school that would have memorialized the suffering of homosexuals during the Nazi period and the holocaust of Armenians at the hands of Turks during World War I. One Knesset member protested against the departure from the uniqueness of Holocaust Memorial Day as a remembrance of Jewish suffering. Another protested that it was impossible to compare the slaughter of six million Jews in the Holocaust to the sufferings of other groups.[16]

The Armenian community of Jerusalem demonstrated at the office of the prime minister. They protested what they saw as increasingly close diplomatic relations between Israel and Turkey, which gave legitimacy to the Turkish government and its denial of an Armenian holocaust.[17]

Orthodoxy and Other Judaisms

Israeli Jews, including former mayor Teddy Kollek of Jerusalem, occasionally say that the problems between religious and secular Jews are more serious than the conflicts between Arabs and Jews. It is never easy to sort out deprecatory humor from serious statement. In this case, the truth may derive from the willingness of Israeli authorities to let Jewish conflicts play themselves out, expecting that they are not likely to threaten the state or even bring serious injury to the participants. A confrontation between Jews and either Muslims or Christians is more serious and must be kept below the level where the concept of Crusade may again become relevant.

One incident involving a Jerusalem institution of Reform Judaism had roots going back more than 300 years. It concerned the transfer of writings by the Dutch philosopher Baruch Spinoza from New York to the Hebrew Union College–Jewish Institute of Religion in Jerusalem. Spinoza was excommunicated in 1656 because of his radical views about Judaism. The dean of Hebrew Union College made the point that the transfer of papers to Jerusalem was a symbol of struggle against the monopoly of Jewish interpretation by Orthodox Jewry.[18]

Somewhat more serious was an episode in an ongoing dispute between Orthodox and liberal Jews about the rituals permitted at the Western Wall. Reform Jews wish to have joint prayers, with no separation between men and women, and to allow women to read from the Torah and don prayer shawls. Israel's Supreme Court had ruled that the women would receive protection for their prayers at the Western Wall on the condition that they did not read from the Torah or wear prayer shawls. Despite the women's compliance with those conditions, a confrontation occurred that involved verbal abuse, spitting, and shoving. Police had been stationed near the wall but did not intervene. A police spokesman cited the responsibility of the rabbinate's ushers to keep order at the holy site.[19] Later the Supreme Court heard a case brought by Reform Jewish women who demanded to pray as they wished. Against their petition were Orthodox Jews who did not want their own prayers disturbed by the presence of women. The court decided that it was not possible to respond positively to the Reform women.[20]

Several organizations dedicate themselves to dealing with tensions among the Judaisms and the Jews who affiliate with them. Despite their claim of good intentions, none of these organizations is ensured an uncritical reception. Shorashim (roots) introduces Jewish culture to immigrants, especially those from the former Soviet bloc who lack a religious background. The founder of Shorashim describes how one day he left a Bnei Brak yeshiva, changed his clothes, divorced his ultra-Orthodox wife, began to learn secular Hebrew, and sought his way in secular Israel.[21] Gesher (bridge) supports a noncoercive effort to bring together Jews of different religious predilections.[22]

Rabbi David Hartman has argued that there is no such thing as a secular Jew who lives in Israel. Hartman is an Orthodox rabbi, professor of philosophy at Hebrew University, and director of the Shalom Hartman Institute. He believes that the secular versus religious tension in the country comes from nonobservant Israelis' fear that their private life will be invaded. In keeping with his role as a teaching rabbi, Hartman has sought to combat such fears by establishing a dialogue about the Jewish content of the state. However, many of those who attend the rabbi's seminars are overseas visitors and Israelis from Anglo-Saxon countries.

Interchanges about Orthodox, Reform, and secular Judaism in the pages of the *Jerusalem Post* are notable for their emotional content. In one interchange the deputy mayor of Jerusalem in charge of cultural affairs revealed his intentions to promote dialogue across the religious and secular divide. He identified himself as a secular Jew but not antireligious, yet his membership in the Meretz political party creates an identity that is easily mistaken as antireligious. He reinforced that identity by saying that a secular majority in Jerusalem was held hostage by a powerful religious minority.[23]

The director of the Israel Religious Action Center (IRAC) of the Israel Movement for Progressive Judaism is a Reform rabbi who also seeks a dialogue between liberal and Orthodox Judaism. He threatened to sue the SHAS party's mentor, Rabbi Ovadia Yosef, for libel on account of deprecatory remarks about the Reform movement.[24]

A series of angry exchanges in the *Jerusalem Post* began when the head of the Jewish Agency (a quasi-governmental body meant to link Israel with Diaspora Jewry) said that Reform Zionists "measure their Zionist activity by attending synagogue once a year for Yom Kippur services." This brought a challenge by a reader that was answered by a passionate member of the *Post*'s editorial staff.

> American Reform rabbis are often dynamic speakers, compassionate family counselors or great Temple administrators. But they aren't religious leaders. . . . Israelis know that to compare shrimp-eating "rabbis" who marry Jews to Gentiles with the "blackest of haredi black-hats" is like comparing witch doctors with competent surgeons. Both carry the name rabbi/doctor, but that's as far as it goes.[25]

One newspaper article began: "Israeli Jews are ready to die for each other, but are incapable of living with each other." It proceeded to report that religious Israelis are not willing to be neighbors with secular Israelis even after death. People scheduled for burial in a Tel Aviv cemetery have the option of being located according to religiosity. The burial society asks families of Sabbath-observant Jews if they prefer to place their loved ones in plots especially reserved for the religious.[26]

Tensions between ultra-Orthodox and secular Jews were prominent in the Rabin government that took office after the election of 1992. In a Knesset of 120 members, Rabin put together a coalition of 44 Labor Party members, 12 from left-wing Meretz, and 6 from the Sephardi ultra-Orthodox party SHAS. SHAS's affiliation was strained from the beginning. Many SHAS voters were uncomfortable with the compromising stances taken by Labor and Meretz in negotiating with the Palestinians and Syrians. The parliamentary leader of SHAS, Ariyeh Deri, was investigated by the police and eventually indicted and put on trial for irregularities during his previous tenure as interior minister. As a condition of becoming interior minister in the Rabin government, he agreed to resign once an indictment was formally initiated.

A major irritant for SHAS was what it perceived as the outrageous behavior and remarks of the head of Meretz, Shulamit Aloni. Aloni had long campaigned to break the monopoly of religious authorities on marriages and divorces. As Rabin's minister of education and culture, she infuriated religious leaders. Their dossier against her included:

- A 1993 photograph of Aloni sitting at a restaurant table laden with bread and beer in the Arab city of Nazareth during Passover
- A proposal that the name of God be removed from the memorial prayer at military ceremonies
- Opposition to teaching that the world was created in six days
- A reference to the chief rabbis of Israel as Israel's two popes and her observation that most Orthodox Jews do not accept their rulings
- Comments that it was no longer necessary to keep kosher in Israel since Jews now live in their own sovereign state and that the laws of kashruth were meant to distance Jews from non-Jews
- A reference to a site revered by some religious Jews as the Tomb of Joseph as the tomb of Sheikh Yusuf. (She based her assertion on archaeological evidence that it was the tomb of an Arab sheikh, perhaps no more than 200 years old.)[27]
- A statement that the government is excessive in bribing the ultra-Orthodox or paying them to move toward a religious fundamentalist, "Khomeinistic" state[28]

Aloni also directed her barbs at the religious Zionists who settle in parts of the West Bank and Gaza. She called on the government to stop the "vile, contemptible methods of rioting and Jewish intifada" that endanger not only the peace process but Israeli society.[29] When the army declared a curfew against Arab residents of Nablus so that religious settlers, along with two Likud members of Knesset, could pray at Joseph's tomb, she said:

> This is human rights? That they put 120,000 people under house arrest [curfew] for 24 hours, so that [Likud MKs] Tzahi Hanegbi and Dov Shilansky could dance with a Torah scroll on Sheikh Yusuf's tomb near Nablus and say "It's all mine," without anyone interfering? This is human rights?[30]

On another occasion, she said:

> The [Jewish] settlement in Hebron should never have happened. . . . Kiryat Arba was established so that Jews would not move into Hebron. Hebron was broken into illegally. . . . Some of the people

living there are racists who want to expel the Arabs. . . . We remember how in the night they threw out the people who were living there. They urinated on them, destroyed their houses and shot at them.

Aloni made this statement after Prime Minister Rabin had given in to religious demands, taking the education portfolio from Aloni and demoting her to minister of culture and communications. A Knesset member of the NRP responded with a call for Aloni's dismissal from the latter position and referred to her as "mentally unstable." He made the point that her remarks about Hebron settlers came only a day after the funeral procession for two victims of Arab terror in Hebron had been stoned by Arabs.[31]

Eliezer Schach is an aged Ashkenazi rabbi and head of an ultra-Orthodox congregation who directs his Yiddish against various groups of religious and secular Israelis. When Shulamit Aloni was appointed minister of education and culture, Rabbi Schach prophesied that she would do to Israeli youth what Hitler had done to one million Jewish children fifty years earlier.[32]

The Sephardim have a reputation of moderation in religion. A large number of them identify themselves as traditional rather than religious. A survey of teenagers studying in religious schools found that the Sephardim were more moderate than the Ashkenazim in both their religiosity and their rebellions against religion. The Sephardim were less pedantic in following the commandments than Ashkenazim, and fewer Sephardim than the Ashkenazim expressed a lack of belief in religious doctrines.[33]

A recent addition to the Sephardi reputation is that the SHAS political party and the religious academies associated with it are mimicking the Ashkenazim in the symbols of piety that they adopt. Among the mimicry that outsiders chide are the extremist statements of SHAS spiritual leader Rabbi Ovadia Yosef. In one cassette made available to SHAS followers, the rabbi sounded like a Sephardi Rabbi Schach when he said that he would "declare a celebration and throw a banquet the day that wicked woman Shulamit Aloni dies."[34] (Readers looking for a biblical precedent may check Jeremiah 28–29, where the prophet calls for the death of his rivals.) Aloni's response was to wish the rabbi "a very long life, so that he would one day indeed get to throw the banquet he wished for."[35]

A number of religious Israelis also condemned the SHAS rabbi. A religious Knesset member of the Labor Party asked if the SHAS rabbi was empowered to pass a sentence of death on anyone.[36] According to a Knesset member of the NRP: "What Rabbi Yosef said was narrow-minded, immoral incitement and is distinctly un-Jewish. He should not be seen as a Torah great, no matter how many pages of the Talmud he knows by heart. His words drip with personal hatred and have nothing to do with an ideological disagreement."

In response, SHAS's Rabbi Yosef was hardly modest in condemning the NRP: "The NRP's religion can be dumped in the garbage can—it and the NRP both. . . . This party calls itself a bridge? . . . It's a bridge all right—a bridge straight to hell for teaming up with Labor. They are both bound for hell."[37]

Although Rabbi Schach helped found SHAS, he later split with its leadership. In reference to SHAS's membership in the Rabin government, Rabbi Schach criticized those who "join with the godless or make their work easier."[38] Confrontations between followers of Rabbi Schach and SHAS have proceeded from shouts to fistfights and gushes from a water cannon.[39]

About secular Israelis, Rabbi Schach said, "Why have you detached yourselves from Torah? . . . You don't observe Shabbat, kashrut, tefillin, family purity. You have no connection to God."[40] He also accused Rabin's government of trying to "uproot religion," and he has blamed the "deterioration of religion" for terrorist attacks against Jews.[41]

Rabbi Schach has also opposed settling Jews in the territories occupied in 1967, in order to keep from a sharp dispute with the United States.[42] In so doing, Rabbi Schach expresses a prominent theme in Jewish doctrine, that is, the avoidance of antagonizing a dominant Gentile power that can bring harm to the Jews. His posture also challenges anyone who believes that religious Jews are united in the effort to hold on to all the Land of Israel that came under Israeli control in 1967.

The secular press seems to enjoy exposing ultra-Orthodox personalities in a way that emphasizes the imperfections of a community that portrays itself as morally superior. A lavish bar mitzvah celebrated by a prominent ultra-Orthodox family received attention because it occurred on the memorial day for members of Israel's security forces.[43] At the bar mitzvah were a Knesset member and his son, who was a member of the Jerusalem city council. The newspaper's point was that ultra-Orthodox parties do not honor the institutions of the Israeli state even while they demand military exemptions for their young men. The celebrants responded that a bar mitzvah is a sacred duty that takes precedence over mourning, even in the case of a death in the immediate family. Other Israelis responded that the celebration could have been more modest out of respect for dead soldiers.

The media have also focused on the messy bankruptcy of Carmel Carpets, the family business of Torah Judaism Knesset member Rabbi Avraham Shapira. Early reports mentioned that the business had failed to pay final salaries to low-wage workers in the depressed town where it had a factory. Later stories reported charges that members of the Shapira family had engaged in fraudulent activities to siphon money from the firm, perhaps as much as one billion Israeli shekels (U.S. $333 million).[44]

The press also reports what to secular ears are outrageous proclamations and curses by religious leaders. When a busload of children from Petach Tikva were killed on a school outing at a railroad crossing, the Sephardi rabbi of Rannana (later minister of interior and minister of immigrant absorption) said that the tragedy was the result of Petach Tikva cinemas being open on Friday evening.

The minority status of religious Jews in Israel may explain their failure to dominate policymaking, yet divisions among them also contribute to the failure. To U.S. observers, the most prominent split may be that between Orthodox and non-Orthodox religious Jews. However, because there are only a small number of religious Jews in Israel who are not Orthodox this division is a sideshow to the main action. The vast majority of non-Orthodox Jews in Israel are not members of Conservative or Reform congregations. They described themselves as not religious, although many occasionally attend religious services in a synagogue or perform them at home on the Sabbath or a religious holiday.

Lessening the weight of a religious bloc in Israeli politics are the divisions between the Orthodox and ultra-Orthodox and within the ultra-Orthodox. Within the ultra-Orthodox are ethnic tensions between the Sephardim of SHAS and the Ashkenazim who dominate Agudat Israel–Torah Judaism. There are further tensions among the Lubavitcher of Chabad, between the Mitnagdim of Degel Hatorah and the Hasidim of Agudat Israel, and between each of these groups and ultra-Orthodox congregations that stand apart from political institutions of the secular state. Acerbic communications between ultra-Orthodox communities are transmitted orally in religious academies and by means of posters that are placed on billboards throughout ultra-Orthodox neighborhoods. Details are likely to focus on points of doctrine that to secular Israelis are exotic reminders of another time and place. Even when the language of dispute is Hebrew rather than Yiddish, it is likely to include phrases taken from religious texts that are incomprehensible to secular ears.

One conflict between Degel Hatorah and Agudat Israel developed in the preparations for the 1996 national election. The issue was a conventional political dispute of how much representation on the common party list would be allocated to each member of the coalition, yet there were arguments that one side had insulted the rabbis of another, threats of excommunication, and the curse that rabbis participating in the conflict would threaten their status in paradise if they did not desist.[45]

The strains between the ultra-Orthodox affiliated with Degel Hatorah and those of the Edah Ha-Haredit were revealed shortly before Passover in 1995. The newspaper of Degel Hatorah called upon its readers to burn, along with the *hametz* (remains of unleavened bread and other products that are cleaned from religious homes prior to the holiday), the guide to preparing for Passover produced by the Edah Ha-Haredit. The dispute developed from an earlier insult to a ruling by a Degel Hatorah rabbi. According to rabbis of Edah Ha-Haredit, the ruling, which forbade the use of produce from the Land of Israel grown by Arabs during a Sabbatical year, was too severe and not accepted by its congregation.[46]

A group of Reform rabbis made their own contribution to the holiday spirit by proclaiming that the custom of symbolically selling to an Arab products that Jews cannot eat on Passover and then buying them back after the holiday is a "bluff, swindle, and hypocrisy" by the rabbinate.[47]

Ultra-Orthodox rabbis differed as to whether their followers should drink water during Passover that is carried throughout Israel from the Sea of Galilee. Some ruled that the water was possibly contaminated by *hametz*, while others reasoned that the fish in the sea probably ate the *hametz* and that the water was free from contaminants. An ultra-Orthodox member of the Jerusalem city council saved Jerusalemites from worry by having the city's water supply switched for the duration of the holiday from the Sea of Galilee to underground aquifers. This produced an objection from the leading Meretz representative on the city council, who also protested the symbolic actions taken by city inspectors against businesses selling bread. An organization standing for freedom of science, religion, and culture objected to the "Ayatolization" of the municipality and questioned the deprivations suffered by religious Jews outside Jerusalem who were forced to use suspect water from the Sea of Galilee.[48]

Conflict between ultra-Orthodox congregations is sometimes initiated by an allusion rather than a direct insult. The weekly newsletter of Degel Hatorah wrote about a rabbi who "was once widely accepted in the religious community but then became shunned for bad activities against the opinions of all great Torah sages." Those in the know recognized an allusion to Rabbi Ovadia Yosef of SHAS. In retaliation, SHAS hoodlums threatened and vandalized the offices of Degel Hatorah. The vandals left a note indicating that two Jews who had been killed in what was generally viewed as a terrorist incident had died as punishment for participating in an insulting demonstration against Rabbi Yosef. In response, an NRP member of Knesset said, "I am delighted that we have no connection with that base and primitive organization [SHAS]."[49]

A SHAS member of Knesset reported that he had been assaulted in the vicinity of the Western Wall by youths wearing the clothing of Degel Hatorah. A member of Knesset from Degel Hatorah condemned the violence, which he attributed to hotheads who had not acted under the authority of his movement. He traced the tension between SHAS and other religious parties to SHAS's willingness to join a governing coalition that was antireligious and explained that tensions had eased since SHAS left the coalition. In an effort to further ease tensions, the Knesset member referred to the vandalism at the offices of Degel Hatorah as an exception to the increased cooperation between SHAS and other religious parties.[50]

The onset of the Palestinian uprising (intifada) in 1987 led religious leaders to lower the profile of religious-secular dispute. A lower court had ruled that the municipal bylaws requiring the closing of public entertainment on the Sabbath were flawed. Ultra-Orthodox rabbis called for massive demonstrations against the violation of the Sabbath in an effort to force the enactment of a Sabbath law that would survive a court challenge. However, they called off the demonstrations in response to the spread of Palestinian rioting. Jewish restaurants, cafes, cinemas, and discotheques opened on Friday evenings in all major cities. Either the intifada caused the Jewish religious leaders to lose their momentum, or the leaders had no chance to enact new legislation because secular Israelis controlled veto points in the cabinet and Knesset committees. More than eight years after the court action, many Israelis are used to going out on Friday night, and no law forbidding their activity is in sight.

Under the threat from external enemies, religious Jews have sought divine intervention for the Jewish nation. Iraqi Scud missile attacks on Israel during the Gulf War of 1991 led Agudat Israel's Council of Torah Sages to declare special prayers at the Western Wall. According to one yeshiva student who came up to Jerusalem from Bnei Brak, "Prayer is all that is left. . . . Prayer always helps, doesn't it? What assurance do you have that your gas mask will help?[51]

The arrival of more than half a million immigrants from the Soviet Union and Ethiopia from the late 1980s through the mid-1990s produced a sense of celebration that once again Jews were saving Jews threatened by Gentiles. But it did not take long for the migrations to produce their own variety of religious tension. Competing for attention were the questions of whether the immigrants were Jewish and what kind of religious training they should receive. Orthodox rabbis, Reform and Conservative congregations, and secular movements each provided their own solutions and competed for the control of absorption centers. In April 1995, the interior ministry reported that 20 percent of the 560,000 immigrants who had come from the former Soviet Union since 1989 were not Jews.[52] Some statements were patronizing in the extreme: They implied that immigrants were plastic and passive, capable of being molded into religious or secular, liberal or ultra-Orthodox Jews, depending on who provided them language training and cultural programs and helped them find jobs and permanent housing.

Avram Burg has taken a posture on the borders of religious and secular communities. The religious son of Yosef Burg, a leading member of NRP who was interior minister under both Labor and Likud-led governments, Avram affiliated with the Labor Party and took positions on international and social issues that identified him with its young left wing. (Many left-wing Laborites are overtly secular if not explicitly antireligious.) In 1995 Avram became the chair of the Jewish Agency, a quasi-governmental organization that administers programs in Israel funded by Diaspora communities and recruits immigrants from the Diaspora. Burg has expressed his openness to the continued immigration of non-Jewish family members of Jewish immigrants and has urged the Israeli rabbinate to help them find solutions to their personal problems. As with other individuals who sit on the fence between disparate populations, Burg is suspected by religious Jews as being too secular or too open to non-Orthodox Judaisms and by secular Jews as being too close to the religious.[53]

There is no issue more symbolic than a dispute about a holiday or the contents of a prayer. Eliezer Don-Yehiya has described how Israelis with different political and religious persuasions have shaped the story of the revolt and the celebration of Hanukkah to their own views. Right-wing secular Israelis emphasize the heroic nationalism of those who resisted foreign rule. Not-so-right-wing Israelis stress those aspects of the story that justify violence only under severe provocation. Religious Israelis emphasize the miracle attributed to the Almighty that caused one day's supply of oil for the sacred lamp to burn for eight days[54]

A cluster of national observances occurs every spring. First there is Holocaust Remembrance Day; a week later is Memorial Day, honoring Israelis who died in the service of their country, followed the next day by Israel Independence Day. Prior to Holocaust Remembrance Day in 1995, a rabbi wrote an article for an ultra-Orthodox newspaper that was critical of how the day was observed. The rabbi said that there was no greater denial of the Holocaust than Holocaust Remembrance Day. (A religious position is that the traditional prayer for the dead is a more appropriate memorial than a special day set aside by the secular state.) The chair of the Knesset education committee suggested that the article be ignored: "The haredim are a state within a state. . . . When do they observe general norms?"[55]

There were differing opinions among ultra-Orthodox rabbis about Memorial Day. Several spoke out against the practice of standing at attention during the two-minute period when sirens sound throughout the country. Rabbi Ovadia Yosef ruled that it was appropriate to stand at attention out of respect and to avoid confrontation with those who observe the holiday. The head of the Meretz delegation on the Jerusalem city council compared those who ignore the sirens to Jews who eat sandwiches at the entrances to synagogues on the fast day of Yom Kippur.[56]

Just prior to Independence Day in 1995, a prominent rabbi identified with the NRP proposed a change in the prayer for the safety of the state. It occurred in the context of negotiations with Palestinians about the future of the West Bank and with Syrians about the Golan Heights. The rabbi wanted to alter the prayer that asks the Almighty to protect Israel, the heads of its government, ministers, and their advisers to include a passage that asks the Almighty "to protect the state *from* its heads of government, ministers, and their advisers." The chair of the NRP responded to criticism of the rabbi by saying that spiritual leaders reflect the pain felt on account of government activities against Judaism and the Land of Israel.[57]

The Holocaust also has a role in Jewish disputes. For a number of religious Jews, a key question is, Why did the Almighty bring such punishment on his people? A biblical parallel is the destruction of Jerusalem and the expulsion of its people to Babylon in 586 B.C.E. According to the prophet Jeremiah, the Lord used the forces of Babylon to punish the Judeans for following foreign gods, adultery, blasphemy, a lack of righteousness, and a failure to heed the warnings of his prophet. As yet, there is no accepted formulation of the sins that brought on the Holocaust by the Germans and their allies. The wounds are still fresh in the minds of survivors and the relatives of victims. A number of rabbis assert that no sin imaginable could justify the extent of the Holocaust. Ultra-Orthodox commentaries about the Holocaust reveal both soul-searching by European rabbis who failed to advocate flight in time for their congregants to avoid the Nazis and a conclusion by some rabbis that the Zionist and Reform movements provoked God into causing the destruction.[58]

Commentaries in ultra-Orthodox newspapers on the eve of the sixtieth anniversary of the Nuremberg Laws returned to the question about the source of the Holocaust. One rabbi concluded that the Reform movement that was strong in Germany violated Jewish prohibitions against acting like Gentiles. The result was that the Gentiles were enraged far beyond their normal hatred of the Jews. A commentary in the newspaper of Agudat Israel made a connection between current controversies and the Holocaust, concluding that leftist Israelis who urge greater concessions to Palestinians are the descendants of Jews who cooperated with the Nazis. A Reform rabbi viewed the commentaries as a modern version of the *Protocols of the Elders of Zion,* an anti-Jewish pamphlet fabricated in czarist Russia that continues to circulate among anti-Semites. He mixed his condemnation with a bit of Zionism: Instead of looking to others for responsibility for the Holocaust, the ultra-Orthodox should face up to the responsibility of their own rabbis who opposed the movement of European Jews to Palestine in the 1930s, which could have saved thousands from the death camps.[59]

The Land of Israel

Intense nationalist sentiments join religious doctrines concerned with the Land of Israel. The importance of both was heightened by the peace process between the Israeli government and the Palestine Liberation Organization and by the transfer to the Palestinians of substantial parts of the territory occupied by Israel as a result of the Six Day War of 1967. The assassination of Prime Minister Yitzhak Rabin by a religious nationalist signaled the Land of Israel as the most explosive issue with a religious content. In the aftermath of the killing, the Israeli media and security forces examined religious and nationalist organizations that had proclaimed Rabin and his government to be traitors and murderers, depicted Rabin as a Nazi, and recited religious curses that called for his death. Rabin's death led a number of religious leaders to examine their souls and insist that killing was beyond the range of proper behavior. It also led the security forces to allocate significantly more resources to dangerous activities within the Jewish sector of Israel and to investigate rabbis and their religious academies.

Despite the drama of the killing and the danger that the Land of Israel presents as a spark to Jewish civil war, it resembles other religious issues in that it is not a doctrinal matter of absolute clarity. Norms of peace and the protection of life compete among Judaic doctrines with the sanctity of the Land of Israel. Not only do many secular Israelis favor territorial concessions to Palestinians, but they are joined by rabbis who emphasize peace and life over territory.

Rabbi Haim Druckman has no doubt that God was at work in Israel's return to Jerusalem, Judea, Samaria, and Gaza.[60] Druckman was one of the earliest Jewish settlers in the new community of Kiryat Arba—established alongside Hebron after the 1967 war—a founder of Gush Emunim, and a member of Knesset for the NRP. More recently, he has offered a religious interpretation of the peace process with the Palestinians. To Druckman, the concessions of the Rabin government reflect the weakness of Israel's Jews. They have not risen to the occasion and made the most of the opportunities that God granted them. The victory of 1967 was a miracle, but Israel is led by people with little faith who are unable to see the miracle. Druckman maintains that Jews will eventually reign sovereign over all the Land of Israel but that the struggle will be long and difficult. He is also confident that talk of uprooting Jewish settlements for the sake of an agreement with the Palestinians will produce an awakening of Judaism and Zionism: "People will see that the country has lost touch with its values, that secularism does not offer the answers. They will see that it is important to return to their roots, for without these roots, without Torah values, there is no reason to be here."[61]

The widely translated novelist and left-of-center political activist Amos Oz fears that the power of religious Jews will spread outward if they are victorious on the territorial issue.

> People think, mistakenly, that this sect is struggling for our sovereignty in Hebron and Nablus, that it wants the Greater Land of Israel, and this end justifies all the means at their disposal—including those dripping with blood. But the truth is that, for this cult, the Greater Land of Israel is merely a sophisticated ploy to disguise its real aims: the imposition of an ugly and distorted version of Judaism on the State of Israel. Nablus and Hebron are just means to an end, way-stations along the course ... towards the spread of their savage conception over Tel Aviv, Jerusalem, Dimona and Beit She'an.[62]

Many rabbis support the *halachic* rulings that forbid the transfer of the Land of Israel to non-Jews, or to non-Jews who threaten to expand their control over Jews or who have a history of violence against Jews.[63] An early proponent of this view was the late Rabbi

Shlomo Goren, who was rabbi of the Israel Defense Forces with the rank of major general and Ashkenazi chief rabbi. He caused a stir by proclaiming that a soldier should refuse to obey an order to remove Jewish settlers from any part of the Land of Israel.[64]

The issue of land transfer surfaced again in the summer of 1995, when the Israeli government and the PLO were nearing an agreement to remove Israeli military positions from the West Bank. A day after a *halachic* ruling against withdrawal signed by eighty rabbis appeared in Israeli newspapers, the Meretz chair of the Knesset legal committee said that he would ask the civil service commissioner to institute actions against rabbis who are state employees and take stands on politically sensitive issues.[65] (This was the same civil service commissioner who was forced to back down from an action against the justice ministry adviser on Hebrew law who compared homosexuality to sex between humans and animals.) It may have been wiser for the Meretz parliamentarian to rely on disputes between Orthodox rabbis to settle the issue rather than sending into the fray a secular official already identified as antireligious. However, that is not the only wisdom appropriate to Israel's kulturkampf; there is also the wisdom of scoring even small and temporary points in an ongoing struggle.

Soon after, a group of rabbis ruled that it was against Jewish law to turn over military positions or land in Israel to non-Jews. (The rabbis' ruling gained prominence because some of them were affiliated with military units that recruit religious Jews and provide them an opportunity to continue their religious studies along with army service.) Yet other rabbis were quick to take postures against their colleagues. They argued that the rabbis' ruling against vacating army posts was mistaken, considering the issues at stake, and that the decision to vacate was more clearly an issue of political judgment than of religious law. They said that it was unseemly to impose on eighteen- and nineteen-year old soldiers the task of determining the morality of military orders pronounced in response to the lawful decisions of a properly elected government. They warned against a split in the people and the danger of a civil war. They elevated the importance of well-disciplined Israeli Defense Forces to such a degree that they strengthened the argument that the army had replaced the Almighty in the central role of Israel's civil religion.[66]

A lack of agreement within both religious and secular camps confuses the conflict. Religious Israelis join secular Israelis in supporting territorial concessions. Rabbi Yehuda Amital is dean of the Har Etzion yeshiva in Gush Etzion, in the West Bank between Bethlehem and Hebron, and head of a movement of religious Jews that is left of center on territorial issues (Meimad, "the Movement for Religious Zionist Renewal"). Amital speaks moderately and rejects the prediction of crisis. He believes that Zionism is strong enough to support the removal of a few Jewish settlements for the sake of peace. According to Amital, a small proportion of the settlers may have problems, but most will adapt to the new reality. He urges settlement leaders to discard delusions that they will overthrow the government and to work within the framework of the agreement with the PLO to include as many settlements as possible into the boundaries of the new map of Israel. For him, the spiritual values associated with the Land of Israel are more important than where exactly within the land the Jews can settle.[67]

The Golden Mean, a group of American Orthodox rabbis, opposes what it perceives as the hawkish sentiment among other American Orthodox Jews.[68] The present Ashkenazi chief rabbi of Israel, Yisrael Law, has sought to distance the official rabbinate from any posture that generates intense disagreement.

> We are just like judges. We can't take a stand on a political issue. . . . although in principle the Jewish people has a right to the Land of Israel, operationally it is a different matter. . . . this is a situation like that in which one doctor says you are saving life by amputating a limb, and another doctor says you are endangering the patient. . . . it is the role of the chief rabbis to encourage the various factions within Israel to speak to one another.[69]

The same rabbi responded to acts of Palestinian violence after the signing of an Israel-PLO accord by saying that the Palestinians do not seem to be ready for peace and urging Prime Minister Yitzhak Rabin to suspend the peace process.

After the assassination of Prime Minister Rabin, religious and secular leaders called for a national period of soul-searching. Some politicians of the Labor and Meretz parties seemed to appropriate the assassination for their own purposes by demanding soul-searching from right-wing and religious Jews. In turn, right-wing party politicians and religious leaders insisted on their right to oppose by nonviolent means the policies of the government. A number of religious leaders urged a revision of religious education to thwart violence among Jews and to lessen the use of religious law as an element in political disputes. When Shimon Peres became prime minister after Rabin's death, he included in his government the accommodationist Rabbi Amital as a minister without portfolio. This was part of Peres's effort to bring religious Jews within the purview of government policy.

Prior to the assassination, it seemed that most rabbis who took public postures on the conflict about the Land of Israel opposed withdrawal. After the assassination, the picture was less certain. In any case, rabbis have traditionally operated by the weight of argument and the reputation of advocates rather than by simple majorities.[70] A biblical passage warns against the passions of an unjust majority: "You shall not be led into wrongdoing by the majority, nor, when you give evidence in a lawsuit, shall you side with the majority to pervert justice."[71]

Prominent among the religious Jews who acquired the label extremist because of their uncompromising postures on the Land of Israel were activists of the Kach movement, created by the late Rabbi Meir Kahane, and its spinoffs or national Zionists from settlements in the occupied territories, especially Kiryat Arba outside of Hebron. (Kach translates as "Thus!" or "That's it!" with an implication of "Take it our way or go to hell!")

While many of the ultra-Orthodox appear to concentrate on Sabbath observance and other issues not linked to territory per se, there are sectors that take extreme postures not significantly different from those of the Kahane camp or other nationalist Zionists. One source of extremism was an ultra-Orthodox weekly newspaper, which publicized charges that likened Prime Minister Rabin to the Jews who cooperated with the Nazis, termed him a psychopath and murderer, and proclaimed on him a curse of death.[72]

If any religious issue is capable of producing violence among the Jews of Israel, it is the Land of Israel. An assertion frequently heard is that religious and nationalist settlers in the territories occupied in the war of 1967 will oppose with force any efforts to remove them. The death of Prime Minister Rabin at the hand of a religious Jew has threatened a spread of violence in place of politics. But the effect of the shock of his death on a number of religious Jews, and their reexamination of postures that have proved to be incendiary, may head off that possibility.

Jerusalem

Jerusalem's status as a Holy City of Judaism, Christianity, and Islam ensures a high intensity of religious dispute.[73] Its role in Jewish memory begins with the stories of its capture by David about 1000 B.C.E., and his unrestrained joy in bringing the Ark of the Lord to the city.[74] I Kings describes Jerusalem as a world center of opulence and wisdom during the period of Solomon (c. 965–927 B.C.E.).[75] When the northern Kingdom of Israel was destroyed by the Assyrians about 722 B.C.E., the prophet Isaiah saw Zion (Jerusalem) as the salvation of God's people:

> Your country is desolate, your cities lie in ashes. Strangers devour your land before your eyes. . . . Only Zion is left, like a watchman's shelter in a vineyard. . . .
> In days to come the mountain of the Lord's house shall be set over all other mountains. . . . All the nations shall come streaming to it. . . . out of Jerusalem comes the word of the Lord.[76]

One of the oldest subjects of Jewish dejection is Jerusalem's destruction by the Babylonians in 586 B.C.E. By rabbinical tradition, Jeremiah wrote the Book of Lamentations at that time. Years later, after Jerusalem was rebuilt and destroyed again by the Romans and the Jews were forbidden to enter the city, Jewish pilgrims would gather on the hills overlooking the site of the Temple and weep as they recited: "How solitary lies the city, once so full of people! Once great among nations, now become a widow; once queen among provinces, now put to forced labor!"[77]

Early Christians viewed Jerusalem as cursed rather than holy. They interpreted its destruction by the Romans in 70 C.E. as the Lord's punishment of the Jews for rejecting Jesus. It became sacred after the Emperor Constantine converted to Christianity in 324 C.E. His mother, Helena, claimed she had located the sites of Christ's crucifixion and burial, and initiated construction of the Church of the Holy Sepulcher. For Muslims, Jerusalem is the site of Muhammad's ascent to heaven and a religious center of an Arab region.

The emotion of the Crusaders was apparent in a passage attributed to a knight who participated in the purge of the city in 1099:

> Some of our men—and this was the more merciful course—cut off the heads of their enemies; others shot them with arrows so that they fell from the towers; others tortured them longer by casting them into the flames. . . . men rode in blood up to their knees and bridle reins. Indeed, it was a just and splendid judgment of God that this place should be filled with the blood of unbelievers, since it had suffered so long from their blasphemies.[78]

The hyperbole of twentieth-century Muslims is hardly less extreme. Arab publicists have sought to reshape history in order to give themselves monopoly of legitimacy.

> The native inhabitants, Christian and pagan, were descended from the original Carmel Man of Palestine, and from the Semitic Arab

tribes of Amorites, Canaanites, and others who had entered the land from Arabia in migratory waves. . . . the Hebrews of the Old Testament were a limited group, [whose] rule in Jerusalem as a city-state was of short duration. . . . Despite Israeli propaganda, there are in fact no important Jewish monuments of religious significance in Jerusalem. It is true that there is a Jewish ritual of mourning at the Wailing Wall, but this in fact is a portion of the wall of the Haram Esh-Sharif, and is actually Muslim property.[79]

Modern Jews are also expansive about Jerusalem. The 1967 victory has been described as "an act of God, providential, irreversible, final."[80]

We could see the Western Wall, through an archway. . . . It was like new life. . . . I could see them, men who were too tired to stand up any more, sitting by the Wall, clutching it, kissing the stones and crying. We all of us cried. That was what we had been fighting for.[81]

An editorial in the *Jerusalem Post* justified Jewish control over Jerusalem by both aged religious texts and recent history.

For Moslems it is one of many holy sites called "the third most important to Islam" after Mecca and Medina. But there is not a single mention of Jerusalem in the Koran, and it is mostly in response to the Arab-Israeli conflict that Arabs have arbitrarily elevated the city's religious importance. When the Temple Mount was under Jordanian rule, only the Jordanian royal family visited it. No other Arab ruler, including those who still call for a jihad to "liberate" the city from the Jewish infidels, ever bothered to visit the city and worship in its mosques.[82]

Religion overlaps with ethnicity in the modern city. Jews are about 72 percent of the municipal population, Muslims 26 percent, and Christians 3 percent. Almost all Muslims and many Christians are Palestinians. Voluntary segregation is the norm in housing and schooling. Most ultra-Orthodox Jews and almost all Palestinians live in their own neighborhoods. Jewish education is divided into secular and religious schools, with the religious schools further subdivided between those that are modern Orthodox, ultra-Orthodox, Conservative, or Reform. Palestinians choose between schools with the Arabic curriculum of the Israeli Ministry of Education, those providing a Jordanian curriculum, those affiliated with Muslim religious authorities, and schools operated by overseas Christian congregations.

The prominence of ultra-Orthodox Jews in Jerusalem is apparent in their parties' polling 22 percent of the vote in the city, compared with only 8 percent of the vote nationwide, in the 1992 election for the Knesset. Fifteen years earlier, in the election of 1977, ultra-Orthodox parties counted for only 8 percent of the vote in Jerusalem. The large families and the growing number of ultra-Orthodox in Jerusalem are evident in changing primary school enrollments over the 1972–1992 period: The number of students in ultra-Orthodox primary schools increased from 17 to 42 percent of the Jewish total, while those in Jewish secular schools dropped from 53 to 32 percent.[83]

The most notable ethnic-religious division in the city is between Jews on the one hand and Muslim and Christian Palestinians on the other. Tensions are apparent in surveys taken in the Palestinian community and in the Palestinians' boycott of the political opportunities offered to them by the Israeli regime. Eighty-six percent of a sample of Palestinians living in Jerusalem answered "no" or "not at all" when asked if they were satisfied with the services rendered by the municipality. When asked, "If confronted with a choice, which would you choose: Palestinian state, economic well-being, family and community, or religion?" almost 90 percent chose "Palestinian state." Fifty-five percent of the Palestinian respondents said that the city should be divided between east (Palestinian) and west (Jewish).[84] At the time the survey was taken, all major political parties in Israel opposed the creation of a Palestinian state and insisted that Jerusalem remain the undivided capital of the Jewish state.

The Israeli government offered but did not impose Israeli citizenship on the Palestinians living in former Jordanian sections when the city was unified in 1967. Participation by residents in the Knesset election of 1988, for which citizenship was required, shows the small percentage of Palestinians who accepted that offer. In predominantly Muslim neighborhoods that were absorbed into the city in 1967, the participation varied from 0.4 to 1.7 percent of the norm in predominantly Jewish areas. Participation in the Christian quarter of the Old City (whose population is 85 percent Christian and 15 percent Muslim) showed the slight degree to which Christian Palestinians exceed Muslim Palestinians in their rapport with Israeli institutions. However, the election participation of residents in the Christian quarter was only 3 percent of the norm in predominantly Jewish areas.[85]

Palestinians can be candidates for the municipal council and vote in municipal elections by virtue of being city residents even if they have not accepted Israeli citizenship. Yet Palestinians have refused to stand as candidates, no Palestinian political party has emerged in local elections, and the number of Palestinians voting in local elections has ranged between 3 and 22 percent of those eligible.[86] By their boycotts, Palestinians have given up the possibility of translating more than a quarter of the city's population into a significant voting bloc. With the power they could achieve in the city council and the Knesset, they might enhance the economic and social conditions of their community. By choosing to put almost all their efforts into the issue of whose city Jerusalem is, Palestinians have surrendered leverage that might aid them in the more conventional struggle over who gets what in Jerusalem.

Historic schisms in the Christian and Muslim communities of Jerusalem are still viable. The clergy of Roman Catholic, Greek Orthodox, and Coptic churches quarrel about the Church of the Holy Sepulcher. The Russian Ministry of Foreign Affairs has reasserted a historic claim as patron of the city's Orthodox congregation, although so far not in language as strong as that of its prerevolutionary predecessors. In the nineteenth century one conflict about Jerusalem holy places involving Russian postures in behalf of the Greek Orthodox and French demands in behalf of Roman Catholics escalated to the Crimean War.[87]

Palestinians and the royal families of Jordan and Saudi Arabia argue about control of Islamic holy places. In 1994 the Palestinian Authority and the Jordanian government each appointed a different mufti for Jerusalem. The Palestinian's appointee occupied the main office, while Jordan's mufti settled into an anteroom, and Yasir Arafat accused the Israelis of favoring Jordanian claims over Jerusalem.

In order to appease foreign governments whose constituencies are sensitive to religious issues regarding Jerusalem, Israeli officials have conceded the administration of Christian and Muslim holy sites to non-Jews, without giving up formal sovereignty. And they have sought to appease prominent Jews from the Diaspora who do not always approve of what the Israelis do in the city. When an issue pits Orthodox and Reform Jews against one another, it puts Israeli officials in a difficult squeeze between the Orthodox position likely to be favored by interests represented in the Knesset and the position of non-Orthodox Jews represented among overseas communities that contribute substantial funds to Israeli programs and support Israel's interests with their national governments.

Jerusalem has been a focus of travelers since ancient times, and many pilgrims have reported on their spiritual experiences in what they perceive to be a holy place.[88] Not a few have gone beyond the normal range of religious ecstasy: *Jerusalem syndrome* is a label used by medical personnel who treat people with fantasies of participating in wondrous events. For example, a young woman with academic credentials was in the city with a Christian tour group. A few days into her trip, she began to run wild, shouting at everyone in the group to dress in white and follow her to the Garden Tomb to pray for the Messiah. A woman from Argentina was found wandering late at night, stark naked, singing and praying aloud. She said that God had given her a secret message and that she alone could bring world peace. An Australian Christian tourist with a record of mental instability set fire to al-Aqsa Mosque. (Al-Aqsa had been built by the Muslims in the eighth century. It was used as a hostel, stable, and latrine by the Crusaders during their occupation of the city from 1099 and was resanctified by the Muslims in 1187. It sits on Mount Moriah, or Haram Esh-Sharif, which some Jews and Christian fundamentalists want to clear for the reerection of a temple. Protestant advocates see such an event as a prerequisite for the Second Coming, and Mormons the Third Coming. Israeli authorities believe the plans portend disaster, and they have set the police against those who try to implement them.)

The Jerusalem syndrome is said to manifest itself differently with Christians and Jews. Christians tend to see themselves as John the Baptist, the Virgin Mary, Satan, or even God and are likely to experience such visions at places associated with the last days of Jesus: the Church of the Holy Sepulcher, Golgotha, or along the Via Dolorosa. Jews are more likely to choose the role of Messiah, Abraham, or King David; many of them manifest the syndrome at the Western Wall or in the Jewish cemetery on the Mount of Olives.[89]

The prospect of ethnic and religious violence is part of the local scene. Jews worry about enraged Muslims who kill Jews while shouting "God is great!" When that occurs, the police mobilize to protect Arabs (and Jews who look like Arabs) on main roads near working-class Jewish neighborhoods. There the chant is "Death to the Arabs," and some crowds have shown their willingness to implement the slogan.

Jewish politics in the Jerusalem municipality are not free of baiting and sniping on issues of religion. At the end of Passover in 1995, the head of the Meretz delegation on the city council accused the mayor of having eaten in a nonkosher restaurant during the holiday. The council member made a point of the mayor's affiliation with a coalition of the ultra-Orthodox and called on him to release the city from a religious siege. He said that the leaders of the council's religious bloc would have to stand before the Almighty as judge in heaven to give an account for every shrimp and every bite of pork that the mayor ate, because they had crowned him king of the Jews in Jerusalem. One ultra-Orthodox political leader said he did not believe the accusation was true. Another was more cautious: He said that if the accusation was true, the mayor's behavior was not wise.[90]

Teddy Kollek

Teddy Kollek was one of Israel's international stars during his 1966–1993 tenure as Jerusalem's mayor. He had the good fortune to be elected to head a small holy city that changed its strategic configuration a year after he entered office. As a result of the Six Day War of 1967, Jerusalem was no longer at the end of a narrow corridor, isolated from Jewish settlements along the coast. It became the center of a Jewish country after a hiatus of 1,900 years. Kollek seized the opportunity for all it was worth. The mayor led the overseas fund-raising for the Jerusalem Foundation, which supported the construction and programming of facilities to the equivalent of some 15 percent of the city's regular budget. During his tenure, the city's population more than doubled, from 268,000 to 557,000. The building of public structures and private residences surpassed in quantity and perhaps in opulence that which occurred during the periods of Solomon or Herod.

Kollek sought to create an image of moderation amid contending communities. He respected each community's right to voluntary segregation even while admitting that every resident had a right to live anywhere in the city. He noted that just as secular Jews avoided living in ultra-Orthodox neighborhoods, he wanted Jews to avoid choosing a residence in the Muslim or Christian quarters of the Old City.[91] He described segregated schooling, with separate Arab and Hebrew curricula and languages of instruction, as a vital component of communal peace. This stand caused him problems with potential overseas donors to the Jerusalem Foundation who were convinced that integration was the key to Jerusalem's future.

Kollek protested against the efforts of nationalist and religious Jews to take too much, too quickly, and with too much bravado. In his view, they inflamed passions in a city that was destined by history for intergroup suspicion. Tension disturbed Kollek's city and the foreign donors and investors whose money he sought to attract. He said many times that religious Jews caused him more trouble than Arabs. At a party for his retirement in 1993, he laughed when the leader of the ultra-Orthodox bloc on the city council recalled newspaper reports twenty-eight years earlier that Kollek had sold out to the religious parties.[92]

Kollek cautioned that his efforts would not produce a solution to Jerusalem's problems in the near term:

> Here it is clear beyond all doubt that Arabs will continue to speak Arabic and be educated with the Koran. The same for the

Armenians or other Christian Churches that have guarded their languages and their doctrines over the generations. We have no aspiration to integrate. That would not be good for us, and it is not possible.[93]

We entertain no illusions that this will defuse the existing political contradictions; these, with patience and tolerance, may be solved in another generation or two. . . . We pursue our goals expecting neither sympathy nor gratitude from a population which cannot alienate itself from its national emotions.[94]

Life in the cross pressures occasionally weakened Kollek's moderation. When one constituent threatened not to vote for him, the mayor responded, "Kiss my ass."[95] When the city council was considering the municipal budget in 1989, a member from Agudat Israel charged that the budget kept up the tradition of slighting the religious population; by his reckoning, the budget allocated more money for orchestras than for facilities in religious neighborhoods. "Learn to enjoy classical music!" the mayor responded, adding that many religious Jews attended musical events. "The fact is that you [ultra-Orthodox] get more than you deserve from the city."[96] He said that "the Cabinet was shit" at a time when the Ministry of Housing and Construction was talking about plans to build additional housing for Jews in Palestinian neighborhoods.[97]

* * *

This chapter has described the tensions that surround religion and politics in Israel, with a focus on the Jews who dominate the population and the government. The next chapter turns to the question of what difference does it make for public policy. The two chapters provide the essential material to justify the central theme of this book: that religion is a topic of continuing and intense dispute among Israelis, but that neither religious nor antireligious activists are strong enough to dominate or to silence their antagonists.

NOTES

1. *Ha'aretz* (in Hebrew), June 14, 1995, p. 7.
2. *Ha'aretz* (in Hebrew), March 7, 1995, pp. 8–9.
3. Leviticus 20:13–15.
4. *Ha'aretz* (in Hebrew), July 11, 1996, p. 5.
5. *Jerusalem Post*, December 21, 1993, p. 2.
6. *Jerusalem Post*, December 24, 1993, p. 4B.

7. *Ha'aretz* (in Hebrew), April 9, 1995, p. 4.
8. *Jerusalem Post*, December 1, 1993, p. 1.
9. *Jerusalem Post*, December 17, 1992, p. 14.
10. *Jerusalem Post*, May 18, 1990, p. 7.
11. *Jerusalem Post*, January 28, 1992, p. 6.
12. *Jerusalem Post*, January 11, 1993, p. 2.
13. *Ha'aretz* (in Hebrew), April 19, 1995, p. 6.
14. *Ha'aretz* (in Hebrew), April 24, 1995, p. 7.
15. *Ha'aretz* (in Hebrew), April 24, 1995, p. 1.
16. *Ha'aretz* (in Hebrew), April 24, 1995, p. 7.
17. *Ha'aretz* (in Hebrew), April 24, 1995, p. 7.
18. *Jerusalem Post*, June 1, 1990, p. 9.
19. *Jerusalem Post*, June 8, 1989, p. 4.
20. *Ha'aretz* (in Hebrew), October 6, 1995, p. 5.
21. *Jerusalem Post*, June 4, 1993, p. 8.
22. *Jerusalem Post*, July 7, 1989, p. 10.
23. *Jerusalem Post*, April 5, 1993, p. 8.
24. *Jerusalem Post*, April 5, 1993, p. 8.
25. *Jerusalem Post*, February 21, 1992, p. 7.
26. *Jerusalem Post*, August 2, 1989, p. 5.
27. *Jerusalem Post*, May 10, 1993, p. 2.
28. *Jerusalem Post*, December 3, 1993, p. 1.
29. *Jerusalem Post*, November 12, 1993, p. 2.
30. *Jerusalem Post*, January 27, 1993, p. 1.
31. *Jerusalem Post*, December 9, 1993, p. 14.
32. *Jerusalem Post*, July 17, 1992, p. 1B.
33. Avraham Leslau and Mordechai Bar-Lev, "Religiosity Among Oriental Youth in Israel," *Sociological Papers* 3, no. 5 (December 1994) (Bar-Ilan University, Sociological Institute for Community Studies).
34. *Jerusalem Post*, February 8, 1993, p. 2.
35. *Jerusalem Post*, February 5, 1993, p. 1.
36. *Jerusalem Post*, February 5, 1993, p. 1.
37. *Jerusalem Post*, February 8, 1993, p. 2.
38. *Jerusalem Post*, December 28, 1992, p. 1.
39. *Jerusalem Post*, October 23, 1992, p. 2.
40. *Jerusalem Post*, June 18, 1992, p. 2.
41. *Jerusalem Post*, April 20, 1993, p. 2.
42. *Ha'aretz* (in Hebrew), April 7, 1995, p. 4.
43. *Kal Ha'ir* (in Hebrew), April 19, 1991.
44. *Jerusalem Post*, December 15, 1994, p. 8; *Ha'aretz* (in Hebrew), July 11, 1996, p. 1.
45. *Ha'aretz* (in Hebrew), May 7, 1995, p. 7.
46. *Ha'aretz* (in Hebrew), April 13, 1995, p 9.
47. *Ha'aretz* (in Hebrew), April 13, 1995, p 9.
48. *Ha'aretz* (in Hebrew), April 17, 1995, p. 5.
49. *Ha'aretz* (in Hebrew), April 2, 1995, p. 3; April 5, 1995, p. 7.
50. *Ha'aretz* (in Hebrew), April 9, 1995, p. 6.
51. *Jerusalem Post*, January 15, 1991, p. 2.
52. *Ha'aretz* (in Hebrew), April 19, 1995, p. 1.
53. *Ha'aretz* (in Hebrew), April 19, 1995, p. 1.
54. Eliezer Don-Yehiya, "Hanukkah and the Myth of the Maccabees in

Zionist Ideology and in Israeli Society," *The Jewish Journal of Sociology* 34, no. 1 (June 1992): 5–23.

55. *Ha'aretz* (in Hebrew), April 26, 1995, p. 6.
56. *Ha'aretz* (in Hebrew), May 5, 1995, p. 6.
57. *Ha'aretz* (in Hebrew), May 2, 1995, p. 10.
58. Menachem Friedman, "The Hasidim and the Holocaust," *Jerusalem Quarterly* 53 (Winter 1990): 86–114.
59. *Ha'aretz* (in Hebrew), October 10, 1995, p. 6.
60. *Judea* and *Samaria* are the terms Israel uses for the southern and northern portions of the West Bank occupied during the 1967 war.
61. *Jerusalem Post*, November 25, 1994, p. 6.
62. *Jerusalem Post*, June 8, 1989, p. 4.
63. For example, *Ha'aretz* (in Hebrew), April 17, 1995, p. 5.
64. *Jerusalem Post*, December 20, 1993, p. 1.
65. *Ha'aretz* (in Hebrew), April 18, 1995, p. 3.
66. *Ha'aretz* (in Hebrew), July 13, 1995, pp. 1ff.
67. *Jerusalem Post*, November 25, 1994, p. 6.
68. *Jerusalem Post*, December 16, 1994, p. 9.
69. *Jerusalem Post*, September 8, 1993, p. 2.
70. Roger Brooks, *The Spirit of the Ten Commandments: Shattering the Myth of Rabbinic Legalism* (New York: Harper and Row, 1990); and Stuart A. Cohen, *The Three Crowns: Structures of Communal Politics in Early Rabbinic Jewry* (Cambridge: Cambridge University Press, 1990).
71. Exodus 23:2. See Joel Roth, *The Halakhic Process: A Systemic Analysis* (New York: Jewish Theological Seminary of America, 1986), especially chaps. 5–7.
72. *Ha'aretz* (in Hebrew), November 12, 1995, p. 6.
73. Portions of this section borrow from Ira Sharkansky, *Governing Jerusalem: Again on the World's Agenda* (Detroit: Wayne State University Press, 1996).
74. II Samuel 6. The episode portrays the king as so ecstatic that he provoked his wife to carp at him for an unseemly display before the servant girls.
75. I Kings 10. For a view that the biblical portrayal of Jerusalem was exaggerated, see J. Maxwell Miller and John H. Hayes, *A History of Ancient Israel and Judah* (Philadelphia: The Westminster Press, 1986), p. 190.
76. Isaiah 1:7–8; 2:2–4.
77. Lamentations 1:1.
78. F. E. Peters, *Jerusalem: The Holy City in the Eyes of Chroniclers, Visitors, Pilgrims, and Prophets from the Days of Abraham to the Beginnings of Modern Times* (Princeton: Princeton University Press, 1985), pp. 285–286.
79. M. A. Aamiry, *Jerusalem: Arab Origin and Heritage* (London: Longman, 1978). The quotations come from the preface and pp. 1–12.
80. Terrence Prittie, *Whose Jerusalem?* (London: Frederick Muller Ltd., 1981), p. 1.
81. Quoted from Henry Near, ed., *The Seventh Day* (London: Andre Deutsch, 1970), by Ronald Segal, *Whose Jerusalem? The Conflicts of Israel* (London: Jonathan Cape, 1973), p. 135.
82. *Jerusalem Post*, May 20, 1993, p. 6.
83. *Jerusalem Statistical Data* (Jerusalem: Municipality of Jerusalem and the Jerusalem Institute for Israel Studies, 1983), p. 176; and *Statistical Yearbook*

of Jerusalem, 1992 (Jerusalem: Municipality of Jerusalem and the Jerusalem Institute for Israel Studies, 1994), p. 257.

84. Abraham Ashkenasi, "Opinion Trends Among Jerusalem Palestinians" (Jerusalem: Hebrew University, Leonard Davis Institute, 1990).

85. *Statistical Yearbook of Jerusalem, 1988* (Jerusalem: Municipality of Jerusalem and the Jerusalem Institute for Israel Studies, 1990), Tables 3:4, 19:2; and Mayn Choshen, "The Elections to the Knesset in Jerusalem: Statistical Outlet" (in Hebrew) (Jerusalem: Jerusalem Institute for Israel Studies, 1990). The data presented here are not direct indicators of Israeli citizenship. They are also not conventional measures of voting turnout insofar as they do not take into account age differentials within the various sectors of the population. Nonetheless, the stark findings indicate the small percentage of Palestinians living in neighborhoods absorbed into Jerusalem by Israel in 1967 who have accepted Israeli citizenship.

86. Michael Romann and Alex Weingrod, *Living Together Separately: Arabs and Jews in Contemporary Jerusalem* (Princeton: Princeton University Press, 1991); Abraham Ashkenasi, "Israeli Policies and Palestinian Fragmentation: Political and Social Impacts in Israel and Jerusalem," (Jerusalem: Hebrew University, Leonard Davis Institute, 1988); and Ashkenasi, "Opinion Trends Among Jerusalem Palestinians."

87. On the competing allegations about the contribution of holy sites to that war, see Norman Rich, *Why the Crimean War? A Cautionary Tale* (Hanover, NH: University Press of New England, 1985); Brison D. Gooch, ed., *The Origins of the Crimean War* (Lexington, MA: D. C. Heath & Co., 1969).

88. Robert L. Wilken, *The Land Called Holy: Palestine in Christian History and Thought* (New Haven: Yale University Press, 1992); John Wilkinson, *Jerusalem Pilgrims: Before the Crusades* (Jerusalem: Ariel Publishing House, 1977); and F. E. Peters, *Jerusalem: The Holy City in the Eyes of Chroniclers, Visitors, Pilgrims, and Prophets from the Days of Abraham to the Beginnings of Modern Times* (Princeton: Princeton University Press, 1985).

89. *Jerusalem Post*, September 6, 1991, p. 24.

90. *Ha'aretz* (in Hebrew), April 24, 1995, p. 7.

91. Supplement for the twenty-fifth anniversary of the Jerusalem Foundation, *Kal Ha'ir* (in Hebrew), May 24, 1991.

92. *Jerusalem Post*, December 3, 1993, p. 8B.

93. Supplement for the twenty-fifth anniversary of the Jerusalem Foundation, *Kal Ha'ir* (in Hebrew), May 24, 1991.

94. Teddy Kollek, "Foreword," in David Kroyanker, *Jerusalem: Planning and Development 1982–1985: New Trends* (Jerusalem: The Jerusalem Committee and the Jerusalem Institute for Israeli Studies, 1985).

95. Abraham Rabinovich, *Jerusalem on Earth: People, Passions and Politics in the Holy City* (New York: Free Press, 1988), p. 17.

96. *Jerusalem Post*, June 23, 1989, p. 2.

97. *Kal Ha'ir* (in Hebrew), April 17, 1992.

6
RELIGION AND PUBLIC POLICY

One reason that religious issues are chronically on Israel's agenda is that basic controversies are not finally resolved. Individual problems may be solved, but the same issue will come back in another setting. Demands to stop a construction project that has uncovered ancient bones may be answered, but sooner or later another project will uncover bones. Requests to close a particular road on the Sabbath and religious holidays will be resolved, but the issue will come up again at another site. If some rabbis are satisfied with a particular resolution, other rabbis may seize the opportunity to demonstrate that they are more observant of Jewish religious law.

In general the secular interests of Israel, like those of other Western democracies, are able to keep religious interests from determining outcomes of heated issues. The discordant nature of the religious sector—with its disputes on matters of principle; competition between religious parties, yeshivot, and congregations; and personal animosities between rabbis—gets in the way of a solid religious front. Religion is strong enough to ensure its respect and occasional victories, but it falls short of defining the tangible substance of important policy issues in Israel or even in the Holy City of Jerusalem.

The ambiguous status of religion in Israeli politics appears in Knesset debates, which reveal the sensitivities of some religious politicians and the willingness of others to engage in ritualized disputes. Some rabbis who represented religious parties in the Knesset in 1990 expressed rage, and others laughed, when, in opposition to their proposal to strengthen the laws against pornography, a secular member read from the Song of Songs: "Thy neck shall be as a tower of ivory . . . thy breasts shall be as clusters of the vine."[1] A left-wing Knesset member provoked an outburst from religious parliamentarians when she referred to the love between David and Jonathan in support of homosexual rights.[2] Foreign Minister Shimon Peres set off a shouting match when he said he could not defend all that King David had done, especially with respect to Bathsheba. Religious members of the Knesset asserted that this was an unacceptable insult to the author of Psalms, and one participant went to the Knesset clinic with what he claimed was a heart attack.[3] Calmer observers noted that God's prophet Nathan considered David a sinner and that rabbis have pondered the different implications of David's activities over the centuries.[4]

Events like these point to the importance of Jewish symbols in the political discourse of Israel, yet they do not reflect the dominance of religious interests. On the contrary, they show religious politicians struggling against secular politicians in a competitive field, each side seeking to advance its perspectives. Sometimes it is difficult to distinguish between angry and humorous outbursts. Shouts of protest and ridicule reflect a standoff and continuing tension rather than the clear dominance of one side or another.

Just what is meant by "the tangible substance of important policy issues" is a matter of some dispute, especially in the context of religion. There is no doubting the power of religion to affect issues with high symbolic content.[5] What is less certain is the capacity of religious interests to determine the outcome of issues with significant material implications, which include detailing the programs that citizens receive from government, imposing controversial normative standards on an unwilling population with the force of law, and determining the way in which substantial public resources will be divided among the claimants.

RITUALS OF DISPUTE ABOUT RELIGION AND PUBLIC POLICY

The prospect of violence across religious and ethnic lines is part of Israel's past and present. The term *crusade* conveys something more worrisome than it does in other countries, where it may be used by publicists wanting to keep the streets clean or to expand the network of parks. Israeli security forces view Arab demonstrations as a potential threat to the state. Christian and Muslim demands that touch issues of religion are likely to be handled by communal leaders, who seem willing to get what they can from the authorities and minimize mass action. In order to keep from provoking Muslims, the police have prevented religious Jews from praying on the Temple Mount.

Religious disputes among Jews are most likely to cause visible disturbances. So common as to be ritualized are charges by religious or antireligious activists that there has been a violation of the status quo. This accepted policy of no change on matters involving religion was designed to limit disputes, but the status quo is vulnerable to contrasting interpretations. The policy explicitly accepts conditions that were in place in 1948, when Israel declared its independence. But what about activities in cities or neighborhoods created since 1948 or technologies introduced thereafter? When a dispute catches hold, there is likely to be an escalation in rhetoric: proclamations from one side that the other side has provoked the confrontation by threatening the status quo; charges of anti-Semitism made both by religious and antireligious activists; and street demonstrations with overturned trash receptacles, fistfights, and mounted police trying to minimize the damage.

One of the mysteries of religious conflict is why certain issues arise and catch hold at a particular time. Many construction excavations uncover old bones, but only some of them attract national attention. Brigham Young University had a Jerusalem program for several years before Jewish activists criticized the proselytizing doctrine of the Church of Jesus Christ of Latter-day Saints. The Yad Vashem memorial to the victims of the Holocaust displayed photographs of nude concentration camp inmates for decades before ultra-Orthodox Jews made an issue of modesty and threatened to construct their own Holocaust memorial if authorities did not remove the pictures. Major roads alongside ultra-Orthodox neighborhoods have carried Sabbath and holiday traffic for years between sporadic efforts to close the roads. Ultra-Orthodox demonstrators have suddenly protested advertising posters, without any indication that the posters are less modest than in the past. Butcher shops and restaurants sold tons of pork, often under the euphemism of "white steak," before ultra-Orthodox protesters congregated daily outside their doors.

There are persuasive explanations for the escalation of some protests. At many construction projects, the discovery of bones is not made public. Workers have a strong incentive to ignore them, insofar as publicity may stop the project and their paychecks. When a construction project serves religious interests, such as housing for a religious neighborhood or schooling for an Orthodox congregation, the contractor and the community may quickly reach an agreement to build around the location of the bones or to reinter them elsewhere. The formal requirement to involve the archaeologists of the Antiquities Authority at a public site often provokes the ultra-Orthodox. The archaeologists want a period to study the site and the bones before reburial, while Orthodox practice requires immediate burial.

The proselytizing of Mormons became an issue when the Jerusalem Center of Brigham Young University was constructing a striking new building at a prominent site overlooking the Old City. (Earlier, the center had gone unnoticed in temporary quarters.) Mass demonstrations stopped construction, and the late rabbi and member of Knesset Meir Kahane proclaimed that the partly finished building should be completed as a rabbinical academy. Senators from the Mormons' home state of Utah expressed their support for Israel but worried about the rule of law in Jerusalem. Teddy Kollek supported the project's continuation. An Israeli court ruled in favor of the university, and construction continued. A committee chaired by an official of the justice ministry was given the responsibility to supervise the university's commitment not to proselytize in Israel.

Although an assessment of recent disputes in the Jewish sector of Jerusalem reveals chronic conflict about religion, and sporadic outbursts of public demonstration, neither religious nor secular interests have been dominant. Table 6.1 summarizes many of these incidents.

The construction of roads and a new stadium that were opposed by religious activists have been delayed or altered rather than abandoned. Generally major thoroughfares are not closed to traffic on Sabbath or religious holidays. With respect to one new highway, it was decided to close an exit that led through a religious neighborhood on Sabbath and holidays and to construct a wall to screen the sight and sound of the main artery from the religious neighborhood.

The issue of "indecent" advertising left the public agenda after many bus shelters were burned and negotiations had begun between advertising companies and religious representatives. Such negotiations seemed futile after the burning of a shelter that displayed an advertisement for mayonnaise that had not pictured any human form. It is too early to assess the protest against Yad Vashem's display of photographs showing nude concentration camp inmates. The museum seems to be standing by statements that the pictures are an important part of exhibits depicting the humiliations that were part of Nazi policy toward Jews. Ultra-Orthodox threats to open their own Holocaust memorial may prove to be rhetorical bluster; it is cheap to threaten such actions but costly to implement them.

There was a clear secular victory in the opening of restaurants, discotheques, and cinemas on the Sabbath. The municipal bylaws that had kept them closed were deemed flawed in a 1987 court decision, and religious politicians have not succeeded in enacting a new measure.

Laws prohibiting the sale of nonkosher food have been enacted but generally not enforced. A newspaper report of May 1995 indicated a significant increase in the number of shops selling pork in response to the immigrant population from the former Soviet Union.[6]

Table 6.1 Outcomes of Religious-Secular Disputes in the Jewish Sector of Jerusalem

Dispute	Outcome
Construction of roads and other public works that would disturb what were said to be ancient Jewish graves	Relocation of construction to avoid the graves, construction of bridges over the grave sites, or relocation of the graves.
Closing of major roads that pass through religious neighborhoods on Sabbath and religious holidays	In the case of a limited access divided highway, the municipality and national Ministry of Transportation constructed a wall between the main road and the religious neighborhood and agreed to close for Sabbath and religious holidays an exit that led through the religious neighborhood.
Sabbath closings of restaurants, discotheques, and cinemas	Court struck down the municipal bylaws by which the closings were mandated; restaurants, discotheques, and cinemas have remained open on Sabbath despite occasional protests.
Construction of a sports stadium	Construction delayed by several years, and stadium relocated to site where events would not disturb the Sabbath observance of religious neighborhoods.
Demands of non-Orthodox Jewish congregations and rabbis for legal status and resources	Increase in the number of Reform and Conservative synagogues and schools, with allocations of public resources, but no official status for non-Orthodox rabbis to perform marriages, divorces, or conversions to Judaism in Israel.
Demands to cease the sale of non-kosher food in Jewish neighborhoods	Laws enacted, but enforcement is lax.
Advertising posters said to be indecent	Issue left the public agenda after negotiations were conducted by representatives of the municipality between representatives of the religious community and advertising companies.
Expansion of religious neighborhoods, schools, and other institutions	Religious neighborhoods and institutions expand in the presence of growth in the ultra-Orthodox population.

A month later, there was an announcement that a newly formed association of pork venders would convene at a meeting organized by the head of the Meretz faction of the Jerusalem city council. Not surprisingly, ultra-Orthodox activists announced that they would demonstrate outside the meeting.[7]

Demands by non-Orthodox rabbis for recognition and funds for their congregations are viewed as challenges to the Orthodox religious establishment. The outcomes have been mixed. The status quo remains with respect to marriages and divorces performed in Israel, providing Orthodox rabbis a monopoly of these official functions. In November 1995, the Supreme Court found a flaw in the procedure that had given Orthodox rabbis a monopoly of conversions to Judaism performed in Israel. The court did not recognize conversions by non-Orthodox rabbis but indicated that the Knesset should consider a revision of existing legislation.[8] There has been an increase in the number of Reform and Conservative synagogues and schools that receive financial support from government and quasi-governmental organizations. The Ministry of Education has added instruction in Conservative and Reform Judaism to religious programs in Jewish secular schools. Several actions initiated by the minister of religious affairs who served in the Rabin cabinet in 1995 provoked a protest by Orthodox rabbis. The minister had opened to public scrutiny the rabbinate's list of Jews forbidden to marry in Israel, demanded that individuals placed on the list be given an opportunity to appeal their designation, and proposed public funding for them to travel overseas in order to obtain a secular marriage.

There has been a continued expansion of ultra-Orthodox neighborhoods and an increased allocation of public resources to schools and other institutions of ultra-Orthodox communities. A great deal of rhetoric surrounds these material benefits. Secular politicians charge that the religious parties inflate their demands and receive excessive material rewards by virtue of their importance in governing coalitions and their capacity to disturb the public with demonstrations. Religious politicians insist that they continue to receive less than their fair share of resources, and what they do receive is the result of legitimate politicking. Absolute truth eludes systematic research. Financial allocations for housing and infrastructure in religious neighborhoods and support for religious schools and other institutions come from a variety of ministerial and quasi-governmental budgets under many program headings. Complex bookkeeping discourages a comprehensive and persuasive record of who gets what.[9]

National politics reinforces the lack of clear religious or secular victories. One religious party, the ultra-Orthodox SHAS, was in and out of the government coalition that served after the election of 1992. Another ultra-Orthodox party, Torah Judaism, declined to join in coalition with what it perceived to be an antireligious Meretz party. Torah Judaism occasionally said that it supported the government from the outside, that is, by not voting against it on certain no-confidence motions. Pundits speculated that governing parties made financial concessions to religious programs and institutions in order to keep SHAS and Torah Judaism from being more firmly in opposition. The NRP staked a posture in opposition to the Rabin government, particularly in regard to the party's support for Jewish settlements and other issues in the occupied territories. However, there is no clear indication that NRP-related settlements had been allowed to dry up during negotiations with the Palestinians, as some party activists claim. No Israeli government would lightly take an overt posture against religious parties, because religious parties have served as coalition partners of both major political parties (Labor and Likud) in the past and will likely be needed in the future.

The muddled standoff between religious and secular Jews is similar to the deadlock of the late 1970s and early 1980s. At that time, religious parties controlled the balance of power between the government and the opposition. Prime Minister Menachem Begin was inclined to add religiosity to the Jewish nationalist programs of his Likud bloc. Religious politicians demanded the cessation of abortions and postmortems, archaeological digs (which they said despoiled ancient Jewish graves), and Sabbath flights of El Al Israel Airlines. They wanted to liberalize further the army's policy of exempting religious women from service, to define the question of who is a Jew according to religious law, and to give more money to religious institutions.

On several of these issues, the religious parties won symbolic victories. El Al ended its Sabbath flights, but other Israeli airlines expanded theirs. The army eased its procedures for exempting religious women from military service: It became the responsibility of a military board to demonstrate that a candidate who claimed an exemption was not entitled to one. (Previously a claimant had had to convince authorities that she was entitled to an exemption.) The criteria for allowing abortions in public hospitals were changed to exclude "social distress," but the Ministry of Health rejected the demand that a representative of the rabbinate be included on the boards that applied the criteria to individual cases. (Participants in the process learned to explain their problem as one of "emotional distress.") The religious parties did not succeed in changing the Law of Return, which evades an explicit definition of who is a Jew and allows the immigration of non-Jewish relatives of Jews. Then as now, the clearest victory of religious parties seemed to be in the pragmatic politics of money. They won increased allocations for religious schools and housing in religious neighborhoods.[10]

The muddled standoff, without clear religious or secular victories, infuriates purists of both camps. However, it parallels the existence of numerous options for those pragmatic religious or secular Israelis who are willing to make do. Sabbath provides a weekly demonstration of the situation. State-operated radio and television broadcast despite periodic demands by religious parties that they cease. (The willingness of religious personalities to be interviewed for programs that will be aired on the Sabbath suggests the ritualized character of these demands. Although such interviews may have been taped on a weekday, their inclusion in a program to be broadcast on Sabbath is not free of *halachic* problems; they are part of programs that cause their Jewish producers and audiences to violate the Sabbath.) With few exceptions, public buses in the Jewish sector do not operate on the Sabbath, but taxis do. Almost all Jewish stores are closed on Sabbath, but the Palestinian and Armenian merchants in the Old City of Jerusalem, Jaffa, and Acco do a thriving business, typically at prices a bit lower than those in Jewish business districts. In recent years, some Jewish-owned stores have risked boycotts by the religious population by staying open on the Sabbath. Restaurants, cinemas, cafes, and discotheques have operated on the Sabbath since 1987, when laws forbidding Sabbath openings were found to be flawed. Sabbath afternoon is also the time when Israel's most popular mass spectator sport is played. Football (soccer) stadiums in the major cities can attract more than 10,000 spectators. Many of the fans are Jews from North African or Asian communities who consider themselves to be traditional with respect to religion. They may observe laws of kashruth, pray often at Orthodox Sephardi synagogues, vote for SHAS, and send their children to SHAS schools, but on the Sabbath, these attributes do not keep them from driving or using electrical appliances, cheering on their home team at the football stadium, or having cookouts in the park or at the beach.

More delicate are problems that have reached serious proportions with the arrival of more than half a million immigrants from the former Soviet Union since the late 1980s. Many Jews came with non-Jewish spouses as allowed under the Law of Return. Other wholly non-Jewish families arrived, either by deception or because of an oversight. When the wife in a mixed marriage is not Jewish, the children are also not Jewish according to Jewish law. Complications arise when non-Jews wish to marry or when they die. Those wanting to marry Jews may have to leave the country for the ceremony. (This is not a great expense in the age of cut-rate air travel.) The interior ministry will record the couple as married on the basis of a certificate obtained elsewhere. Alternatively, they can live together and have their union recognized if it comes to a dispute over property, child support, or inheritance.

Not so easily solved are questions of where to bury the bodies of persons not recognized as Jewish according to religious law. A number of families have been unable to bury their relatives in Jewish cemeteries, despite the fact that they thought of themselves as Jewish and suffered as Jews in the Soviet Union. Bodies have languished for days in hospital morgues and become topics of media attention while relatives sought a solution. Some are accepted by Christian cemeteries, and some by cemeteries at kibbutzim that have room and no concern for religious background. As the problem mounted during the mid-1990s, state authorities moved to create nonreligious cemeteries that would accept the remains of individuals whose religion was not clarified to the satisfaction of the Orthodox burial societies that administer the municipal cemeteries for Jews. The new cemeteries would also accept those Jews who did not wish a religious ceremony at the end of their lives. The government appointed a ministerial committee to deal with the problem of burial, but its implementation was slowed by local planning committees with a role in approving the sites for such cemeteries.

The issue of burying non-Jews, individuals whose Jewish origins could not be established to the satisfaction of Jewish burial societies, and secular Jews was not without religious-secular tensions. As in several other cases of dispute, it was also clouded by erratic behavior and allegations difficult to verify. Antireligious activists alleged that religious activists on local planning commissions were delaying the creation of secular cemeteries. In response, a number of Orthodox Jewish rabbis spoke out in favor of establishing secular cemeteries.

The issue of religious and secular cemeteries did not pass without an exchange between Shulamit Aloni and the ultra-Orthodox. In response to Aloni's comment that the establishment of secular cemeteries would prevent blackmail by Orthodox burial societies, a SHAS member of Knesset said that when the time comes, the societies should refuse to bury Aloni's body, and that it should be cremated and the ashes thrown into the wind.[11]

There remains the problem of Jews who are committed to the doctrines of Reform or Conservative congregations and do not want to compromise on a matter of principle or find a pragmatic solution to a personal problem. They may be concerned about their own conversion by a non-Orthodox rabbi, or that of a spouse, or the designation of children who are not Jewish according to the Orthodox rabbinate. Such persons can live in Israel but may have to jump through the hoops described above in order to marry or be buried. For one convinced that non-Orthodox Judaism ought to be legitimated in Israel, the practical steps may be so humiliating as to lead them to avoid Israel altogether. The state provides options to help individuals fit into the complexities created by Jewish history. Justice, if that is what is being pursued, is not likely to be complete in a situation of religious dispute complicated by an intensity of views.

WHO WINS? TIED SCORE, MORE OR LESS

Several problems stand in the way of a systematic, quantitative reckoning of who wins in individual religious confrontations or whether religious or antireligious interests have been dominant in recent Israeli history. We have already seen the problems in sorting a religious issue from an issue that is nationalist in character, and likewise in deciding whether to accept the posture of a religious authority as to what is an issue of religious importance or what is the correct view of the religious interest. We have seen disputes even among rabbis of the ultra-Orthodox and Orthodox communities, and among those of non-Orthodox Judaisms. There is also a lack of unity among religious authorities in Christian and Muslim communities, which may be endemic to spiritual issues: "One special problem has been the otherworldly orientation of these deeply religious people; another problem has been religious particularism, where theological disputes have inhibited political cooperation."[12]

Additional problems derive from judging the outcomes of individual confrontations. How does one record success if one side has won the enactment of a law, but the measure is seldom enforced or is implemented in ways that are criticized by those who supported its enactment? And how does one reach a conclusion when the same general problem (e.g., public modesty, Sabbath observance, the availability of nonkosher food) returns time and again—with variations in the character of the demands and subtle nuances in the ways that issue is resolved—or when individual episodes disappear from the public agenda without a resolution?

The weight of argument is that neither side has won. The score is tied, more or less. The conclusion rests on numerous cases that illustrate the large gaps between the rhetoric and the accomplishments of both religious and antireligious sectors, the lack of final resolution of issues that keep returning to the political agenda, and the lack of satisfaction expressed by both religious and antireligious interests.

The examination of individual religious-secular conflicts shows the problems in determining who won and by how much. When excavation for a two-level intersection in the French Hill neighborhood of Jerusalem was well advanced, contractors uncovered grave sites from the period of the Second Temple (535 B.C.E.–70 C.E.). Thus began a process of political-religious ritual. Some rabbinical sources were cited in support of moving the remains to other grave sites in order to facilitate the city's development, while other rabbinical sources were cited as opposing any disturbance of the dead. Secular observers asked why these graves should prove a barrier to the city's development when contractors managed to find solutions for grave sites found while building housing in ultra-Orthodox neighborhoods. Hundreds of yeshiva students gathered at the construction site every day, and some spent the night guarding the site.

A third factor was Israel's archaeologists, who inserted themselves between those wanting to leave the graves as is and those wanting a new intersection as soon as possible. The country's laws provide for a halt to construction when ancient sites are discovered and a period for archaeologists to ascertain the importance of the findings and to make provision for preservation or removal. When archaeologists demanded their rights for the site in question, they triggered memories of many previous conflicts with religious Jews over the excavations of grave sites. Some religious leaders seemed willing to move the remains to other graves but not to have them pass through the hands of the archaeologists. Archaeologists insisted on the implementation of laws allowing them to examine ancient graves and to preserve the stone coffins for further research or exhibition.

A committee appointed to deal with the problem recommended that the planned intersection be moved eight meters westward in order to avoid the grave sites, which would add some ten million shekels (U.S. $3.5 million) to the cost of the project and further delay its completion. The proposal did not satisfy the archaeologists, who began a suit to realize their rights to excavate the grave sites. The proposal satisfied religious leaders only until another grave site was discovered along the revised roadway. Then, in a process that ends numerous controversies, the matter was delayed, helping to cool tempers. Work eventually continued, with neither the religious protesters nor the archaeologists receiving what they demanded.

A different road project to contend with traffic alongside an ultra-Orthodox neighborhood generated opposition from the same cluster of archaeologists and religious Jews. There was also opposition from Arabs who objected to construction close to their properties and from the Likud Party, whose leaders thought the highway would follow the pre-1967 east-west border, emphasizing the division of Jerusalem between Jewish and Arab sectors.

A protracted protest by church authorities that the project would despoil Christian holy sites brought an outburst by Mayor Teddy Kollek. He announced that he was angry and insulted at their criticism of Israel's treatment of their holy sites and their threat to appeal to the UN if the project continued. Kollek told leaders of the Greek Orthodox, Armenian, Greek Catholic, Anglican, and Arab Lutheran churches:

> Your behavior was antagonistic and totally out of proportion. . . . The antiquities found are being treated responsibly and professionally. . . . We let you know about the work. We could have simply covered it up and avoided all the problems, but this is not our way. . . . After all the years of dialog and cooperation, I am angry and insulted that you went to the press with complaints about the Israeli authorities without speaking to me.

The gravesite and bones believed to have been those of Saint Stephan were turned over to the Armenian church. Other artifacts were removed from the site for preservation. Antiquities Authority officials concluded that the site was not important enough from an archaeological point of view to warrant building the highway elsewhere.[13]

Jewish religious opposition reached its peak as the road was completed. It was not enough that road planners had included a wall to screen the road and its noise from the religious neighborhood and agreed to close on the Sabbath an exit that led through a religious neighborhood. Antireligious Jewish politicians accused the ultra-Orthodox of trying to break the status quo by demanding the closing on Sabbath of major roads near their neighborhoods, while religious activists responded that the status quo has already been broken by the city's secular community, with many pubs, discos, and restaurants open seven days a week. Several Sabbaths saw the subsequent stages of the usual ceremony: masses of ultra-Orthodox; shouts about the sanctity of the Sabbath; overturned garbage receptacles; stones directed at Sabbath traffic; mounted police; some injuries among the protesters, the police, and secular counterprotesters; short-term arrests of protesters; and proclamations about the rule of law by Teddy Kollek and police officials and about the sanctity of the

Sabbath by Orthodox rabbis. Then the police toughened their posture, asking the rabbis to accept a limited period for protests. Sabbath traffic continued, but not via the exit that led through the religious neighborhood, and the protests died.

An interview granted by Jerusalem's mayor Ehud Olmert to an ultra-Orthodox newspaper on the eve of Passover in 1995 revealed a prominence of religious symbols against a background of few tangible actions. Earlier in the year the city had been affected by Sabbath demonstrations about the closing of a major road that bisected an ultra-Orthodox neighborhood. Among the charges heard from both religious and antireligious camps was that the mayor had promised to abide by the leadership of religious parties with respect to road closings in exchange for the support of those parties in his 1993 election campaign. A committee appointed by the mayor produced a cumbersome compromise: The road would be closed to traffic during the period just prior to and after the onset of the Sabbath, when there is a great deal of pedestrian traffic to and from synagogue. This proposal would not be easy to implement: The timing of the Sabbath changes from week to week and the road was used by out-of-towners and foreign tourists who might be surprised by a major road suddenly being closed. In any case, the Ministry of Transportation, which had the authority to rule on the closing of major roads, said that the road in question would be kept open.

In the interview the mayor explained the failure to close the road and asserted that he had never promised that it would be closed. Olmert's speech also indicated the importance of symbolic issues to the ultra-Orthodox community: his frequent use of religiously correct terminology (e.g., "with the help of God") and his assertion that the upcoming celebration of Jerusalem's 3,000-year anniversary would feature programs of religious content and would not include the erection of statues that violate the injunction against graven images. When asked whether he read Psalms regularly, the mayor responded with the first line of Psalms: "Blessed is the man that walketh not in the counsel of the ungodly, nor standeth in the way of sinners, nor sitteth in the seat of the scornful." He said that as mayor he was obligated to utter that phrase each day on account of all the temptations that come to someone with his responsibilities.[14]

Ultra-Orthodox congregations are not without means of enforcing rules on wayward individuals within their communities. "Modesty patrols" exist in Bnei Brak and ultra-Orthodox neighborhoods of Jerusalem; their purpose is to keep those areas free of immoral influences.

Each neighborhood has its own community leader and neighborhood rabbi. If somebody notices one of the neighborhood children misbehaving, he talks to the parents. If a woman whose husband is out of town starts having male visitors, the husband is advised to keep an eye on his wife. . . . a man who worked in a kiosk here in Bnei Brak started giving kids money and gifts in exchange for sexual favors. . . . We turned to the police but were told that the children would have to testify and be subjected to the defense lawyer's cross-examination. We decided to take care of the guy ourselves. We stopped the guy in a dark alley, knocked him around a little. The next day he closed his kiosk and left town for good.[15]

Secular critics note that the modesty patrols do not intervene when ultra-Orthodox activists threaten kiosk owners who dare to sell secular newspapers in their neighborhoods and vandalize those kiosks whose owners do not desist.[16] In April 1995, the kiosk of a 92-year-old newspaper vender was destroyed in Bnei Brak. The vender was religious but had withstood for decades repeated demands and threats to stop selling the two most popular Israeli daily newspapers, Ma'ariv and Yediot Aharonot. In response to religious claims of moral superiority, secular critics point to cases in which ultra-Orthodox organizations claim credit for the desecration of archaeological artifacts from the Byzantine or Crusader periods in Israel. Supporters of the vandals say they are concerned with removing remnants of Christian domination from Israel.[17]

Through their economic power, Ultra-Orthodox Israelis achieved a partial victory in the excavation for the construction of a shopping center close to the seashore in Jaffa. When the digging uncovered human bones, students from Jerusalem and Bnei Brak religious academies congregated daily at the site to demand a halt to the project. The police intervened when the numbers reached into the thousands and blocked traffic on neighboring streets. A resolution emerged when ultra-Orthodox rabbis declared a boycott on Bank Hapoalim, which was financing the project. The project's developers felt not only the threat to their financing but also the economic power of the religious community that could be directed against potential tenants. The developers reached an agreement with religious interests, pausing construction and allowing religious men access to the site, where they could search for and remove bones for burial elsewhere. The developers also indicated that continued negotiations would focus on provisions to be made in the construction to take account of the remains found on the site. Perhaps oblivious to the agreement, or not satisfied by it, a group of religious youths was apprehended setting fire to cash machines at a Jerusalem branch of Bank Hapoalim.

The Jaffa project gained attention again some months later when a developer in his mid-thirties died suddenly of a heart attack. One ultra-Orthodox rabbi saw in his death the appropriate punishment of the Lord. Another ultra-Orthodox rabbi expressed sorrow about the man's death but linked it to his wrongdoing in Jaffa. A Reform rabbi said that those who spoke out in such a way were hypocrites who failed to judge similarly the deaths of prominent figures in the ultra-Orthodox community.[18]

Another controversy involved a Chinese restaurant owned by a Jew on the border of an ultra-Orthodox neighborhood in Jerusalem. It was torched in 1991, apparently by someone who objected to its serving pork and shrimp. In response, the owner obtained the approval of the local planning authority to build a four-story shopping center. At one point, he offered his religious neighbors the choice of "a Chinese restaurant that serves pork chops, or a four-story commercial center with movie theaters and pinball arcades open on Sabbath." But he also had to obtain the approval of the regional planning authority, responsible to the interior ministry, which was controlled by the ultra-Orthodox SHAS party. There the process stopped, and the restaurant changed hands, reopening as a *glat kosher* (kosher to the extreme) Chinese restaurant.[19]

Sometimes the attainment of rights is lost, at least temporarily, in the cracks between government bureaucracies. One case involved an Israeli Jew who married a non-Israeli Christian in a civil ceremony in a U.S. Christian church. The local office of the interior ministry in the Israeli's hometown of Eilat refused to record the marriage or to bestow Israeli citizenship on the bride. The reason offered was that the Israeli had abandoned Judaism by virtue of marrying in a Christian church and therefore the Law of Return would not confer benefits on his wife. The Israeli filed a suit with the assistance of the Civil Rights Organization. In response, the interior ministry agreed to record the marriage and to grant the citizenship. For some time, however, the local clerk continued to refuse to record the actions on the grounds that a written order had not been received.[20]

Occasionally, even an inured observer can be impressed with the stupidity of official action. The Ministry of Housing and Construction demanded that contractors who bid to construct apartments in a newly opened section of Beit Shemesh must agree not to sell them to individuals who appear to be ultra-Orthodox. It did not take long for religious activists to accuse the ministry of anti-Semitism and racism. One newspaper account about the policy was coupled with the report of another project supposedly closed to non-Jewish purchasers. It told how an Arab couple overcame the policy by threatening to begin a court action.[21]

In 1993 the subject of indecent advertisements returned to the religious agenda in Bnei Brak when the area's bus company was charged with displaying Pepsi-Cola posters that showed women with bare arms. This brought a threat of a boycott and a march of 300 men and children. The bus company promised a solution: "We respect all groups from all sectors of society and do not differentiate between religion, race or color. We find no reason to hurt people's feelings or break their trust. . . . We intend to contact . . . the company responsible for the ads, and reach an agreement with them whereby we will operate public transport in B'nei Brak without hurting residents' feelings."[22]

Some ultra-Orthodox believe that the video recorder is the greatest threat of our generation. A group calling itself the Committee for the Purity of Our Community in the Holy City of Jerusalem proclaimed that religious Jews must not travel on the buses between Jerusalem and Tel Aviv installed with video players. For the spokesman of the group, it was not enough that the bus company yielded to earlier demands and disconnected the devices; as long as they remain in the buses, there is a danger that they will be used.[23]

The issue of Jewish access to the Temple Mount has been argued by religious and secular, Jewish and Muslim, and Israeli and international sources. Israeli authorities have followed a more or less consistent policy of forbidding Jews to pray on the Temple Mount. This posture follows Israeli policy of avoiding incitement of Muslim religious authorities and Arab masses with respect to this especially sensitive site, and it has at least the tacit support of numerous religious Jews. Leading rabbis support the ruling that Jews must not enter the Temple Mount because they would risk treading on areas that—when the Temple was in place—were forbidden to all but the High Priest, and then only after he had passed through ritual purification. (Modern scholars quarrel as to just where on the Temple Mount those areas were.) Other rabbis have ruled that only certain areas of the Temple Mount are closed to Jews. The chief Sephardi rabbi recently ruled against establishing a small synagogue alongside the Temple Mount or allowing Jews to enter the Mount. He reasoned that the status quo of avoiding the Temple Mount is an indication that the entire Mount should be Jewish but that current realities prevent the implementation of what is desirable.[24] Jewish tourists are allowed to enter the Temple Mount, against the advice of a sign erected by religious Jews urging them to avoid it. Jews are not allowed on the Mount during occasions of Muslim prayer (Fridays and other holy days) or when circumstances indicate to Israeli security authorities that a Jewish presence would be provocative.

At least three groups have missions concerning the Temple Mount: Establish the Temple, Kahane Lives, and Temple Mount Faithful. Establish the Temple and Temple Mount Faithful have sought to pray on the Mount and advocate building a Jewish temple on the site. A close examination of the groups reveals differences in membership and style. However, none have a large following or have succeeded in producing more than occasional disturbances.

One member of both Establish the Temple and Kahane Lives has served time in jail for attempting to blow up the Muslim holy places that currently occupy the Temple Mount. The members of Temple Mount Faithful are more placid: They assemble at the gates of the Temple Mount, typically on occasions in the religious calendar when Jews traditionally visited the Temple, and demand the right to pray. At times the group has been accompanied by members of Knesset who assert their parliamentary immunity from arrest. Occasionally, a demonstration gains them limited rights to pray. More often, the police prepare for a confrontation. A typical scene on the nightly news is a squad of police blocking the entrance to the Temple Mount, with angry-looking Jews on one side, a few angry-looking Muslims on another side, and a number of bored-looking Arabs walking past the commotion, whose lack of concern seems to express best the ritualized character of the event.[25] (Members of Kahane Lives are younger and more physical than those of Temple Mount Faithful and are more likely to struggle with the police.) Prior to Passover 1995, the Temple Mount Faithful petitioned the Ministry of Religious Affairs to allow a Passover sacrifice and prayer on the Temple Mount. The petition contained the standard rhetoric: How can the Jewish state deny only to Jews the opportunity of carrying out a religious ritual on the site that is most holy to Jews?[26]

The issue of the Temple Mount illustrates several themes of this book: the lack of clarity as to matters of Jewish religious doctrine (to pray on the Temple Mount or to avoid it altogether out of fear of treading on a site forbidden to common people); the ritualized drama in which some Jews participate in order to demonstrate their demands; the emotions surrounding a particular site holy to both Muslims and Jews; and the imperfect political accommodation chosen by state authorities whose motives are more political than religious. The Temple Mount Faithful's demand for an animal sacrifice also highlighted contrasting traditions within the Jewish communities of Israel. During the same Passover season, Reform Jews planned an interfaith vegetarian seder. Participants included Buddhists, Hindus, and Christians, as well as Jews, and they refrained from eating meat in order to "improve the ecology of the world and prevent killing."[27]

The complex reality of loud religious and secular demands and tenuous accomplishments exists alongside stereotypes that are much more simple and contradictory. In the spiritual atmosphere of religious and antireligious communities, beliefs can range in several directions and are oblivious to objective reality.

On the one hand are the stereotypes of religious and antireligious Israelis that describe their opponents as the source of aggressive, chronic, and successful challenges to the status quo. Each community is likely to describe the other as anti-Semitic. Religious Israelis point to incidents of abortion, autopsies, violations of Sabbath observance, heavily traveled roads near religious neighborhoods, or many other abominations. Antireligious Israelis counter with charges of religious efforts to close major roads, vandalism to bus shelters displaying advertisement posters that to secular eyes are inoffensive, and governmental crises caused by religious parties seeking to maximize their political leverage.

There is also optimism in religious communities. Religious Jews speak of the flow of secular Jews to religiosity and indications that religious congregations are becoming ever more strict in their observances. They believe the conquest of the Land of Israel continues and will survive the temporary ascendance of one or another misguided political party. The decision of an Israeli court that resulted in the opening of cinemas and other places of entertainment on the Sabbath was insignificant. Religious neighborhoods are free of such filth, and that is what is important.

Antireligious Israelis mix their stories of cunning by religious politicians with stories of primitive religiosity: pilgrimages to the graves of zaddikim (holy men) reputed to be sources of healing and other miracles, the conviction of many members of the Lubavitcher congregation that their late rebbe was the Messiah, and anecdotes of religious Jews who are profoundly ignorant of science or non-Jewish societies. One firsthand account was of a Jew in ultra-Orthodox clothing who was listening to the news on the radio while riding in a Jerusalem bus. "What is Libya?" he asked. "A country in Africa" was the response. "What is Africa?" was the next question. "Libya is a country next to Egypt. Have you heard of Egypt?" "Of course," came the reply. "Everyone knows that the Lord took us out of Egypt."

There are no surprises in these stereotypes to those familiar with the strength of religious beliefs and secular ideologies. Individuals who intensely believe in doctrines are not likely to test them by systematic analyses of objective reality. When faced with counterexample, the deeply committed have no trouble in challenging their truth or reducing their importance. Such strongly held beliefs appear in all societies, and they recall the Hebrew term for the faculties of humanity: *madei haroach*. One translation is the science of the spirit; another is the science of wind. If there is such a science, even it would have trouble sorting out the wind and the spirit, the winners and losers in Israel's religious disputes.

Whether wind or spirit, strongly held religiosity and antireligiosity are part of the Israeli scene. Within both religious and antireligious camps there are complex and contradictory beliefs, attitudes, and doctrines, as well as individuals who are more or less intense in their commitments. Religious and secular communities add to the tensions of Israeli society. The partial successes and failures of each community stimulate their opponents and contribute to their own frustrations, and they fuel continued cycles of competition that remain unresolved and unsatisfied.

HOW DIFFERENT IS ISRAEL?

Several questions left at the end of this book are, How different from the situation in other countries are the tensions between religious and secular interests in Israel and the impact of religious interests on public policy? Compared to which countries? How should the comparison be made?

The comparison offered here will not be in-depth or systematic, but it will touch on a number of points that have already been discussed. Israel may not be substantially different from other Western democracies that many Israelis choose for their own standards of comparison on traits as diverse as public morality, levels of economic development, health, education, and the quality of science and technology.

On the dimension of expressed belief, Israel would appear to fit somewhere among the countries listed in Table 1.1, which assembles surveys from twenty-one countries (not including Israel). The results reflect a range of religiosity among the countries surveyed: Between 2 and 82 percent of the respondents reported that they attend church weekly; between 24 and 81 percent feel religious; and between 39 and 96 percent express a belief in God. Surveys reported in Chapter 4 indicate that 49 percent of Israelis define themselves as ultra-Orthodox, Orthodox, or traditional; and 79 percent place themselves on a continuum between "strictly observant" and "somewhat observant."

Regarding government support for religion, Israel also finds itself in company with many other countries. The various modes of support complicate any effort at systematic international comparison; in Israel as elsewhere, material aid flows from public authorities to religious bodies in several ways. Even in the United States, with its official separation of church and state, substantial benefits flow to religious organizations via tax exemptions, and there is direct public support for hospitals, schools, and other institutions affiliated with religious bodies. While there is no established church in the United States, religiosity appears to be the national creed. In Utah, it is Mormon authorities who speak out on issues of policy and occasionally seem to influence the decisions of government officials. It may be a cardinal of the Roman Catholic church who is prominent in New York, Boston, Chicago, or Philadelphia or the preacher of a Baptist megachurch in a southern city. Like the rabbis of Israel, none of these Christian authorities can be assured of influencing government on a matter of religious importance or even producing anything close to uniform behavior among the faithful.

The religious symbol on its national flag groups Israel with the United Kingdom, Finland, Sweden, Norway, Denmark, Iceland, Switzerland, Greece, Australia, and New Zealand. The flag of the United States is secular, but coins and currency, as well as the Pledge of Allegiance, proclaim the importance of God. Perhaps every democracy's list of national holidays is heavily affected by religion, especially Good Friday, Easter, and Christmas, and other holidays with a residue of religion attached to them: St. Patrick's Day, Valentine's Day, New Year's Day, Easter Monday, Boxing Day, and Halloween.

The prominence of religious issues on Israel's national agenda also foils systematic international comparison. I have already addressed the problems of sorting out a religious issue from an issue that is said to involve religion. Israel has no shortage of disputes affected by religion that reach the mass media. However, many of the cases reviewed here appeared mostly on the inner pages of the national and local newspapers. They are news but not the most important issues. Topics with elements of religion that have surfaced in other countries with no less emotion include abortion, euthanasia, prayer in schools, the wearing of religious garb in schools or the military, ritual slaughter of animals, the rights of homosexuals, provisions for divorce and birth control, and the status of children born out of wedlock.

A SUMMARY OF THE ARGUMENT AND A LOOK TO THE FUTURE

I have argued that several traits of Israel's society and history heighten the importance of religious issues on the political agenda, but other traits moderate their intensity and do not lead to victory for either side. The amorphous nature of doctrines and beliefs invites numerous assessments, some of them tendentious and most of them open to dispute. Among the possible explanations of the standoff between religious and secular interests is Judaism's character as a national religion, which permits a wide range of postures. Individuals can remain members of the community no matter what their beliefs. The complexity began early in Jewish history. The Hebrew Bible is a collection of stories, laws, moral precepts, bits of theology, social criticism, and other wisdom accumulated over the centuries rather than clearly ordered theology. Rabbinical teaching has endorsed dispute at least as much as it has imposed order on Judaism. Jewish culture became even more complex as European Jews left the isolation of closed religious communities for the experience of the Enlightenment in the nineteenth century.

Along with much cultural variety and a tendency toward intracommunal dispute, certain rules of the game have developed that limit the extent of conflict. Rabbinical admonitions against sectarian conflict have their roots in the Jewish civil wars of the late biblical period. In order to cool tempers during religious-secular tension, religious and secular leaders cite the threats to Jews as a minority in the Diaspora and a beleaguered population in Israel. Stones, sticks, fists, garbage, screams, and terrible curses are usually the weapons of confrontation. The lack of guns and knives and the low incidence of serious injury may reflect how Jews relate to one another generally and the ritualized character and limited intensity of their religious disputes.

The plurality that is built into Jewish history is reinforced by the character of Israeli democracy. Jews dominate the political system, but individual Jewish factions have been unable to dominate the polity. No party has ever won a majority in a national election. Religious and secular parties have learned to bargain in a setting of inevitable coalition. The struggle between religious and antireligious activists is often loud, but neither camp has been able to overcome the other. Even the Holy City of Jerusalem illustrates the theme of chronic tension rather than victory by religious or secular forces.

The conflict between religious and secular interests in Israel is an insoluble problem. The roots of current disputes go back at least as far as the Enlightenment, and they also appeared in clashes between Jewish cosmopolitans and zealots during the periods of Greek and Roman rule. The longevity of the problems and their insolubility may reflect the moderation exhibited by most religious and secular Israelis. For the past 2,000 years, an earlier bloody history has helped Jews avoid communal violence. The threat of civil war has not led

Jews to solve their problems, but it has kept their lack of solution from boiling over into warfare. The continued presence of one anti-Jewish movement or another has strengthened the incentive to keep internal disputes from violating the protections that the community has provided against outside hostility.

The chronic tensions and occasional outbursts are the price that Jews must pay for living in a Jewish state. Both religious and secular activists express dissatisfaction with unresolved issues and the annoying monotony with which one incident replaces another in disputes about ancient graves or Sabbath observance. The problems have been chronic, perhaps, because they are tolerable and have been ritualized at a low level of suffering. The old and repetitious conflict about religion among the Jews of Israel hardly seems to be on the verge of solution. Competing doctrines—such as those of tribal separatism and cosmopolitan humanism, which have been in Judaism since the Bible was composed—seem likely to generate disputes as the community continues to evolve through one controversy after another.

THE IMPLICATIONS OF
INTERNATIONAL PEACE FOR DOMESTIC PEACE

Israel's international relations may also affect its religious politics. What if peace really occurs in the Middle East? What will happen if the peace process is derailed? As these words are being written, the peace with Egypt seems cool but durable, and that with Jordan warm and inviting. Some wits suggest that if King Hussein offers himself as Israel's ruler, he could be elected both prime minister and king. The agreement with the Palestinian Authority is more complex and has religious implications. On the one hand, agreements between the Israeli government and the Palestinian Authority have produced a transfer of substantial territory to Palestinian administration. On the other hand, a wave of suicide bombings that peaked in March 1996, with some 60 deaths and more than 100 wounded in a period of eight days, resulted in the Israeli army returning to some of the territories previously turned over to the Palestinians. The events threatened the peace process directly, and further changes may occur after the Israeli elections of May 1996. The implications of the election for both peace and religious dispute were inconclusive as this book went to press. While negotiations with Syria may produce a treaty of peace and result in a treaty between Israel and Lebanon as well, these negotiations may also fall victim to escalating violence.

There are several alternative scenarios. One emerges from the possibility of an Israel at peace and asks the question, If Israel succeeds in formalizing agreements with each of its neighbors, will this lessen external pressures so that internal religious conflicts will produce violence among the Jews? The answer to this question is easy insofar as it hardly seems likely that cultural fears or suspicions of outsiders will soon dissipate, especially when Arab rejectionists of peace with Israel can launch violent attacks no matter how strongly Arab governments seek to restrain them.

More difficult is the scenario that the efforts toward peace will lead religious and nationalist Israeli extremists to engage in violence in order to frustrate the implementation of international agreements, especially those that may require the dismantling of Jewish settlements in the Land of Israel or their transfer to Arab rule. This scenario emerged in November 1995 with the killing of Prime Minister Yitzhak Rabin. In the week after the assassination, the Israeli media provided an extended discussion, often at an impressive intellectual level, of the implications of the killing and the various individuals, groups, and social conditions that contributed to it. The picture that emerged from police reports was that the Jew who killed the prime minister was a law student at Bar-Ilan University (governed by religious nationalists) and was part of a conspiracy among individuals from the extreme wing of religious nationalists.

Hatred against the Israeli government and especially the prime minister derived from arrangements made with the Palestinian Authority. Much of the discussion following the killing concerned the significance of the biblical Land of Israel, how much of it could be bargained away to recent terrorists for the promise of peace, and how Jews should conduct their disputes about these issues. The assassination and the soul-searching that followed showed the passions that Jews can allocate to political issues with biblical roots.

At this point it is too early to make serious conclusions about the killing and its implications for the future of Judaism and Israel. It may depend on whether Israel's rabbis and secular leaders dissuade their followers from violence and lead them to conduct disputes via persuasion and whether Israel's security forces deal adequately with those who cannot be dissuaded from violence.

A much different possibility is that the violence of Muslim extremists can lead the Jews to bury their religious conflicts, at least for the time being. The government's response to a wave of suicide bombings was to declare war against terrorism. The prime minister was severely critical of the Palestinian Authority for its failure to control the violence of its own people, and he raised the prospect of postponing indefinitely any further transfer of territory to the Palestinians. These actions suggested at least a temporary solution to what Israel's religious nationalists viewed as a threat to the Land of Israel.

Both religious and secular figures representing a wide spectrum of opinion called on the Jews to put aside their quarrels in order to unite against a common enemy. The call echoed ancient sentiments in a people whose existence once again seemed to be threatened. The context of the violence furthered the sentiment. The victims of one suicide bomber included Jewish children who had come to Tel Aviv to observe the holiday of Purim, which celebrates survival against evil forces bent on Jewish extermination.

According to one Jewish belief, there has been no prophet who has spoken for the Lord since Malachi, who preached about 500 B.C.E. According to another Jewish belief, the prophets spoke to their times. They criticized the political and economic elites and the priests at least as much as they spoke about the future. The biblical Amos may have been trying to distance himself from fortune tellers, magicians, and hired sycophants of the royal court when he proclaimed that he "was no prophet, nor a prophet's son, but a herdsman and a tender of sycamore trees."[28]

Rather than falling afoul of these beliefs and risking a prediction, it seems wisest to conclude with the concession that issues of peace or war will test the viability of this book's central analysis. In the contest of peace, the book will pass the test if rules of moderate conflict developed to deal with such issues as Sabbath observance, kosher foods, and ancient grave sites manage to keep peace in a society challenged by concessions over land that some consider to be holy. If the immediate future is war or a suspension of the peace process, that test may be postponed. It hardly seems likely that religious and secular Jews will live in harmony with one another. The quality of their peace may depend not only on what emerges from domestic conflict but on what comes to their society from outsiders committed to either hostility or accommodation.

NOTES

1. Song of Songs 7:5–8; a report about the different responses of the rabbis who were members of Knesset appears in *Ma'ariv* (in Hebrew), November 21, 1990.
2. The relevant passage is II Samuel 1:26.
3. *Ha'aretz* (in Hebrew), December 15, 1994.

4. See II Samuel 12:9. For a summary of rabbinical writings, see Yehuda Kil, *The Book of Samuel: Second Samuel* (in Hebrew) (Jerusalem: Mossad Harav Kook, 1981), pp. 420 ff.

5. Murray Edelman, *The Symbolic Uses of Politics* (Urbana: University of Illinois Press, 1964).

6. *Ha'aretz* (in Hebrew), May 3, 1995, p. 1.

7. *Ha'aretz* (in Hebrew), June 2, 1995, p. 6.

8. *Ha'aretz* (in Hebrew), November 13, 1995, pp. 1, 7.

9. *Ha'aretz* (in Hebrew), April 19, 1995, p. 6.

10. See Ira Sharkansky, *What Makes Israel Tick? How Domestic Policy-makers Cope with Constraints* (Chicago: Nelson Hall, 1985), chap. 4.

11. *Ha'aretz* (in Hebrew), April 26, 1995, p. 6.

12. John C. Green, "The Christian Right and the 1994 Elections: A View from the States," *PS: Political Scence and Politics* 27, no. 1 (March 1995): 5–8.

13. *Jerusalem Post*, January 16, 1992, p. 1.

14. *Ha'aretz* (in Hebrew), April 14, 1995, p. 6.

15. *Jerusalem Post*, December 22, 1993, p. 7.

16. As described in *Ha'aretz* (in Hebrew), April 12, 1995, p. 7.

17. *Kal Ha'ir* (in Hebrew), March 31, 1995, p. 35; *Ha'aretz* (in Hebrew), June 6, 1995, p. 14.

18. *Ha'aretz* (in Hebrew), May 24, 1995, p. 9.

19. *Jerusalem Post*, November 14, 1991, p. 3.

20. *Ha'aretz* (in Hebrew), April 10, 1995, p. 9.

21. *Kal Ha'ir* (in Hebrew), June 2, 1995, p. 31.

22. *Jerusalem Post*, June 13, 1993, p. 2.

23. *Ha'aretz* (in Hebrew), April 18, 1995, p. 6.

24. *Ha'aretz* (in Hebrew), May 28, 1995, p. 4.

25. *Jerusalem Post*, November 30, 1994, p. 2.

26. *Ha'aretz* (in Hebrew), April 6, 1995, p. 6.

27. *Kal Ha'ir*, April 7, 1995, p. 25.

28. Amos 7:14.

BIBLIOGRAPHY

Aamiry, M. A., *Jerusalem: Arab Origin and Heritage* (London: Longman, 1978), pp. 1–12.

Aaron, Henry J., Thomas E. Mann, Timothy Taylor, eds., *Values and Public Policy* (Washington, DC: Brookings Institution, 1994).

Alt, Albrecht, "The God of the Fathers," in Albrecht, *Essays on Old Testament History and Religion,* trans. R. A. Wilson (Garden City, NY: Doubleday & Company, 1967).

Armstrong, Karen, *A History of God: The 4,000-Year Quest of Judaism, Christianity and Islam* (New York: Ballantine Books, 1993).

Arrington, Leonard J., and Davis Bitton, *The Mormon Experience: A History of the Latter-day Saints* (New York: Knopf, 1979).

Ashkenasi, Abraham, "Israeli Policies and Palestinian Fragmentation: Political and Social Impacts in Israel and Jerusalem" (Jerusalem: Hebrew University, Leonard Davis Institute, 1988).

Ashkenasi, Abraham, "Opinion Trends Among Jerusalem Palestinians" (Jerusalem: Hebrew University, Leonard Davis Institute, 1990).

Ault, James, "Family and Fundamentalism: The Shawmut Valley Baptist Church," in Jim Obelkevich, Lyndal Roper, and Raphael Samuel, eds., *Disciplines of Faith: Studies in Religion, Politics and Patriarchy* (London: Routledge & Kegan Paul, 1987), pp. 13–36.

Aviad, Janet, "The Messianism of Gush Emunim," in Jonathan Frankel, ed., *Jews and Messianism in the Modern Era: Metaphor and Meaning. Studies in Contemporary Jewry: An Annual* (Jerusalem and New York: Institute of Contemporary Jewry, Hebrew University and Oxford University Press, 1991), pp. 197–213.

Banfield, Edward C., *The Moral Basis of a Backward Society* (Glencoe, IL: Free Press, 1958).

Barak, Gregg, "Toward a Criminology of State Criminality," in Barak, ed., *Crimes by the Capitalist State: An Introduction to State Criminality* (Albany: State University of New York Press), 1991, pp. 3–16.

Beckford, James A., *Cult Controversies: The Societal Response to the New Religious Movements* (London: Tavistock Publications, 1985).

Bell, Daniel, "The Return of the Sacred? The Argument on the Future of Religion," *British Journal of Sociology* 28, no. 4 (December 1977): 419–449.

Beltz, Walter, *God and the Gods: Myths of the Bible,* trans. Peter Heinegg (Harmondsworth, England: Penguin Books, 1983).

Benvenisti, Meron, *The Shepherds' War: Collected Essays (1981–1989)* (Jerusalem: Jerusalem Post, 1989).

Benvenisti, Meron, *The Sling and the Club: Territories, Jews and Arabs* (in Hebrew) (Jerusalem: Keter Publishing House, Ltd., 1988).

Benvenisti, Meron, *The West Bank Data Project: A Survey of Israel's Policies* (Washington, DC: American Enterprise Institute for Policy Research, 1984).
Ben-Yehuda, Nachman, *Political Assassinations by Jews: A Rhetorical Device for Justice* (Albany: State University Press of New York, 1993).
Bergen, A. E., "Religiosity and Mental Health: A Critical Reevaluation and Meta-Analysis," *Professional Psychology: Research and Practice* 14 (1983): 170–184.
Biggar, H. Nigel, Jamie S. Scott, and William Schweiker, eds., *Cities of Gods: Faith, Politics and Pluralism in Judaism, Christianity and Islam* (New York: Greenwood Press, 1986).
Bloom, Harold, *The American Religion: The Emergence of the Post-Christian Nation* (New York: Simon & Schuster, 1992).
Brams, Steven J. *Biblical Games: A Strategic Analysis of Stories in the Old Testament* (Cambridge: M.I.T. Press, 1980).
Bright, John, *A History of Israel* (London: SCM Press Ltd., 1980).
Bright, John, *Jeremiah: The Anchor Bible* (Garden City, NY: Doubleday & Company, 1965).
Brooks, Roger, *The Spirit of the Ten Commandments: Shattering the Myth of Rabbinic Legalism* (New York: Harper and Row, 1990).
Butler, Jon, *Awash in a Sea of Faith: Christianizing the American People* (Cambridge: Harvard University Press, 1990).
Campbell, Robert A., and James E. Curtis, "Religious Involvement Across Societies: Analysis for Alternative Measures in National Surveys," *Journal for the Scientific Study of Religion* 33, no. 3 (1994): 215–229.
Cantor, Norman F., *The Sacred Chain: The History of the Jews* (New York: Harper Collins, 1994).
Carmy, Shalom, "A View from the Fleshpots: Exploratory Remarks on Gilded *Galut* Existence," in Chaim I. Waxman, ed., *Israel as a Religious Reality* (Northvale, NJ: Jason Aronson Inc., 1994), pp. 1–42.
Casanova, José, *Public Religions in the Modern World* (Chicago: University of Chicago Press, 1994).
Choshen, Maya, "The Elections to the Knesset in Jerusalem: Statistical Outlook" (in Hebrew) (Jerusalem: Jerusalem Institute for Israel Studies, 1990).
Coelho, George V., David A. Hamburg, and John E. Adams, eds., *Coping and Adaptation* (New York: Basic Books, 1974).
Cohen, Stuart A., *The Three Crowns: Structures of Communal Politics in Early Rabbinic Jewry* (Cambridge: Cambridge University Press, 1990).
Collins, John J., *Between Athens and Jerusalem: Jewish Identity in the Hellenistic Diaspora* (New York: Crossroad Publishing Company, 1986).
Croft, Q. Michael, "The Influence of the L.D.S. Church on Utah Politics, 1945–1984" (Ph.D. diss., University of Utah, 1985).
Dart, John, *The Jesus of Heresy and History: The Discovery and Meaning of the Nag Hammadi Gnostic Library* (San Francisco: Harper and Row, 1988).
Dershowitz, Alan M., *Chutzpah* (New York: Touchstone, 1991).
Dery, David, *Data and Policy Change* (Boston: Kluwer Academic Publishers, 1990).
Dimont, Max I., *Jews, God and History* (New York: Signet Books, 1964).
Don-Yehiya, Eliezer, "Does Place Make a Difference? Jewish Orthodoxy in Israel and the Diaspora," in Chaim I. Waxman, ed., *Israel as a Religious Reality* (Northvale, NJ: Jason Aronson Inc., 1994), pp. 43–74.

Don-Yehiya, Eliezer, "Hanukkah and the Myth of the Maccabees in Zionist Ideology and in Israeli Society," *The Jewish Journal of Sociology* 34, no. 1 (June 1992): 5–23.
Durkheim, Emile, *The Elemental Forms of Religious Life* (London: Allen and Unwin, 1915).
Edelman, Murray, *The Symbolic Uses of Politics* (Urbana: University of Illinois Press, 1964).
Editors of *Commentary* Magazine, *The Condition of Jewish Belief: A Symposium* (New York: Macmillan, 1966).
Elliott, Russell R., *History of Nevada* (Lincoln: University of Nebraska Press, 1987).
El-Or, Tamar, *Educated and Ignorant: On Ultra-Orthodox Women and Their World* (in Hebrew) (Tel Aviv: Am Oved, 1992).
Ferraro, Kenneth F., and Cynthia M. Albrecht-Jensen, "Does Religion Influence Adult Health?" *Journal for the Scientific Study of Religion* 30, no. 2 (1991): 193–202.
Ferraro, Kenneth F., and Jerome R. Koch, "Religion and Health Among American Black and White Adults: Examining Social Support and Consolation," *Journal for the Scientific Study of Religion* 33, no. 4 (1994): 362–375.
Fishman, Aryei, and Yaaqov Goldschmidt, "The Orthodox Kibbutzim and Economic Success," *Journal for the Scientific Study of Religion* 29, no. 4 (1990): 505–511.
Folkman, Susan, "Personal Control and Stress and Coping Processes: A Theoretical Analysis," *Journal of Personality and Social Psychology* 46, no. 4 (1984): 839–852.
Folkman, Susan, et al., "Dynamics of a Stressful Encounter: Cognitive Appraisal, Coping, and Encounter Outcomes," *Journal of Personality and Social Psychology* 50, no. 5 (1986): 992–1003.
Foucault, Michel, *Discipline and Punish: The Birth of the Prison*, trans. Alan Sheridan (New York: Vintage Books, 1979).
Frankel, Jonathan, *Prophecy and Politics: Socialism, Nationalism, and the Russian Jews, 1862–1917* (Cambridge: Cambridge University Press, 1981).
Freedman, David Noel, "'Who Is Like Thee Among the Gods?' The Religion of Early Israel," in Patrick D. Miller, Jr., Paul D. Hanson, and S. Dean McBride, eds., *Ancient Israelite Religion* (Philadelphia: Fortress Press, 1987), pp. 315–336.
Friedman, Menachem, *Haredi Society: Sources, Goals, and Procedures* (in Hebrew) (Jerusalem: Jerusalem Institute for Israel Studies, 1991).
Friedman, Menachem, "The Hasidim and the Holocaust," *Jerusalem Quarterly* 53 (Winter 1990): 86–114.
Frisch, Hillel, "State Ethnicization and the Crisis of Leadership Succession amongst Israel's Druze," (manuscript, Department of Political Science, Hebrew University of Jerusalem, 1995).
Frye, Northrop, *The Double Vision: Language and Meaning in Religion* (Toronto: University of Toronto Press, 1991).
Garbini, Giovanni, *History and Ideology in Ancient Israel* (New York: Crossroad Publishing Company, 1988).
Georges-Abeyie, Daniel E., "Piracy, Air Piracy, and Recurrent U.S. and Israeli Civilian Aircraft Interceptions" in Gregg Barak, *Crimes by the Capitalist State: An Introduction to State Criminality* (Albany: State University of New York Press), pp. 129–144.

Gilkey, Langdon, *Society and the Sacred: Toward a Theology of Culture in Decline* (New York: Crossroad Publishing Company, 1981).
Gitelman, Zvi, ed., *The Quest for Utopia: Jewish Political Ideas and Institutions Through the Ages* (Armonk, NY: M.E. Sharpe, Inc., 1992).
Goldscheider, Calvin, and Jacob Neusner, eds., *Social Foundations of Judaism* (Englewood Cliffs, NJ: Prentice Hall, 1990).
Gooch, Brison D., ed., *The Origins of the Crimean War* (Lexington, MA: D. C. Heath & Co., 1969).
Gordis, Robert, *Koheleth: The Man and His Work: A Study of Ecclesiastes* (New York: Schocken Books, 1968).
Gottlieb, Robert, and Peter Wiley, *America's Saints: The Rise of Mormon Power* (New York: Harcourt Brace Jovanovich, 1986).
Grant, Frederick C., *Ancient Judaism and the New Testament* (Westport, CT: Greenwood Press, 1959).
Grant, Michael, *The Jews in the Roman World* (New York: Dorset Press, 1973), p. 14.
Grant, Robert M., with David Tracy, *A Short History of the Interpretation of the Bible* (Philadelphia: Fortress Press, 1984).
Green, John C., "The Christian Right and the 1994 Elections: A View from the States," *PS: Political Science and Politics* 28, No. 1 (March 1995): 5–8.
Gunn, David M., *The Fate of King Saul: An Interpretation of a Biblical Story*, Journal for the Study of the Old Testament Supplement Series, no. 14 (Sheffield, 1984).
Hamilton, Malcolm B., *The Sociology of Religion: Theoretical and Comparative Perspectives* (London: Routledge, 1995).
Harkabi, Yehoshafat, *The Bar Kokhba Syndrome: Risk and Realism in International Relations*, trans. Max D. Ticktin, ed. David Altshuler (Chappaqua, NY: Rossel Books, 1983).
Harkabi, Yehoshafat, *Israel's Fateful Hour*, trans. Lenn Schramm (New York: Harper & Row, 1988).
Harrington, Michael, *The Politics at God's Funeral: The Spiritual Crisis of Western Civilization* (New York: Penguin Books, 1983).
Hertzke, Allen D., *Representing God in Washington: The Role of Religious Lobbies in the American Polity* (Knoxville: University of Tennessee Press, 1988).
Hofnung, Menachem, *Israel-State Security Against the Rule of Law 1948–1991* (in Hebrew) (Jerusalem: Nero Publisher, 1991).
Holtz, Barry W., ed., *Back to the Sources: Reading the Classic Jewish Texts* (New York: Summit Books, 1984).
Horowitz, Dan, and Moshe Lissak, *Trouble in Utopia: The Overburdened Polity of Israel* (Albany: State University of New York Press, 1989).
Johnson, Paul, *A History of Christianity*, pt. 1 (New York: Atheneum, 1976).
Johnson, Stephen D., and Joseph B. Tamney, eds., *The Political Role of Religion in the United States* (Boulder, CO: Westview Press, 1986).
Jonas, Frank H., "Utah: Crossroads of the West," in Jonas, ed., *Western Politics* (Salt Lake City: University of Utah Press, 1961), p. 273.
Josipovici, Gabriel, *The Book of God: A Response to the Bible* (New Haven: Yale University Press, 1988).
Kahane, Rabbi Meir, "Forty Years," (Brooklyn, NY: The Institute of the Jewish Idea, 1983).
Keller, Chaim Dov, "Modern Orthodoxy: An Analysis and a Response," in Reuven P. Bulka, ed., *Dimensions of Orthodox Judaism* (New York: KTAV Publishing House, 1983), pp. 253–271.

Keren, Michael, *Ben Gurion and the Intellectuals: Power, Knowledge, and Charisma* (Dekalb: Northern Illinois University Press, 1983).
Kochan, Lionel, *Jews, Idols and Messiahs: The Challenge from History* (Oxford: Basil Blackwell, 1990).
Kosmin, Barry A., and Seymour P. Lachman, *One Nation Under God: Religion in Contemporary American Society* (New York: Crown Publishers, 1993).
Kraft, Robert A., and George W. E. Nickelsburg, eds., *Early Judaism and Its Modern Interpreters* (Philadelphia: Fortress Press, 1986).
Kroyanker, David, *Jerusalem: Planning and Development 1982–1985: New Trends* (Jerusalem: The Jerusalem Committee and the Jerusalem Institute for Israel Studies, 1985).
Lacey, Michael J., ed., *Religion and Twentieth-Century American Intellectual Life* (New York: Cambridge University Press, 1989).
Lederhandler, Eli, *The Road to Modern Jewish Politics: Political Tradition and Political Reconstruction in the Jewish Community of Tsarist Russia* (New York: Oxford University Press, 1989).
Leege, David C., and Lyman A. Kellstedt, eds., *Rediscovering the Religious Factor in American Politics* (Armonk, NY: M. E. Sharpe, 1993).
Lehman-Wilzig, Sam, *Stiff-necked People, Bottle-necked System: The Evolution and Roots of Israeli Public Protest, 1949–1986* (Bloomington: Indiana University Press, 1991).
Lehman-Wilzig, Sam, and Bernard Susser, eds., *Public Life in Israel and the Diaspora* (Ramat Gan: Bar-Ilan University Press, 1981).
Leibowitz, Yeshayahu, *On Just About Everything: Talks with Michael Shashar* (in Hebrew) (Jerusalem: Keter Publishing House, Ltd., 1988).
Lensen, Larry C., Janet Jensen, and Terrie Wiederhold, "Religiosity, Denomination, and Mental Health Among Young Men and Women," *Psychological Reports* 72 (1993): 1157–1158.
Leslau, Avraham, and Mordechai Bar-Lev, "Religiosity among Oriental Youth in Israel," *Sociological Papers* 3, no. 5 (December 1994) (Bar-Ilan University, Sociological Institute for Community Studies).
Lichtenstein, Aharon, "The Israeli Chief Rabbinate: A Current Halakhic Perspective," in Chaim I. Waxman, ed., *Israel as a Religious Reality* (Northvale, NJ: Jason Aronson Inc., 1994), p. 131.
Liebman, Charles S., and Steven M. Cohen, *Two Worlds of Judaism: The Israeli and American Experiences* (New Haven: Yale University Press, 1990).
Liebman, Charles S., and Eliezer Don-Yehiya, *Civil Religion in Israel: Traditional Judaism and Political Culture* (Berkeley: University of California Press, 1984).
Lijphart, Arend, *Democracies: Patterns of Majoritarian and Consensus Government in Twenty-one Countries* (New Haven: Yale University Press, 1984).
Lindblom, Charles E., and David K. Cohen, *Usable Knowledge: Social Science and Social Problem Solving* (New Haven: Yale University Press, 1979).
Magleby, David B., "Religion and Voting Behavior in a Religiously Homogeneous State" (paper delivered at the 1987 Annual Meeting of the American Political Science Association).
Mauss, Armand L., John R. Trijan, and Marth D. Esplin, "The Unfettered Faithful: An Analysis of the *Dialogue Subscribers Survey*," *Dialogue: A Journal of Mormon Thought* 20 (April 1987): 27–53.
McCarter, P. Kyle, Jr., "Aspects of the Religion of the Israelite Monarchy: Biblical and Epigraphic Data," in Patrick D. Miller, Jr., Paul D. Hanson,

and S. Dean McBride, eds., *Ancient Israelite Religion* (Philadelphia: Fortress Press, 1987), pp. 137–156.
McKenzie, John L., S.J., *The Two-Edged Sword: An Interpretation of the Old Testament* (Garden City, NY: Image Books, 1966).
Medding, Peter Y., *The Founding of Israeli Democracy 1948–1967* (New York: Oxford University Press, 1990).
Medding, Peter Y., ed., *A New Jewry? America Since the Second World War. Studies in Contemporary Jewry: An Annual* (Jerusalem and New York: Institute of Contemporary Jewry, The Hebrew University and Oxford University Press, 1992).
Melzar, Fibal, *The Five Scrolls* (in Hebrew) (Jerusalem: Mossad Harav Kook, 1973).
Mendelsohn, Ezra, *On Modern Jewish Politics* (New York: Oxford University Press, 1993).
Mettinger, Tryggve N. D., *Solomonic State Officials: A Study of the Civil Government Officials of the Israelite Monarchy* (Lund, Sweden: CWK Gleerup, 1971).
Meyers, Carol, "David as Temple Builder," in Patrick D. Miller, Jr., Paul D. Hanson, and S. Dean McBride, eds., *Ancient Israelite Religion* (Philadelphia: Fortress Press, 1987), pp. 357–376.
Michel, Patrick, *Politics and Religion in Eastern Europe: Catholicism in Hungary, Poland and Czechoslovakia*, trans. Alan Braley (Cambridge: Polity Press, 1991).
Miller, J. Maxwell, and John H. Hayes, *A History of Ancient Israel and Judah* (Philadelphia: The Westminster Press, 1986).
Miller, Timothy, ed., *America's Alternative Religions* (Albany: State University of New York Press, 1995).
Mintz, Jerome R., *Legends of the Hasidim: An Introduction to Hasidic Culture and Oral Tradition in the New World* (Chicago: University of Chicago Press, 1968).
Moore, R. Laurence, *Selling God: American Religion in the Marketplace of Culture* (New York: Oxford University Press, 1994).
Moos, Rudolf H., and Jeanne A. Schaefer, "Life Transitions and Crises: A Conceptual Overview," in Moos in collaboration with Schaefer, eds., *Coping with Life Crises: An Integrated Approach* (New York: Plenum Press, 1986).
Near, Henry, ed., *The Seventh Day* (London: Andre Deutsch, 1970).
Nelson, Geoffrey K., *Cults, New Religions and Religious Creativity* (London: Routledge & Kegan Paul, 1987).
Neusner, Jacob, *Death and Birth of Judaism: The Impact of Christianity, Secularism, and the Holocaust on Jewish Faith* (New York: Basic Books, 1987).
O'Dea, Thomas Francis, and Janet O'dea Aviad, *The Sociology of Religion* (Englewood Cliffs, NJ: Prentice-Hall, 1983).
Orlinsky, Harry M., *Essays in Biblical Culture and Bible Translation* (New York: KTAV Publishing House, Inc., 1974).
Oz, Amos, *A Journey in Israel: Autumn 1982* (in Hebrew) (Tel Aviv: Am Oved, 1986).
Penchansky, David, *The Betrayal of God: Ideological Conflict in Job* (Louisville, KY: Westminster/John Knox Press, 1990).
Peters, F. E., *Jerusalem: The Holy City in the Eyes of Chroniclers, Visitors, Pilgrims, and Prophets from the Days of Abraham to the Beginnings of Modern Times* (Princeton: Princeton University Press, 1985), pp. 285–286.

Powell, G. Bingham, Jr., *Contemporary Democracies: Participation, Stability, and Violence* (Cambridge: Harvard University Press, 1982).
Prittie, Terrence, *Whose Jerusalem?* (London: Frederick Muller Ltd., 1981).
Rabinovich, Abraham, *Jerusalem on Earth: People, Passions and Politics in the Holy City* (New York: Free Press, 1988).
Ramet, Pedro, ed., *Religion and Nationalism in Soviet and East European Politics* (Durham, NC: Duke University Press, 1989).
Rich, Norman, *Why the Crimean War? A Cautionary Tale* (Hanover, NH: University Press of New England, 1985).
Richardson, James T., "The 'Old Right' in Action: Mormon and Catholic Involvement in an Equal Rights Amendment Referendum," in David G. Bromley and Anson Shupe, eds., *New Christian Politics* (Macon, GA: Mercer University Press, 1984), pp. 214–233.
Richardson, James T., and Sandie Wightman Fox, "Religious Affiliation as a Predictor of Voting Behavior in Abortion Reform Legislation," *Journal for the Scientific Study of Religion* 11 (1972): 347–359.
Richardson, James T., and Barend Van Driel, "Public Support for Anti-Cult Legislation," *Journal for the Scientific Study of Religion* 23 (1984): 412–418.
Robbins, Thomas, *Cults, Converts and Charisma: The Sociology of New Religious Movements* (London: Sage Publications, 1988).
Romann, Michael, and Alex Weingrod, *Living Together Separately: Arabs and Jews in Contemporary Jerusalem* (Princeton: Princeton University Press, 1991).
Roof, Clark Wade, and William McKinney, *American Mainline Religion: Its Changing Shape and Future* (New Brunswick, NJ: Rutgers University Press, 1987).
Rosenblatt, Jason P., and Joseph C. Sitterson, Jr., *"Not in Heaven": Coherence and Complexity in Biblical Narrative* (Bloomington: Indiana University Press, 1991).
Ross, Jeffrey Ian, ed., *Controlling State Crime* (New York: Garland Press, 1995).
Roth, Joel, *The Halakhic Process: A Systemic Analysis* (New York: Jewish Theological Seminary of America, 1986).
Safire, William, *The First Dissident: The Book of Job in Today's Politics* (New York: Random House, 1992).
Sanford, John A., *King Saul, The Tragic Hero: A Study in Individuation* (New York: Paulist Press, 1985).
Scholem, Gershom, *Sabbatei Sevi: The Mystical Messiah*, trans. R. J. Zwi Werblowsky (Princeton: Princeton University Press, 1973).
Segal, Ronald, *Whose Jerusalem? The Conflicts of Israel* (London: Jonathan Cape, 1973).
Seltzer, Robert M., *Jewish People, Jewish Thought: The Jewish Experience in History* (New York: Macmillan, 1980), p. xi.
Shalev, Meir, *The Bible Now* (in Hebrew) (Jerusalem: Schocken, 1985), pp. 65–73.
Sharkansky, Ira, *Governing Jerusalem: Again on the World's Agenda* (Detroit: Wayne State University Press, 1996).
Sharkansky, Ira, *Israel and Its Bible: A Political Analysis* (New York: Garland Publishing Company, 1996).
Sharkansky, Ira, *The Political Economy of Israel* (New Brunswick, NJ: Transaction Books, 1987).
Sharkansky, Ira, *What Makes Israel Tick? How Domestic Policy-makers Cope with Constraints* (Chicago: Nelson Hall, 1985).

Shimshoni, Daniel, *Israeli Democracy: The Middle of the Journey* (New York: Free Press, 1982).
Silberstein, Laurence I., ed., *Jewish Fundamentalism in Comparative Perspective: Religion, Ideology, and the Crisis of Modernity* (New York: New York University Press, 1993).
Silver, Abba Hillel, *Where Judaism Differs: An Inquiry into the Distinctiveness of Judaism* (New York: Collier Books, 1989).
Silver, Daniel Jeremy, *A History of Judaism*, vol. 1 (New York: Basic Books, 1974).
Simon, Herbert, *Administrative Behavior* (New York: Free Press, 1976).
Smith, Jonathan Z. *Imagining Religion: From Babylon to Jonestown* (Chicago: University of Chicago Press, 1982).
Soloveitchick, Haym, "Rupture and Reconstruction: The Transformation of Contemporary Orthodoxy," *Tradition* 28, no. 4 (1994): 64–131.
Sprinzak, Ehud, *The Ascendance of Israel's Radical Right* (New York: Oxford University Press, 1991).
Sprinzak, Ehud, *Between Extra-Parliamentary Protest and Terror: Political Violence in Israel* (in Hebrew) (Jerusalem: Jerusalem Institute for Israeli Research, 1995).
Stark, Rodney, and William Sims Bainbridge, *The Future of Religion: Secularization, Revival, and Cult Formation* (Berkeley: University of California Press, 1985).
Steinsaltz, Adin, *Biblical Images: Men and Women of the Book* (New York: Basic Books, 1984).
Stone, A. A., and J. M. Neale, "New Measure of Daily Coping: Development and Preliminary Results," *Journal of Personality and Social Psychology* 46, no. 4 (1984): 892–906.
Stone, Deborah A., *Policy Paradox and Political Reason* (Glenview, IL: Scott, Foresman and Company, 1988).
Tabory, Ephraim, "Avoidance and Conflict: Perceptions Regarding Contact Between Religious and Nonreligious Jewish Youth in Israel," *Journal for the Scientific Study of Religion* 31, no. 2 (1992): 148–162.
Tarnas, Richard, *The Passion of the Western Mind: Understanding the Ideas That Have Shaped Our World View* (New York: Ballantine Books, 1991).
Tcherikover, Victor, *Hellenistic Civilization and the Jews* (New York: Atheneum, 1959).
Tsimhoni, Daphne, "Continuity and Change in Communal Autonomy: The Christian Communal Organizations in Jerusalem, 1948–1980," *Middle East Studies* 22 (July 1986): 398–417.
Visotzky, Burton L., *Reading the Book: Making the Bible a Timeless Text* (New York: Anchor Books, 1991).
Waetjen, Herman C., *A Reordering of Power: A Sociopolitical Reading of Mark's Gospel* (Minneapolis: Fortress Press, 1989).
Wald, Kenneth D., *Religion and Politics in the United States* (Washington, DC: CQ Press, 1992).
Walker, Sheila S., *The Religious Revolution in the Ivory Coast: The Prophet Harris and the Harrist Church* (Chapel Hill: University of North Carolina Press, 1983).
Waxman, Chaim I., *America's Jews in Transition* (Philadelphia: Temple University Press, 1983).
Werblowsky, J. Zwi, *Beyond Tradition and Modernity: Changing Religions in a Changing World* (University of London: The Athlone Press, 1976).

Wildavsky, Aaron, *The Nursing Father: Moses as a Political Leader* (University: University of Alabama Press, 1984).

Wilken, Robert L., *The Land Called Holy: Palestine in Christian History and Thought* (New Haven: Yale University Press, 1992).

Wilkes, Paul L., *And They Shall Be My People: An American Rabbi and His Congregation* (New York: Ballantine Books, 1995).

Wilkinson, John, *Jerusalem Pilgrims: Before the Crusades* (Jerusalem: Ariel Publishing House, 1977).

Williams, J. D., "The Separation of Church and State in Mormon Theory and Practice," *Dialogue: A Journal of Mormon Thought* 1, no. 2 (Summer 1966): 30–54.

Wolfensohn, Abraham, *From the Bible to the Labor Movement* (in Hebrew) (Tel Aviv: Am Oved, 1975).

Wolfsfeld, Gadi, *The Politics of Provocation* (Albany: State University of New York Press, 1988).

Wuthnow, Robert, "Religious Movements and Counter-Movements in North America," in James A. Beckford, ed., *New Religious Movements and Rapid Social Change* (London: Sage Publications, 1986), pp. 1–28.

Wuthnow, Robert, *The Restructuring of American Religion* (Princeton: Princeton University Press, 1988).

Yaniv, Avner, ed., *National Security and Democracy in Israel* (Boulder, CO: Lynne Rienner Publishers, 1993).

Young, Brad H., *Jesus and His Jewish Parables: Rediscovering the Roots of Jesus' Teaching* (New York: Paulist Press, 1989).

INDEX

Absalom, 47
Achish, 56
Adherence to a religion, 23
Agudat Israel, 39, 90–93, 104, 113, 115, 118, 129
Aloni, Shulamit, 93, 104–105, 109–111, 141
American Jewry. *See* United States
Amital, Rabbi Yehuda, 120–121
Amorphous character of religion, 29
Anticlericalism, 2, 5, 21, 31
Arafat, Yassir, 40, 126
Archaeologists, 135, 144
Armenian community, 107
Assimilation, 65
Association of Sephardi Observants of the Torah (SHAS), 39, 89, 90–95, 109–115, 138–140, 147

Barak, Ehud, 89
Begin, Menachem, 94, 140
Benefits of religion, 23
Ben-Gurion, David, 77, 83
Benvenisti, Meron, 79
Ben-Yehuda, Nachman, 85
Bible, 6–8, 24–30, 31, 45–68, 69, 83–84, 96, 153–154
Bloom, Harold, 3
Bnei Brak, 9, 39, 65, 108, 116, 146, 147, 149
Brigham Young University, 135
Burg, Avram, 116
Burials, 142

Cantor, Norman F., 38
Carmy, Rabbi Shalom, 66
Carter, President Jimmy, 66
Changing religion, 23
Christianity, 8, 9, 12, 21, 28, 62, 68, 123
Christians, 2, 9, 10, 13, 21, 23, 28, 30, 32, 37, 62, 68, 79, 88, 101, 103–107, 122–127, 134, 141–142, 144, 147, 149, 152, 167
Church of the Holy Sepulcher, 105
Civil libertarians, 79
Civil Service Commission, 102
Commager, Henry, 65
Commentary magazine, 43
Conservative Judaism, 7, 8, 9, 23, 28, 43, 44, 64, 66, 86, 90, 113, 116, 124, 138, 141
Coping, 15, 16, 52–61, 76, 96–97
Costs of dispute, 16
Cult, 6, 22, 119

Declaration of Independence (Israel), 6, 75
Degel Hatorah, 39, 92, 106, 114, 115
Democracy, 3, 5, 23, 50, 76–83, 152–154
Democratic Party: loyalty to, 66
Dershowitz, Alan M., 65
Divorce, 2, 27, 79, 91, 93, 101, 152
Don-Yehiya, Eliezer, 116
Druckman, Rabbi Haim, 119
Druze, 10, 79, 88, 101, 106
Durkheim, Emile, 3

Ecclesiastes, 60
Economic management, 77
Edah Ha-Haredit, 40, 114
Eisenhower, Dwight D., 32
Enlightenment, 3, 5, 22, 64, 81, 96, 101, 153
Ethnocentric, 43, 84
Ethnocentrism, 7, 27, 84
Excommunication, 29, 31, 114

Factionalism, 81

God, 2–5, 6, 7, 8, 9, 21–28, 30–33, 41, 43–45, 48, 50–52, 53–55, 57, 59–61, 62, 67, 83–84, 101, 110, 112, 118, 119, 123,

169

124, 127, 134, 145, 151–152; insecurity of, 55
Golden calf, 26–27
Greek Orthodox, 105, 106, 126, 144
Gush Emunim, 40, 44, 92, 119

Hanukkah, 116
Harkabi, Yehoshafat, 79
Hartman, Rabbi David, 108
Hebrew law, 102
Heresy, 21, 29, 31
Holocaust, the, 6, 15, 39, 63, 65, 68, 76, 77, 80, 91, 92, 106, 107, 117, 118, 135, 136
Holocaust Remembrance Day, 106, 117
How Different Is Israel?, 151–152

Immigration, 16, 37, 76, 77, 96, 116, 136, 140
Insoluble problems, 13
Intifada, 110, 115
Israel: compared to other countries, 5, 151
Israelite monarchy, 7, 50, 52
Israel Religious Action Center, 109

Jaffa, 103, 140, 147
Jeremiah, the prophet, 58
Jerusalem, 1, 6, 9, 10, 11, 12, 15, 41, 49, 57, 58, 63, 64, 79, 87, 92, 103–107, 108, 109, 114, 115, 117, 119, 122–127, 128, 133, 136, 137(tab), 140, 143–146, 147–149, 153; syndrome, 126, 127
Jewish: ethnicity, 9, 68; humanism, 44, 62
Joab, 47
Job, 60–62
Josipovici, Gabriel, 8
Judaism: defined, 6, 10, 37, 44–45; kinds of, 5

Kahane, Rabbi Meir, 28, 41, 84, 122, 136, 149
King David, 40, 45–48, 55–56, 82
King Hussein, 40, 154
King Josiah, 56–57
King Saul, 51–52
King Zedekiah, 57–58
Knesset, 9, 12, 16, 39, 76, 80, 84, 88, 91, 93, 95, 102, 105, 107, 109–112, 115, 117, 125–126, 133–134, 136, 138, 149
Kochan, Lionel, 8

Kollek, Teddy, 103, 105, 107, 128–129, 136, 144

Labor Party, 88–89, 93–95, 109, 111–112, 116
Land of Israel, 1, 10, 13, 33, 40, 63, 92, 103, 112, 114, 117, 118–122, 150, 155–156
Latin patriarch of Jerusalem, 104
Latter-day Saints, 28, 135. *See also* Mormons
Law, Rabbi Yisrael, 121
Leibowitz, Yeshayahu, 80
Likud, 92–95, 107, 110, 116, 139, 144
Lubavitcher, 39, 92, 113, 150
Lustiger, Cardinal Jean-Marie, 106

Marriage, 2, 15, 31, 37, 42, 79, 84, 88–89, 91, 101–102, 138, 140, 147
Memorial Day, 107, 117
Meretz, 93–96, 109–110, 114, 117, 120–121, 127, 138–139
Ministry of Education, 80, 89–90, 124, 138
Ministry of Housing and Construction, 90, 129, 147
Ministry of Interior, 79, 89
Ministry of Religious Affairs, 88–90, 149
Modesty patrols, 145
Mormons, 10, 30–31, 127, 135
Moses, 7–8, 26–27, 31, 50, 53–56, 62
Muslims, 1, 10, 41, 68, 101, 103, 107, 123–124, 125, 127–128, 134, 149

Nathan, the prophet, 47–48
National Religious Party (NRP), 40, 86, 87, 88, 89, 90, 91, 92, 93, 94, 95, 106, 111, 112, 115, 116, 117, 119, 139
Nature of Judaism, 67
Neturei Karta, 40
Neusner, Jacob, 6
Nixon, President Richard, 66
NRP. *See* National Religious Party

Olmert, Ehud, 145
Opportunities for non-Jews, 78
Orthodox, 1, 2, 5, 6, 9, 10, 11, 15, 23, 24, 29, 38–45, 62, 65–68, 75, 78, 86–95, 102–129, 135–151
Oz, Amos, 44, 119

Palestine Liberation Organization, 13, 40, 79, 118
Palestinian Authority, 1, 126, 154, 155
Paul, 62
Peace process and religion, 154
Pepsi Cola posters, 148
Peres, Shimon, 89, 104, 121, 133
Peres, Yohanan, 86–87
Political views: associated with religion, 87–88
Power of faith, 31
Protest, 78
Public policy, 1, 2, 11, 12, 29, 31, 65, 101, 129, 134, 151

Rabbinate, 29, 75, 90, 93, 102, 108, 114, 116, 138, 139
Rabin, Yitzhak, 1, 32, 85, 89, 93, 110, 118, 121, 122, 155
Reagan, President Ronald, 66
Reform Judaism, 7, 8, 9, 23, 28, 43, 44, 62, 64, 66, 86, 90, 102, 107, 108, 109, 113, 114, 116, 118, 124, 126, 137, 138, 141, 147, 149
Religion: defined, 6
Religious: creativity, 5, 21, 22, 24, 28, 29, 31, 62, 63; doctrines, 30; law, 7, 10, 15, 40, 65, 75, 79, 81, 101, 121, 133, 139, 140, 141; vs. antireligious in Israeli society, 143
Rituals, 134, 149
Ruth, 84

Sabbath, 2, 9, 10, 12, 15, 45, 49, 84, 91, 109, 114, 115, 133, 136, 137, 139, 140, 142, 144, 145, 147, 150, 154, 156
Sartre, Jean-Paul, 22
Schach, Rabbi Eliezer, 111, 112
Schneerson, Rabbi Menachem Mendel, 39
Scopes, John T., 3
Sea of Galilee, 114

Sect, 6, 119
Security, 78
Sephardim, 5, 39, 92, 111, 113
SHAS. *See* Association of Sephardi Observants of the Torah
Shorashim, 108, 109
Silver, Rabbi Abba Hillel, 8
Soviet Union, 2, 16, 21, 22, 29, 31, 96, 108, 115, 116, 136, 140, 141
Spinoza, Baruch, 107
Standoff, 95, 97, 140
State comptroller, 80, 81
Stereotypes, 38, 68, 87, 88, 150
Stresses, 15
Surveys, 86
Symbolic issues, 12, 94, 114, 116, 134, 139, 145

Tamar, 29
Temple Mount, 124, 134, 148–149
Traditional Israeli Jews, 9, 42, 44, 68, 86, 87, 111, 140, 151
Tsomet, 95, 96

Ultra-Orthodox, 1, 5, 6, 9, 11, 15, 39, 40, 42, 45, 62, 65, 67, 68, 78, 86–95, 102–129, 136–151
United States, 3, 7, 12, 13, 21, 65, 66, 67, 85, 105, 113, 147, 152
Universalism, 27, 68, 84
Utah, 29, 136, 152

Vatican, 104
Vegetarian seder, 149
Violence, 3, 85

Western Wall, 102, 107, 115, 124, 127
Wildavsky, Aaron, 8

Yad Vashem, 106
Yosef, Rabbi Ovadia, 109, 111, 114–115, 117

About the Book

The assassination of Yizhak Rabin and the election of Benjamin Netanyahu as prime minister have highlighted the ongoing political and cultural tensions between religious and secular Israeli Jews. Among the latter, the events have introduced fear about the onset of a new religious war and a dramatic shift in public policy. However, Ira Sharkansky notes that, while religious interests in Israel have been powerful enough to keep their issues on the political agenda, they have, to date, been unable to influence the overall direction of either domestic or foreign policy.

Sharkansky demonstrates that within the communities of both religious and secular Jews, there is division about conceding parts of biblical Israel for the sake of peace. Neither group is unified about how and if government should address other matters important in Judaism, including Sabbath observance, kosher food, secular marriage, divorce, burial, abortion and other medical procedures, the definition of who is a Jew, and the rights of non-Orthodox congregations and their rabbis.

In this timely and insightful work, Sharkansky makes important comparisons about religion and politics in other Western democracies, where some activists warn of the catastrophes that occur in secular, "godless" societies and others see intolerant coalitions of believers. Sharkansky notes that, even where religious disputes thrive most intensely, victories for either religious or antireligious parties are rare; policy tends to favor neither extreme.

IRA SHARKANSKY is a professor of political science and public administration at The Hebrew University of Jerusalem. His other books include *Jerusalem: Again on the World's Agenda; Israel and Its Bible: A Political Analysis; Ancient and Modern Israel: An Exploration of Political Parallels;* and *The Political Economy of Israel.*